Davis, John

Travels of Four Years and a Half in the United States of America During 1798, 1799, 1800, 1801, and 1802

ISBN: 978-1-948837-00-2

This classic reprint was produced from digital files in the Google Books digital collection, which may be found at http://www.books.google.com. The artwork used on the cover is from Wikimedia Commons and remains in the public domain. Omissions and/or errors in this book are due to either the physical condition of the original book or due to the scanning process by Google or its agents.

This edition of John Davis's **Travels of Four years and a Half in the United States of America** was originally published in 1909 (New York).

Townsends
PO Box 415, Pierceton, IN 46562
www.Townsends.us

TRAVELS OF FOUR YEARS AND A HALF IN THE UNITED STATES OF AMERICA DURING 1798, 1799, 1800, 1801, AND 1802.

BY

JOHN DAVIS

WITH AN INTRODUCTION AND NOTES BY
A. J. MORRISON

NEW YORK
HENRY HOLT AND COMPANY
1909

INTRODUCTION

AMONG the number of non-official inspectors who came from Europe to the United States between the year 1776 and the year 1802—the quarter-century elapsed between the Declaration of Independence and the incorporation of the vague West—there was not one whose record of his observations is uninteresting. The great Experiment attracted men of a superior type to see what the new nation was; or, of those who found themselves landed in America at that time it was the man of ordered intellect, open-minded, who set down memoranda. The result is a series of documents, a book for every year almost, which if not an absolute registry for that era of origins is beyond question an extraordinary repository, both as fact and by comparison, for when before have the beginnings of a nation been journalized?

The impulse to the keeping of a day-book may be of several sorts, the purely business, the scientifically objective, the literary—facts for profit, facts as facts, and facts somewhat as drama. This book by John Davis is for that period fairly unique as the work of a Traveller who was professedly literary, who cared little for the political aspects of what he saw and asked no place among statisticians. Crèvecœur and Chateaubriand were sentimentalists, but Crèvecœur is very disquisitional and Chateaubriand might have written his book in his tower. Henry Wansey, in his Journal of a Summer, is the Pepys of this eighteenth century group; Parkinson and Cooper are also, in their way, entirely practical; the others, Robin, Chastellux, Schoepf, Castiglioni, Coke, Bayard, von Bülow, and the rest, are political philosophers, topographers of more or less sprightliness, anecdotal, tabulators, or men interested in natural and applied science, all good, and none like John Davis.

In the first place, John Davis was not at all a heralded foreigner. He came to America a very young man, twenty-two years old, to make a living. He could not inspect except in and between places where he found employment. As it happened, his business led him from New York to South Carolina, and (south of New England) he saw the country as it was along the coast before Ohio was a State. He was a sailor with a literary sense and equipment, resolved after a dozen years of the sea to make literature a profession. Being active and industrious, although a writer of meditative verse, he succeeded: the second edition of his book bears the sub-title, "Travels in Search of Independence and Settlement. Portum Inveni."

John Davis was in the writing business, and he could not afford to be habitually a recluse. From the pages of his book an adequate idea may be had of the status of American authorship at the turn of the eighteenth century. That is perhaps the least worth of the book, but since there is not a great deal of direct evidence on this point, it is to be remarked that Davis took stock of the literary situation at that time, talked with authors at Dickins's shop in Philadelphia, and knew Brockden Brown, the novelist, and Joseph Dennie, the critic. The wherefore of a national literature is not explicable in brief. The opening of the nineteenth century seems to have given promise of such a thing in America, and John Davis saw something of that. He and his learned friend, Mr. George, who said, "Where are their poets?" stated the *pro* and *con* for the year 1799, but Davis was in the right, whether from wisdom, tolerance, or merely because he took the other side.

A certain importance attaches to the beginning of a century, and the Traveller is on the whole fortunate whose notes are made around the rotund zero years. It is a distinction to have seen (year 1800) the author of *Arthur Mervyn* at work, "embodying virtue in a new novel," to have been commended, and also abased, by "that Mammoth of literature," the Editor of the *Portfolio*, to have maintained a literary correspondence, (year 1801 —superscriptions, Long Island and Virginia), full of Pope and the Augustan age, and to have been a spectator at the inauguration of the Federal City. It appears that John Davis was the originator of a Jefferson legend that has persisted a hundred years. And he was the first of the many who, by the interstitial work of fancy, have made of Captain John Smith's story a romance..

The author of these travels walked, with occasional recourse to the stage-coach, the horse, or the sloop; he seems to have been the sole traveller of that time who walked through a great part of the fifteen States. As between the vehicle and foot-passengership there was perhaps no great dissimilarity in the data offering for observation, but the pedestrian must be individual and if he is bookish as well the record of his journeys is apt to give the suggestion of a personality; that is to say, the impressionist writer is usually bookish, and if, being on his travels, he chooses for any reason that mode of transit best fitting his character, the result will likely be a more permanent expression of the man. John Davis believed that, and his own assertion may recommend his book: "This Volume will regale curiosity while man continues to be influenced by his senses and affections." *

John Davis was a vagrant from his youth, and is an interesting figure quite apart from the significance of his activities as international author and observer of young America—it is not to be expected that a seaman will learn the French of books, then Latin, and then become a producing man of letters. In the preface to one of his novels, (*First Settlers of Virginia,* 1805), the author supplies information regarding his career, which no doubt after 1806 was that of a London journalist and book-maker. He was born at Salisbury, Wiltshire, in the year 1776, and was 'reared in the lap of opulence.' He was never at school,

[* The last chapter of this book, an appendix, has been omitted. It was discreetly abridged by the author in his second edition, being merely a heightened log of his voyage from Baltimore to Cowes in the Isle of Wight. The remainder of the text is entire. Supplied footnotes have been enclosed in brackets, as this.]

going to sea from romantic motives at the age of eleven: he had read the story of Robert Drury, the story of Captain Richard Falconer, and other books which fired his imaginations. His first voyage was in 1787, to China and the Dutch Indies; his second (1790) to Bombay, in the *Worcester*, Captain Hall. Off the high land of Chaul the ship was attacked by pirates of Angria. The *Worcester* was taking out a hundred John Company's recruits.

"Among these was a German, Oberstien, of dissipated fortune, but elegant education. Now did my mind first catch a ray of intellectual light: now was it ordained I should not be all my life illiterate. I began to learn French under Oberstien between the tropics; in my watch upon deck my station was in the main top, to haul down the top gallant studding sail at the approach of a squall, or to go up and hand the royal. For our top gallant masts were fidded, and our royal yards rigged across. When the boatswain's mate piped Starbowlines, I walked up the main rigging into the top. I always put Le Sage in my pocket; and in the maintop of an East Indianman, under a cloudless tropical sky, when the breeze was so steady that for days we had no occasion to start either tack or sheet, I began to cultivate the language of the court of Lewis the fourteenth.

"I was several months on shore at Bombay. I lodged at the country tavern. It was kept by Mr. Loudwick, and shaded with cocoa nut and bananna trees. My landlord had a complete set of European magazines; I rather devoured than read them; and it is to the perusal of these volumes that I ascribe that love of *belles lettres* which has always made me loath the mathematicks and other crabbed sciences.

"Neither Mr. Loudwick nor Mrs. Loudwick could talk English. I now thanked my stars that I had learnt French in the maintop of the *Worcester*, and conversed with my host and hostess in their own idiom.

"From Bombay we went twice down the Malabar coast, anchoring at every port. I landed at Cochin where Camoens wrote his Lusiad, and at Anjengo, where Eliza was born;* and I was engaged in the reduction of Cannanore under General Abercrombie. In our passage home I landed at the Cape of Good Hope."

Returning to Salisbury with a love of literature enkindled, Davis directed his attention to the family library, 'a room full of books.' His pleasure in reading an English book was diminished by not knowing the sources of its classical allusions, of which he could be no judge of the propriety or efficacy. By a happy fortune he hit upon Mant's Phædrus, with a parsing index, which 'strewed flowers in his road, and obtained him the rewards of study without its toils.'

"In the beginning of 1793 I was sent into the navy. In the *Active* frigate, Capt. Nagle I went to the Orkneys, Cadiz, and into the Elbe. Being turned over with the ship's company to the *Artois* (her former commander lord Charles

* See Sterne's Letters to Eliza, and Raynals' Apostrophe to Anjengo.

Fitzgerald was given the command of the *Brunswick*, seventy-four) I belonged a year and a half to a flying squadron of frigates; namely the *Pomone*, Sir John Borlase Warren, the *Arethusa*, Sir Edward Pellew, and the *Diamond*, Sir Sidney Smith. Our cruizing ground was the coast of France, and our port of rendezvous was Falmouth.

"The *Artois* was the fastest sailing frigate of the squadron. She could sail round the others. No ship could touch her, whether going large, or close hauled. We were always first up with the chase; and on the twenty-first of October, 1794, after an action close, vigorous, and persevering, the *Revolutionnaire* French frigate hauled down her colors to the *Artois*. Captain Nagle was knighted by his Majesty for the action.

"In 1798 I embarked in a small brig, at Bristol, for the United States. I had before made some progress in Greek, and begun the study of the language of harmony, with the Father of Poetry, and the Bible of the Ancients. In Latin I had looked into every writer of the Julian and Augustan ages; the study of French had always been to me like the cracking of nuts; and in my vernacular idiom I had neglected no writer from Bunyan to Bolingbroke. Lowth had put me *au fait* of all the critical niceties of grammar; and when I read it was always with an eye to new combinations of diction.

"I translated at New York Buonaparte's Campaign in Italy, a considerable octavo, and proceeded to the South. I now experienced the advantage of having educated myself. By imparting what I knew of English, French and Latin to others, I was enabled to gratify my disposition to travel, and to subsist comfortably.

"In 1802 I returned to England. I proceeded to London where my time was divided between pleasure and literature. I published a large volume of my own peregrinations. I wrote an American tale called Walter Kennedy, a Life of Chatterton, and a novel entitled The Wooden Walls Well Manned, or a Picture of a British Frigate. *

"In the winter of 1804 I returned to America. Our passage in the *Cotton Planter* was a rough

---

*The author's books and translations, published in the United States, are as follows:

1) Campaigns of Buonoparte in Italy. New York. H. Caritat. 1798.
2) Ferdinand and Elizabeth. New York. H. Caritat. 1798.
3) Poems. Charleston. 1799.
4) Farmer of New Jersey. New York. Printed by Furman and Loudon. 1800. 70 pp.
5) Wanderings of William. Philadelphia. R. T. Rawle. 1801. xii-299 pp.
6) Poems. New York. H. Caritat. 1801.
7) The First Settlers of Virginia: an historical novel. 2nd ed. New York. G. Riley & Co. 1805. xii-284 pp.
8) Berquin-Duvallon: Travels (1802) in Louisiana and the Floridas. New York. G. Riley. 1806. viii-181 pp.
9) Life and Campaigns of Victor Moreau. New York. David Bliss. 56 Maiden Lane. 1806.
10) Captain Smith and Princess Pocahontas. Philadelphia. B. Warner. 1817. iv-90 pp.

The *Travels of Four Years and a Half*, &c. was issued at London in an amended edition, 1817, 'For J. Davis, Military Chronicle office. 14 Charlotte St., Bloomsbury.'

The author's last book appears to have been "The American Mariners, or the Atlantic Voyage: a Moral Poem. Prefixed is a vindication of the American character from the Aspersions of the Quarterly Reviewers &c." Salisbury. 1822.]

one. I never witnessed severer gales. It was necessary to keep the broad axe sharp, when the ship was lying to, in case she should go on her beam ends; that we might cut away her weather rigging or the masts, in order to enable her to get upon her legs again.

"And now to the keeping of that Great Being, whose protecting arm extends over land and sea, I commend myself and my readers."

A. J. M.

TRAVELS

OF

FOUR YEARS AND A HALF

IN THE

UNITED STATES OF AMERICA;

DURING 1798, 1799, 1800, 1801, and 1802.

DEDICATED BY PERMISSION TO

THOMAS JEFFERSON, ESQ.

PRESIDENT OF THE UNITED STATES.

BY JOHN DAVIS,

> Je ne connais sur la machine rônde
> Rien que deux peuples différens:
> Savoir les hommes bons, & les hommes mechans.
>
> BEAUMARCHAIS.

LONDON:

SOLD BY T. OSTELL, AVE-MARIA-LANE, AND T. HURST,
PATER-NOSTER-ROW; B. DUGDALE, AND J. JONES,
DUBLIN; AND H. CARITAT, NEW-YORK;
FOR
R. EDWARDS, PRINTER, BROAD-STREET, BRISTOL.

1803.

BANKS OF THE OCCOQUAN
August 31, 1801.

SIR,

IN frequent journeyings through your country, I have made remarks on the character, the customs and manners of the people; these remarks I purpose to systematize into a Volume, and to you I should be happy to be allowed the honour of dedicating them. The object of my speculations has been Human Nature; speculations that will lead the reader to the contemplation of his own manners, and enable him to compare his condition with that of other men.

In my uncertain peregrinations, I have entered with equal interest the mud-hut of the negro, and the log-house of the planter; I have alike communed with the slave who wields the hoe, and the task-master who imposes his labour. My motto has been invariably *Homo sum! humani nihil a me alienum puto,* and after saying this, whatever I were to say more, would be idle declamation.

I am, SIR,

Your most obedient, most humble Servant,

JOHN DAVIS

THOMAS JEFFERSON, *Esq.*
President of the United States of America, Monticello, Virginia.

MONTICELLO, *September* 9, 1801.

Sir,

I received duly your letter of *August* 31, in which you do me the honour to propose to dedicate to me the work you are about to publish. Such a testimony of respect from an enlightened Foreigner cannot but be flattering to me, and I have only to regret that the choice of the patron will be little likely to give circulation to the work; its own merit however will supply that defect.

Should you in your journeyings have been led to remark on the same objects on which I gave crude notes some years ago, I shall be happy to see them confirmed or corrected by a more accurate observer.

I pray you to accept the assurances of
my respect and consideration.

TH: JEFFERSON

MR. DAVIS,
    Occoquan, *Virginia.*

PREFACE

HAVING employed four years and a half in travelling through the Southern States of *North America*, I was about to return home content with regulating imagination by reality, when the accidental perusal of those Travellers who had journeyed over the same ground, determined me to become a publisher. Of these some want taste, and others literature; some incapable of observation, count with profound gravity the number of miles from place to place; and others, intent only upon feeding, supply a bill of fare. A family likeness prevails through the whole. Their humour bears no proportion to their morbid drowsiness. We are seldom relieved from the langour of indifference, or the satiety of disgust; but in toiling through volumes of diffusive mediocrity, the reader commonly terminates his career by falling asleep with the writer.

In comparing this Volume with the volumes of my predecessors, the reader will find himself exempt from various persecutions.

1. I make no mention of my dinner, whether it was fish or flesh, boiled or roasted, hot or cold.

2. I never complain of my bed, nor fill the imagination of the reader with mosquitoes, fleas, bugs, and other nocturnal pests.

3. I make no drawings of old castles, old churches, old pent-houses, and old walls, which, undeserving of repair, have been abandoned by their possessors. Let them be sacred to the *Welch* Tourist, the *Scotch* Tourist, and *id genus omne*.

4. In treating common subjects, I do not accumulate magnificent epithets, and lose myself in figures.

That this Volume will regale curiosity while man continues to be influenced by his senses and affections, I have very little doubt. It will be recurred to with equal interest on the banks of the *Thames,* and those of the *Ohio*. There is no man who is not pleased in being told by another what he thought of the world, and what the world thought of him. This kind of biography, when characterized by simplicity and truth, has more charms for the multitude than a pompous history of the intrigues of courts, the negotiations of statesmen, and the devastation of armies.

The Memoirs of *Franklin* the printer, come more home to my feelings than the History of Sir *Robert Walpole's* Administration. I behold the concluding page of the one with the same eye of sorrow, that the Traveller in the woods of *America* casts upon the sun's departing ray; but the other is task-reading, and, in perusing it, I consult more the taste of the public, than my own disposition. Yet even Franklin studied his ease in with-holding his Memoirs from the world till he was beyond the reach of its censure; and I know no writers of eminence who have ventured to encounter the malice of ridicule by the publication of their own biography, but *Wakefield* whose loss the sons of learning are yet deploring, and *Kotzebue* who is still holding the mirror up to nature.

There are some who would conceal the situation to which my exigencies reduced me in *America;* but I should blush to be guilty of such ridiculous pride; and let the insolence of those who scorn an honest calling be repressed by remembering, that the time is not very remote when all conditions will be levelled; when the celebrated and obscure, the powerful and weak, shall all sink alike into one common grave.

Though my mode of life has not been favourable to the

cultivation of an elegant style, yet in what relates to the structure of my sentences, I shall not fear competition with those who have reposed from their youth under the shade of Academic bowers. He who can have recourse to the critical prefaces of *Dryden,* the voluble periods of *Addison,* the nervous sentences of *Johnson,* and the felicitous antitheses of *Goldsmith,* may spare himself the trouble of seeking that purity and decoration of language in a College, which may be found in his closet.*

In the progress of my work it will be discovered that I have not joined myself to that frantic crew of Deists, who would prostrate every institution, human or divine; and, though I dedicate my book to a republican, it is not the magistrate but the man, whom I address. I am no republican! No federalist! I have learned to estimate rightly the value of the *British* Constitution; and I think no system of government so perfect as that of King, Lords, and Commons.

A word more before I conclude. Should the critic de-

---

* While contemporary writers were wandering in imagination with *Ulysses* and *Æneas,* and growing giddy with the violence of poetical tempests, I was performing a sailor's duty in a ship of nine hundred tons, and encountering the gales of the promontory of *Africa.*

I have visited many places in the eastern section of the globe. I have been twice in *India.* I am familiar with *St. Helena,* and *Batavia,* and *Johanna,* and *Bombay,* and *Tillicherry,* and *Goa,* and *Cochin,* and *Anjengo.* I was four months at *Canton;* and I have toiled up the *Table Mountain* at the Cape of *Good Hope.*

Let me be forgiven this impulse *à me faire valoir.* It is what every small Traveller does. Behold the *Welch* Tourist! He crosses the *New Ferry,* enters the ale-house on its border—calls for pen and ink—lugs out his enormous common-place book—awes the family into silence by the profound wisdom of his looks—and solemnly sits down to fill a solemn chapter with the tempests that harassed him in navigating the SEVERN!!!

tect the vanity that not infrequently swells my periods, let him be assured that he cannot be more sensible of it than I. When a man becomes the historiographer of his own actions, he can scarcely avoid this error without degenerating into the opposite one of affected diffidence. I have often caught myself making my own panegyric; the fact is indisputable; yet it is still better to be vain than dull.

ERRATA

[Retained as in original Edition.]

Page 30-32, *dele* the Elegy, because neither gods, nor men, nor the stall of the bookseller, can tolerate mediocrity in poetry.
P. 67, for irrevalent *r.* irrelative. P. 73, for stagnant *r.* turbid. P. 114, for banks *r.* bank. P. 116, *dele* who. P. 204, for Centryphon *r.* Trypho. P. 208, for libere *r.* bibere. P. 257, for midnight *r.* balmy. P. 308, for Ominia *r.* Omnia.

TRAVELS &C

VOYAGE from BRISTOL to NEW-YORK

HAVING formed the resolution of visiting the United States, I repaired, December 15, 1797, from *Salisbury* to *Bristol,* with a view of embarking on board a Snow of two hundred tons, which lay at the Quay, and was bound to *New-York.* The Captain had purposed to sail the 20th of the same month, but it was not before January 7th of the new year, that the vessel moved from the wharf, when the spring-tide enabled her to proceed down the river.

For my passage, which was in the steerage, I had paid seven guineas to the merchants who chartered the vessel, and my mess, which was with two young gentlemen of my acquaintance, cost me only three pounds more. But, with this money, besides provisions, we purchased a stove, which, during the voyage, was a treasure to us. It not only fortified us against the cold, but we cooked our victuals upon it; and the drawer which was designed to hold the ashes, made an admirable oven.

Hence there was never any occasion for us to have recourse to the caboose; but, on the contrary, when the frequent gales of wind which we experienced caused the sea to break over the vessel, the cabin-boy solicited leave to dress his dinner on our fire. In relating these circumstances, I must claim the indulgence of the reader not to rank me among the courtiers of *Alcinous;* men, *fruges consumere nati.* My only motive is to suggest to the enterprising traveller at how small an expence he may be enabled to cross the *Atlantic.*

The cabin was by no means an enviable place. It offered neither accommodation nor society. Its passengers consisted of an Unitarian priest and family, and two itinerant merchants. The steerage groupe was composed of a good, jolly, *Somersetshire* farmer and his housekeeper, who were going to settle in *Pennsylvania,* of the two young gentlemen I have already mentioned, and myself. Having repeatedly crossed the Equator, and doubled the Cape of Good Hope, there is no occasion for me to say that the ocean was familiar to me; and that, while the other passengers were sick and dejected, I was in health and good spirits. To the roll of the vessel I was fully accustomed; but my companions not having gotten their sea legs on board, tumbled grievously about the decks. The library which I had brought with me, consisted of nearly three hundred volumes, and would have endeared me to any place. The Muses, whom I never ceased to woo, blessed me, I thought, not infrequently, with their nightly visitations; and I soothed my mind to tranquillity with the fancied harmony of my verse.

> *Ridentur mala qui componunt carmina: verum*
> *Gaudent scribentes, et se venerantur, et ultro,*
> *Si taceas, laudant; quidquid scripsere, beati.*
> Hor.*

Being an old sailor, I had provided myself with a cot, which, by making me insensible to the roll of the vessel, would, I thought, render my sleep more tranquil and undisturbed than a cabin. But I cannot say my slumbers the first night were very soft; for, hanging in the wake of the hatchway, the breeze from the deck made my situation very unpleasant. Foreseeing also that I was exposed to the deluge of every sea the brig should ship on the passage, I unhung my cot, and put it into a spare fore and aft cabin, which, to my satisfaction, I found, afterwards, was the only dry one in the steerage. The wind being favourable on getting under weigh, we profited from the occasion by shaking out the reefs, and shewing all our canvass to the breeze.

[* *Epist.*, II, 2, 106.]

The old housekeeper, the very type of Dame Leonarda in Gil Blas, was the first among the passengers that began to hold up her head; and the fourth day of our voyage she murdered an old hen to regale a poor sick gentleman, who thought he could relish some chicken broth. We had scarcely been out a week, when we experienced a gale of wind that was not less disastrous than tremendous. A sea which broke over the quarter washed a hencoop from its lashing, and drowned nearly three dozen of fowls. But it is an ill wind that blows nobody any good. The sailors made the fowls into an huge sea-pye of three decks, which they called the United States Man of War, and fed on it eagerly.

There was a carter in the vessel, who came on board to work his passage; but he did very little work. Whenever a porpoise or even a gull was visible, he considered it the presage of a storm, and became himself invisible till it was over. A report being circulated that the rats had left the vessel when in harbour, Coster Pearman concluded that they had done it by instinct; and, as an opinion prevails among sailors that a ship, on such an event, never gets safe to her port of desination, the booby gave himself up for lost. But hearing one night a rat scratch against the vessel's side, he ran upon deck in his shirt to proclaim it to the sailors, calling out with a joyful tone of voice, " Whoa! hoa! hoa! a rat! a rat!"

The two Brothers was a miserably sailing tub, and her passage a most tedious one. Head winds constantly prevailed, and scarcely a week elapsed without our lying-to more than once. To scud her was impracticable, as she would not steer small, and several times the Captain thought she was going to founder. Her cargo, which consisted of mill stones and old iron, made her strain so with rolling, that incessant pumping could hardly keep her free. She seemed to be fitted out by the parish; there was not a rope on board strong enough to hang a cat with. She had only one suit of sails, not a single spar, and her cordage was old. If a sail was split by the wind, there was no other alternative but to mend it; and when, after being out six weeks, we had sprung our fore top mast, we were compelled to reef it. The same day, I remember, we fell in with a schooner from New York, which we spoke. It was on the 18th of February. She was bound to St. Sebastian. The seamen being employed, I volunteered my services to pull an oar on board her, which were readily accepted. Her Captain received us politely, and regaled us with some cyder. She had left port only a fortnight; but it took the ill-fated Two Brothers a month to get thither. We parted with regret. The Captain of her was of a social, friendly disposition. As to our own skipper, he was passionately fond of visiting every vessel that he saw on the passage. If an old salt fish schooner hove in sight, he clamoured for his boarding-boots, and swore he would go to her if it were only to obtain a pint of molasses. Once, having hailed a vessel, he was justly rebuked. He told the Captain of her he would hoist out his boat and go to see him; but the man not approving, I suppose, his physiognomy, hauled aft his sheets and bore round up before the wind. The skipper had contracted these habits during the American war, when he commanded a small privateer; and he could not in his old age reclaim the foibles of his youth.

As we increased our longitude, the priest, in examining his barrels of white biscuit, found one of them emptied by other hands than his own. Suspicion fell on a sailor, whom he one day accused before the passengers, as he was standing at the helm. " Did you not steal my biscuit, sirrah!" said the parson. " I did, Sir," answered the fellow. " And what, pray, can you say in defence of yourself?" " Why, Sir, I can say—that when I crossed the Line, Neptune made me swear I would never eat brown bread when I could get white; and *your* barrel of *white* stood next *my barrel of brown.*" This reply of the sailor was so happy and unexpected, that to remain grave exceeded all powers of face. The roar of the sea was lost in the combined laughter that arose from the Captain, passengers, and ship's company. Farmer Curtis, whom the tythes exacted from him by the parson of his parish had nearly ruined, now revenged himself on the cloth by a peal of laughter that shook the ship from stem to stern; not even the priest could refrain from a smile; though, perhaps, it was rather a sardonic grin; a distortion of the countenance, without any gladness of heart.

On the 8th of March, we saw the Isles of Sile, and three days after weathered the breakers of Nantucket; from whence, coasting to the southward, we made Long Island, and ran up to Sandy Hook. The wind subsiding, we let go our anchor, and the next morning, at an early hour, I accompanied the Captain and two of the cabin passengers on shore. It was Sunday, March 18th.

On the parched spot, very properly called Sandy Hook, we found only one human habitation, which was a public house. The family consisted of an old woman, wife to the landlord, two young girls of homely appearance, a negro man and boy. While breakfast was preparing, I ascended, with my companions, the light house, which stood on the point of the Hook. It was lofty, and well furnished with lamps. On viewing the land round the dwelling of our host, I could not help thinking that he might justly exclaim with Selkirk:

"I'm monarch of all I survey,
My right there is none to dispute,
From the centre all round to the sea,
I am lord of the fowl and the brute."

The morning passed away not unpleasantly. The vivacity of the Captain enlivened our breakfast, which was prolonged nearly till noon; nor do I think we should have then risen from table, had not the Mate, who was left in charge of the snow, like a good seaman, hove short, and loosened his sails in readiness to avail himself of the breeze which had sprung up in our favour. The Captain, therefore, clamoured for the bill, and finished his last bowl of grog with the favorite toast of *Here's to the wind that blows, the ship that goes, and the lass that loves a sailor.*

In our progress to the town, we passed a British frigate lying at anchor. It was sunset, and the roll of the spirit-stirring drum brought to my recollection those scenes, that pomp, pride, and circumstance of glorious war, that makes ambition virtue.* We moored our vessel to one of the wharfs, and I rejoiced to find myself on a kindred shore.

* Shakespeare.

CHAP. I.

Pursuits at New-York. Interview with Mr. Burr. A Walk to Philadelphia. A Tribute to James Logan. Yellow Fever desolating the City. Embark for South-Carolina.

UPON my landing at *New-York*, my first care was to deliver a letter of recommendation which I had been favoured with by a friend to a merchant in the city; together with a volume of Travels from *Boston* to *Philadelphia,* which he had recently published.* But I cannot say that I was received with the urbanity I had anticipated. Neither my friend's letter, nor his book, could soften the features of the stern American; and were the world to read the volume with as little interest as he, it would soon be consigned to the peaceful shelf.

I was now to become the architect of my own fortune. Though on a kindred shore, I had not even an acquaintance to whom I could communicate my projects; the letter had failed me that was to decide my fortune at one blow, and I found myself solitary and sad among the crouds of a gay city.

[* Journal of an Excursion to the United States of North America in the Summer of 1794. By Henry Wansey, F. A. S. Salisbury, 1796.]

But I was not long depressed by melancholy reflections over my condition, for I found a friend in a man, who, having himself been unfortunate, could feel for another in adversity. A concurrence of circumstances had brought me into the company of Mr. *Caritat,** a bookseller, who, being made acquainted with my situation, addressed me with that warmth, which discovers a desire to be useful, rather than a wish to gratify curiosity.

He inquired into my projects. I told him that my scheme was to get into some family as a private tutor. A private Tutor! said he. Alas! the labour of Sisyphus in hell is not equal to that of a private Tutor in *America!* Why your project puts me in mind of young Mr. Primrose. And your exclamations, said I, remind me of his cousin in *London*. Just enough, rejoined Mr. *Caritat,* and let me examine you a little after the manner of his cousin.

Do you write a good hand, and understand all the intricacies of calculation? No. Then you will not do for a private Tutor. It is not your Latin and Greek, but your handwriting and cyphering, that will decide your

[* This was H. Caritat, of the title page, who later removed to Paris. Cf. Sabin, No. 5205. Bibliothèque Américaine & l'analyse des ouvrages scientifiques de ce pays, ainsi que de ceux des Européens qui y ont voyagé &. Paris; Caritat et Barrois Fils. 1807. 3 vols.]

character. Penmanship, and the figures of arithmetic, will recommend you more than logic and the figures of rhetoric. Can you passively submit to be called Schoolmaster by the children, and *Cool Mossa* by the negroes? No. Then you will not do for a private Tutor. Can you comply with the humility of giving only one rap at the door that the family may distinguish it is the Private Tutor; and can you wait half an hour with good humour on the steps, till the footman or housemaid condescends to open the door? No. Then you will not do for a private Tutor. Can you maintain a profound silence in company to denote your inferiority; and can you endure to be helped always the last at table, aye even after the clerk of the counting-house? No. Then you will not do for a private Tutor. Can you hold your eyes with your hands, and cry Amen! when grace is said; and can you carry the childrens' bibles and prayer-books to church twice every Sunday? No. Then you will not do for a private Tutor. Can you rise with the sun, and teach till breakfast; swallow your breakfast, and teach till dinner; devour your dinner, and teach till tea-time; and from tea-time to bed-time sink into insignificance in the parlour? No. Then you will not do for a private Tutor. Do you expect good wages? Yes. Then you will never do for a private Tutor.

No, sir, the place of private Tutor is the last I would recommend you; for as Pompey, when he entered a tyrant's dominions, quoted a verse from Euripides that signified his liberty was gone, so a man of letters, when he undertakes the tuition of a family in *America,* may exclaim he has lost his independence. Though not a countryman of your's, continued Mr. *Caritat,* I am from the same division of the globe, for I was born and educated in *France.* I should be happy to serve you, but I have not the hypocrisy to pretend that my offers of service are disinterested: interest blends itself with all human actions, and you, sir, have it in your power to be useful to me; I know you are skilled in French, because I have conversed with you in that language; of your own idiom you also discover an intimate acquaintance. *Vous etes donc mon homme.* I have just imported Buonaparte's campaign in *Italy,* from *Bourdeaux,* and the people are eager for a translation. Will you undertake the task? Will you translate the work for two hundred dollars? This is not the land of literature; booksellers in this country are not the patrons of authors, and therefore the remunerations for literary labour are not munificent. But the notoriety of Buonaparte will sell the work; and the translation make your name known beyond the mountains of the Blue Ridge. In a word, if you will translate the volume, I will pay you two hundred dollars.

Less declamation would have made me undertake the translation. I could hardly conceal my transports; and hugging the volume to my breast I danced home to my lodgings.

I lodged with a young man, who called himself a Physician, in Ferry-street, a melancholy alley impervious to the sun. Doctor de Bow, however, in huge gilt letters, adorned the entrance of the house:

> "And in his needy shop a tortoise hung,
> An alligator stuff'd and other skins
> Of ill-shap'd fishes; and about his shelves
> A beggarly account of empty boxes;
> Green earthen pots, bladders, and musty seeds,
> Remnants of packthread, and old cakes of roses
> Were thinly scattered to make up a shew." *

Of the medical skill of the Doctor I cannot pretend to judge; but he had little or no practice in his profession, notwithstanding he dressed in black, maintained a profound gravity, and wore green spectacles on his nose.

While the Doctor was reading the Life of Don Quixote, I was to be seen toiling at my translation like *Cruden* at his Concordance. The original was an octavo of four hundred pages, and every time I opened the volume it seemed to increase in bulk; but the golden

[* *Romeo and Juliet*, V, 1, 42-48.]

dream of reputation fortified my diligence, and I corrected the proof-sheets with lively sensibility.

Emolument, and an avidity of reputation, are two powerful incentives to literary industry; and I prosecuted my translation with so much diligence, that on the fourth of June it was ushered into the literary world amidst the acclamations of the Democrats, and the revilings of the Federalists. This was to me extraordinary, for I had professed myself of neither party, but declared my intention never to meddle with the politics of a country, in which I had neither a fixed dwelling, nor an acre of land.

About this period, my friend the Doctor relinquished his house, and rented a little medicinal shop of a Major Howe, who was agreeably situated in Cherry-street. As the Major took boarders, I accompanied the Doctor to his house, determined to eat, drink, and be merry over my two hundred dollars. With some of the well-stamped coin I purchased a few dozen of Madeira, and when the noontide heat had abated, I quaffed the delicious liquor with the Major and the Doctor under a tree in the garden.

Major Howe, after carrying arms through the revolutionary war, instead of reposing upon the laurels he had acquired, was compelled to open a boarding-house in *New-York*, for the maintenance of his wife and children. He was a member of the Cincinnati, and not a little proud of his Eagle. But I thought the motto to his badge of *Omnia reliquit servare Rempublicam,* was not very appropriate; for it is notorious that few Americans had much to leave when they accepted commissions in the army. *Victor ad aratrum redit* would have been better.

In principles, my military friend was avowedly a Deist, and by tracing the effect to the cause, I shall expose the pernicious tendency of a book which is read with avidity. The Major was once commanding officer of the fortress at *West Point,* and by accident borrowed of a subaltern the history of the Decline and Fall of the Roman Empire. He read the work systematically, and a diligent perusal of that part which relates to the progress of Religion, caused him to become a Sceptic, and reject all belief in revelation. Before this period the Major was a constant attendant on the Established Church, but he now enlisted himself under the banners of the Infidel *Palmer,* who delivers lectures on Deism at *New-York,* and is securing for himself and followers considerable grants of land in hell.

My translation introduced me to the acquaintance of some distinguished characters in *New-York,* and among others that caressed me was the celebrated Colonel *Burr,* who was in the late election chosen for the office of Vice-President of the United States. The letters interspersed through this narrative will show my intimacy with Mr. *Burr,* whom I have *seen in his social hour;* and of whose political character I am perhaps enabled to give the prominent features. The slave of no party, and unbiassed by personal affections, my portrait shall be free as it is unprejudiced.

To a genius of singular perspicacity, Mr. *Burr* joins the most bland and conciliating manners. With a versatility of powers, of which, perhaps, *America* furnishes no other example, he is capable of yielding an undivided attention to a single object of pursuit. Hence we find him at the close of the Revolutionary War, in which he took a very honourable part, and in the fatigues of which he bore no common share, practising the law with unrivalled brilliancy and success. Indeed his distinguished abilities attracted so decided a leaning of the Judges in his favour, a deference for his opinions so strongly marked, as to excite in no small degree the jealousy of the bar. So strong was the impression made by the general respect for his opinions, that exclamations of despair were frequently heard to escape the lips of the Counsel whose fortune it was to be opposed by the eloquence of Mr. *Burr.* I am aware that this language wears the colour of panegyric; but the recollections which the facts must excite in the breasts of his candid rivals, will corroborate its accuracy.

For a short period Mr. *Burr* acted as Attorney-General to the State; but his professional reputation, already at the acme of splendour, could derive no new lustre from the office. It however should be remembered that in State prosecutions, a disposition to aggravate the enormities of the accused was never attributed to him.

At length Mr. *Burr* was removed by the Legislature of the State to the Senate of the United States. The deliberations of that body being conducted in secret, the public possessed but slender means of knowing and appreciating the merits of individual members. But it is certain, from the lead he took in some of its most important transactions, and from the deference shewn his opinions by his senatorial colleagues, that the character for ability which he had previously acquired, must have been there well sustained. It was, indeed, universally acknowledged, that no other State was so respectably represented as the State of *New-York,* in the combined talents of Mr. *Burr* and Mr. *King.*

His time of service expiring, Mr. Burr again returned to the exercise of his profession with a facility which would induce a belief that his legal pursuits had never been interrupted.

Such are the outlines of the character of the man who, cultivating literature himself, loved to encourage it in others; and who, with a condescension little known to patrons, sought out my obscure lodgings in a populous city, and invited me to his house.

I found Mr. *Burr* at breakfast, reading my translation over his coffee. He received me with that urbanity which, while it precludes familiarity, banishes restraint; and discovered by his conversation, that he was not less skilled in elegant literature, than the science of graciousness and attraction.

Mr. *Burr* introduced me to his daughter, whom he has educated with uncommon care; for she is elegant without ostentation, and learned without pedantry. At the time that she dances with more grace than any young lady of *New York,* Miss *Theodosia Burr* speaks *French* and *Italian* with facility, is perfectly conversant with the writers of the *Augustan age,* and not unacquainted with the language of the Father of Poetry. *Martel,* a Frenchman, has dedicated a volume of his productions to Miss *Burr,* with the horatian epithet of " *dule decus."* *

[* Probably Michel Martel, who published at New York, 1791, *Elements: New Essays on Education. A Selection of Bon Mots* &c.]

Fortune had now opened to me *les entrées* of the house of Mr. *Burr,* to whose table and library I had the most unrestrained access. But Mr. *Burr* did not stop here; he proposed to me the study of the law, which I imprudently declined, and thus neglected to take that *flood in the tide of my affairs* which led immediately to fortune. A student of the law could not have formed himself on a better model than Mr. *Burr;* for at the same time that he was perhaps the most skilled of any man in the practice, he was also the most eloquent:

Του κ'απο γλωσσης μελιτος γλυκιων ρεεν αυδή.

The favorable reception given to the campaign in *Italy,* of which the whole impression was soon diffused through the different States of the Union, animated *Caritat* with courage for another publication; and few men knew better how to gratify present curiosity, by directing his attention to temporary subjects.

In the preceding winter an occurrence had happened of which the public had not abated their eagerness to know the particulars. A *German* by the name of *Ferdinand Lowenstoff* had become enamoured of a young girl named *Elizabeth Falkenham,* a native of *New York. Ferdinand* was forty, but *Elizabeth* had scarcely seen sixteen summers. *Ferdinand,* notwithstanding the disparity of their years, found means to win the affections of *Elizabeth,* who consented to marry him; but it was judged expedient to defer their marriage till the return of *Elizabeth's* brother-in-law, from *Germany,* who had left his child under her care. In the meantime love prevailed over prudence, and the lover unloosed the virgin zone of his yielding fair. At length the brother returned from *Germany,* but would not consent to the marriage, and to release himself from the importunities of *Ferdinand,* confined his sister-in-law to her chamber. The indignation of the lover was inflamed, and to banish from his mind an object whom he could not obtain, he married a *French* lady from *Guadaloupe,* remarkable for the beauty of her person, and the vivacity of her conversation. But the charms of a newer object, however lovely and eloquent, could not obliterate the impression which *Elizabeth* had made: he pined for her in secret, and became a victim to melancholy.

In this harassed state of mind *Ferdinand* continued some months, when a letter was privately delivered him, in the superscription of which he recognized the hand-writing of *Elizabeth.* It was short but emphatical. *"I am pregnant, and resolved on death!"*

Ferdinand, far from discouraging, fortified *Elizabeth* in her resolution by professing an earnest desire himself to share her fate, and seek an oblivion also of his own woes in a voluntary death. The reply to the letter in which *Ferdinand* desires to die with this unhappy girl, is an injunction to break without delay his union with visible nature, to rush before his Maker " with all his imperfections on his head." It goes further; it proposes to add the crime of murder to that of suicide.

" But why recal your resolution because of
" the child of my womb? Let it not see the
" light of a world that has nothing but misery
" for its portion; come to me this night! Bring
" with thee poison! Bring with thee pistols!
" And when the clock strikes twelve we'll both
" become immortal! "

From this it is plain that *Ferdinand* was at first held in suspense between contrary impulses; but his mind was not long diverted from its purpose, for contriving an interview with *Elizabeth* the same night, he first shot her with a pistol, and afterwards himself. The fatal event took place at a house in the Bowery, where the lovers were found weltering in their blood, and letters explaining the motive of their rash conduct were placed on a table. Such deliberate suicide was perhaps, unexampled, and the letters that had passed between the unhappy pair, I dilated into a volume, which *Caritat* published to the emolument of us both, and, I hope, without injury to the world.

Far be it from me to insult over the ashes of the dead; but I consider it a species of moral obligation to make mention that *Ferdinand* was not only insensible to all the purposes of piety, but rejected all belief in Revelation. Let the reader impress this circumstance on his mind; let him contemplate the wretchedness of Deistical principles. Had he given to piety an early ascendancy over his heart, he might have withheld *Elizabeth* from plungng into the vale of misery; he would have sounded in her ears the holy admonition, *Return and live, for why wilt thou die!*

To the memory of these unfortunate lovers I wrote an elegy, which, produced from sympathy for their fate, may, perhaps, excite the softer emotions in the breasts of my readers.

ELEGY to the Memory of FERDINAND and ELIZABETH.

WHERE wand'ring ghosts their vigils keep at night,
And dance terrific by the moon's pale light;
Where gloomy yews their sable branches wave,
And cast their shadow o'er the rising grave,
Together rest in death's profound repose
These hapless victims to love's tender woes.
  That form which once with every charm was blest,
To touch the heart, and break the gazer's rest;
Those eyes that sparkled once with love's bright fire,
That voice which sung responsive to the lyre:
That face which once, with sweetly-soothing smiles,
Beam'd forth expression, and displayed its wiles,

Now lifeless rests beneath the clay-cold ground,
O'er which grim spectres take their nightly round;
Where the hoarse raven flaps his leaden wing,
Where Philomel was never heard to sing,
But where the owl, with melancholy strain,
Does to the moon in solitude complain.

  O! you, whose breasts have felt the pangs of love,
If e'er my verse your sympathy could move,
Here give your sorrows; o'er the ashes weep
Of these sad lovers, locked in death's cold sleep.

  Sunk are those hearts that once with vivid glow,
Melted in mutual tenderness of woe;
Clos'd are the eyes that, bright with living fire,
Spoke the sweet eloquence of soft desire:
Mute are those lips, that oft-times would disclose
The moving story of impending woes:
Now lifeless rest, yet bleeding from the wound,
This hapless pair beneath the mould'ring ground.

  Ah! cruel brother of a charge too good,
'Twas you who caus'd this pair to shed their blood,
To seek an end to weight of human woe,
To plunge despairing in the vale below,
To court a death that weeping crowds lament,
Ah! could not beauty make thy soul relent?
Could not the plaints of love once reach thy heart?
Could not the weeping eye a grief impart?
Could not ELIZA's voice thy pity move;
But, must her choice thy furious lips reprove?
Oh! when thy eyes death's horrid form shall meet,
And when thy hearse moves slowly through the street,
May not a tear thy memory demand,
But call reproaches from this gen'rous land!
A land, where love's inflicting power extends,
Where the proud youth at beauty's altar bends;
Where the muse smiles, when *Barlow** strikes the lyre,
In bold sublimity of epic fire.

    [* Joel Barlow, author of the *Vision of Columbus.*]

Yet shall each muse her tuneful tribute bring,
Sweep the sad harp, and mournful touch the string;
Rehearse the woes that mingled with their love,
And ev'ry heart to tears of sorrow move.
　Ye swains and nymphs, with health and beauty crown'd,
Scarce let your footsteps press the hallow'd ground,
When the loud bell, slow-echoing from the walls,
Your minds to worship or to prayer calls;
But treading lightly o'er the lovers' grave,
Drop the sad tear their mem'ries from you crave.

My occupations at *New-York*, however agreeable, did not repress my desire to explore the continent before me; and I thought it best to travel while I had some crowns left in my purse. I felt regret at the thought of separating from the Doctor, whom I was attached to from habit; but the Doctor soon relieved me by saying, he would accompany me whithersoever I went; that no man loved travelling better than he, and that he would convert his medicine into money to defray his expences on the road.

But tell me, said the Doctor, are you fond of walking? I assured him no person could be more so. Then, resumed he, let us each provide ourselves with a good cudgel, and begin our journey on foot. I will put a case of instruments into my pocket, and you can slip into your's the campaign of *Buonaparte* in *Italy*.

But whither, replied I, do you propose

to go; and what, I beseech you, is the object of your travelling? To see the world, assuredly, said he; to eat, drink and laugh away care on the road. How, Doctor, said I, would you approve of a walk to *Philadelphia?* I should like it of all things, said the Doctor. In our way to it we should go through the place of my birth; you have heard, I guess, of *Hackinsac;* and at *Philadelphia* I could get somebody to introduce me to the great Doctor *Rush*. All we have to do is to send on our trunks in the coach, and trudge after them on foot.

Our resolution was no sooner taken than executed. The Doctor got an apothecary, who lived opposite, to purchase what few drugs were contained in his painted drawers; and having dispatched our trunks forward by the coach, we began our journey to *Philadelphia*.

Having crossed the *Hudson,* which separates *York-Island* from the shore of the *Jerseys,* we were landed at a Tavern * delightfully situated on the bank of the river. The Doctor having once reduced a fractured leg

---

* Every public-house in the United States, however contemptible, is dignified by the name of Tavern.

[* In Virginia, at this time, taverns were often called Ordinaries. Cf. La Rochefoucauld, *Travels in North America, 1795, 1796,* and *1797*. London. 1799. Vol. II, p. 68—" After having spent nearly the whole day at M. de Rieux's we went ten miles farther on to *Bird-ordinary* "]

for the landlord, proposed dining at the Tavern: he will certainly charge us nothing, said he, for I once reduced his leg, when the Tibia and Fibula were both badly fractured. It was a nice case, and I will put him in mind of it.

But *you charged him, Doctor, did you not,* said I. No matter for that, replied he. I should have been expelled from the College of Whigs had I not put in my claim.

I represented to the Doctor that no man who respected himself would become an eleemosynary guest at the table of another, when he had money to defray his wants. That to remind another of past services discovered a want of humanity; and that a mean action, though it may not torment the mind at the moment it was done, never fails afterwards to bring compunction: for the remembrance of it will present itself like a spectre to the imagination.

The landlord of the tavern was a portly man, who in the middle of the day was dressed in a loose night-gown and mocossins;* he recognised the Doctor, whom he shook heartily by the hand, and turning to a man in company, said, "they may talk of Doctor *Rush,* Doctor *Mitchell,* or Doctor Devil, but I maintain Doctor *De Bow* is the greatest Doctor of them all."

* Mocossins are Indian shoes, made of deer-skin.

It was difficult to refrain from laughing aloud; but the speech of the landlord inspired the Doctor with very different emotions; he made an inclination of his head, adjusted his spectacles, and assumed a profound look that assented to the justness of the remark.

What, gentlemen, said the landlord, would you chuse for your dinner? It is now the hottest part of the day, and if you are walking to *Newark,* you will find the evening more pleasant. How comes on trade, Doctor, at *New-York?* I warrant you have got your share.

Why, Mr. *Clinch,* replied the Doctor, I cannot complain. There have been several cases of fever to which I was called. And the patients were right, said Mr. *Clinch,* for they could not have called a better Doctor had they sent over the four quarters of the globe for him. Well, it is true, God sends this country fevers, but he also sends us Doctors who are able to cure them. It is like the State I was born in: *Virginia* is infested with snakes, but it abounds with roots to cure their bite. Come, walk in, gentlemen, walk in. I will get dinner ready directly.

Our dinner was a miserable one; but the landlord seasoned his dishes with flattery, and the Doctor found it very palatable. We went forward in the cool; nor did my friend hesitate to pay his club towards two dollars for our repast: it was high, the Doctor whispered, but, continued he, when a man's consequence is known at a tavern it always inflames the bill.

It was our original design to have gone through *Hackinsack,* a little village that claimed the honor of my companion's nativity; but it was getting late; the road to it was circuitous, and we wished much that night to travel to *Elizabeth Town.* The Doctor consoled himself for not visiting his family by observing that no man was a prophet at home.

We did not stop long at *Newark,* but prosecuted our walk, after taking shelter from a shower of rain in one of its sylvan habitations.*
The sun, which had been obscured, again gladdened the plains; and the birds which had ceased awhile singing, again renewed their harmony.

We reached *Elizabeth Town* a little while after the stage-coach. My companion, being

---

* The houses at *Newark* are generally shaded by clusters of trees. One of our modern tourists would devote probably a dozen pages to the description of *Newark,* which is famed for the richest cider, and the largest cobbler's stall in the United States of *America.* It supplies also an old house on a hill, which, unworthy of repair, is moulding to dust; but which has enough of the walls remaining to furnish an English tourist with an admirable plate. To such *Tourists* I consign *Newark,* and other places on the road, which the *Traveller* beholds and dismisses from his mind with frigid indifference.

somewhat fatigued, retired early to bed, but I devoted a great part of the night to the refined pleasures of reading and reflection. There is no life so unsettled but a lover of reading will find leisure for the acquisition of knowledge, an acquisition that depends not on either seasons or place. To know the value of time, we must learn to appreciate every particle of it; and remember that moments, however trifling in appearance, form the year by accumulation.

When I went to bed there was little sleep to be obtained; for a huge mastiff in the yard, notwithstanding the Doctor put his head out of the window and vociferated to him repeatedly, did not remit barking the whole of the night. We therefore rose without being called, and pursued our journey to *Princetown*, a place more famous for its College than its learning.

The road from *Prince-town* to *Trenton* offers little matter for speculation. I know that in some places there were battles fought between the British and their revolted Colonists; but the recollection of it tends to no use, and, I am sure, it cannot be pleasing.

At *Trenton*, the Doctor, who was afflicted with sore eyes, declined proceeding any further. It was to no purpose that I expostulated with him on the folly of his conduct, and urged that we had not many more miles to travel. The son of *Paracelsus* was inexorable, and it only remained for me to perform the last office of friendship, which was to tie a bandage over his eyes, and lead him blindfolded to his room; in our way to which, happening to stumble, the Doctor comically enough observed, *When the blind leads the blind, they shall both of them fall.*

From *Trenton* I was conveyed over the *Delaware* in the ferry-boat, with an elderly man, clad in the garb of a Quaker. His looks beamed benignity, and his accents breathed kindness; but, as the great Master of Life observes, there is no art can find the mind's construction in the face.

We had scarce landed on the opposite bank of the river, when a poor cripple in a soldier's jacket, advanced towards the Quaker, holding both his crutches in one hand, and taking half a hat from his head with the other:—Bestow your charity, cried the beggar, on a poor worn-out soldier, who fought for your liberty during a long war, and got wounded by a *Hessian* at the very place you have just left. Refuse not your charity to an old soldier in distress.

Alas! exclaimed the Quaker, this comes of war. Shame on our nature. Beasts live in concord, men only disagree. Had thou taken the advice of scripture, thou wouldest have escaped thy wounds!

What, Master, is that?

Why, Friend, if a man smite thee on one cheek, turn to him the other.

And were you to take the advice of scripture, you would not refuse me your alms.

What, Friend, is that?

Why, when a man wants to borrow of thee, turn not thou away.

I remember no such passage, replied the Quaker.

It is in the New Testament, said the beggar.

The text has been corrupted, cried the Quaker, hastening away through a field.

Won't you give me a copper? bawled the beggar, limping after the Quaker.

Charity begins at home, said the Quaker, accelerating his pace.

The Lord help thee, exclaimed the beggar, halting almost breathless on his crutch. But here perhaps is a gentleman who has more of the milk of human kindness.

To become acquainted with human life, the traveller must not mingle only with the sons of opulence and ease; these know no greater fatigue than the hurry of preparation for a ball, and experience no higher mortification than the disappointment of pride. Such beings who pass their days in solemn pomp and plenty, can display no examples of fortitude, of serenity, or patience; their wishes are anticipated, and their mandates obeyed. It is among the children of adversity that we must look for resignation under misfortune; it is from the indigent only we can be instructed to bear calamities without repining.

Impressed with this conviction, I entered into discourse with the cripple, whom I found to be a man not without reflection. He had seen better days, and hoped for their return. Though my present appearance, said he, shews I am in the most wretched state of poverty, there was a time when I knew the comforts of a home and fireside. These are past, but there is a pleasure in the recollection of them; for no man who has enjoyed the comforts of life is ever without the hope that he shall enjoy them again.

I had walked about a mile along the bank of the *Delaware* when the coach to *Philadelphia* overtook me, and finding the road dusty I complied with the invitation of the driver to get into the vehicle. At *Bristol* we took up two young women, clad in the habit of the Quakers, whom I soon, however, discovered to be girls of the town; and who, under pretence of shewing me a letter, discovered their address.

A spacious road conducted us to *Philadelphia,* which we entered at Front-street. I had expected to be charmed with the animation of the American metropolis;* but a melan-

* *Philadelphia* in 1798 was the Capital of the United States.

choly silence prevailed in the streets, the principal houses were abandoned, and none but *French* people were to be found seeking pleasure in society.

The coach stopped at the sign of the Sorrel-Horse, in Second-street, where I heard only lamentations over the Yellow Fever, which had displayed itself in Water-street, and was spreading its contagion.

It costs no more to go to a good tavern than a bad one; and I removed my trunks, which I found at the Stage-office, to the French Hotel in the same street. Mr. *Pecquet* received me with a bowing mien, and called *Jeannette* for the *passepartout* to shew me his apartments. He exercised all his eloquence to make me lodge in his hotel. He observed that his house was not like an American house; that he did not in summer put twelve beds in one room; but that every lodger had a room to himself, and Monsieur, added he very solemnly, *"Ici il ne sera pas necessaire de sortir de votre lit, comme chez les Americains, pour aller a la fenetre, car Jeannette n'oublie jamais de mettre un pot de chambre sous le lit."*

Monsieur *Pecquet* assured me his dinners were of a superior kind, and finding I was an Englishman, observed with a bow, that he could furnish me with the best porter brewed in the city of *Philadelphia*.

Such professions as these, what unhoused

traveller could resist? I commended Monsieur *Pecquet* on his mode of living, reciprocated compliments with him, chose the chamber I thought the coolest, and the same night found myself at supper with a dozen *French* ladies and gentlemen, who could not utter a word of *English*,* and with whom I drank copious libations of that porter which my host had enlarged upon with such elegance of declamation.

My first visit was to the library. A bust of Doctor *Franklin* stands over the door, whose head it is to be lamented the librarian cannot place on his own shoulders. Of the two rooms the *Franklinian* Library is confined to books in the *English* language, but the *Loganian* Library comprehends every classical work in the ancient and modern languages. I contemplated with reverence the portrait of *James Logan,* which graces the room.

———*magnum et venerabile nomen.*

I could not repress my exclamations. As I am only a stranger, said I, in this country, I

[* Cf. La Rochefoucauld, *Travels in North America* &c. London. 1799. Vol. II, pp. 17-18. "To the port of Norfolk, above any other in the United States, came the greatest number of colonists escaped from Saint-Domingo at the commencement of their troubles. They have dispersed through the other parts of America, where there is hardly a town that does not reckon some of their number among its inhabitants."]

affect no enthusiasm on beholding the statues of her Generals and Statesmen. I have left a church filled with them on the shore of *Albion* that have a prior claim to such feeling. But I here behold the portrait of a man whom I consider so great a benefactor to Literature, that he is scarcely less illustrious than its munificent patrons of *Italy;* his soul has certainly been admitted to the company of the congenial spirits of a *Cosmo* and *Lorenzo* of *Medicis.* The Greek and Roman authors forgotten on their native banks of the *Ilyssus* and *Tiber,* delight by the kindness of *Logan* the votaries to learning on those of the *Delaware.*

It has been observed, I believe, by *Horace,* that there have lived many heroes not inferior in prowess to those of the *Iliad,* but that for want of a bard to sing their feats, they might as well have not achieved them. But how many characters are now unknown, who susceptible only of the social energies, deserve to be remembered more than an *Agamemnon,* or an *Achilles.* What man ever rose from the *Iliad* with an accession of benevolence? but who would not be better for reading the life of a *Kyrle,** of whom nothing can be now known but what is furnished by an episode in a poem.

---

* The Man of *Ross.* [Philanthropist. " Owes his fame largely to the eulogy of him which Pope introduced into his third Moral Epistle (1732) on information supplied by Jacob Tonson."]

Of the readers of this volume there are few who have ever heard mention made of *James Logan* of *Philadelphia;* a man whose benevolent actions aspire far higher than any *Greek* or *Roman* fame.

James Logan was born in *Scotland,* about the year 1674. He was one of the people called *Quakers,* and accompanied *William Penn* in his last voyage to *Pennsylvania.* For many years of his life he was employed in public business, and rose to the offices of Chief Justice and Governor of the Province; but he felt always an ardour of study, and by husbanding his leisure, found time to write several treatises in *Latin,* of which one on the Generation of Plants, was translated into English by *Dr. Fothergill.**

Being *declined in the vale of years,* Mr. *Logan* withdrew from the tumult of public business to the solitude of his country-seat, near *Germantown,* where he found tranquillity among his books, and corresponded with the most distinguished literary characters of Europe. He also made a version of *Cicero de Senectute,* which was published with notes by the late Dr. *Franklin.*† Whether *Franklin* was qualified to write annotations on *Tully's*

[* *Experimenta et Meletemata,* etc. Leyden 1739; London 1747.]

[† *De Senectute.* Philadelphia 1744, 1758, 1812, (the two last in Dr. Franklin's name); London 1750, 1778; Glasgow 1751, 1758.]

noble treatise, will admit of some doubt; for the genius of *Franklin* was rather scientific than classical.

Mr. *Logan* died in 1751, at the venerable age of seventy-seven; leaving his library, which he had been fifty years collecting, to the people of *Pennsylvania;* a monument of his ardour for the promotion of literature.*

It was at this library that during three successive afternoons I enjoyed that calm and pure delight which books afford. But on the fourth I found access denied, and that the librarian had fled from the yellow fever, which spread consternation through the city.

Of the fever I may say that it momentarily

---

* The following extract from Mr. Logan's will cannot fail to interest the curious in literature:

"In my library, which I have left to the city, of *Phila-*
"*delphia*, for the advancement and facilitating of classical
"learning, are above 100 volumes of authors in folio, all in
"*Greek*, with mostly their versions. *All the Roman Classics*
"*without exception*. All the whole *Greek* Mathematicians,
"viz. *Archimedes, Euclid, Ptolemy,* both his Geography and
"Almagest, which I had in *Greek* (with *Theon's* Commentary
"in folio, above 700 pages) from my learned friend *Fabricius,*
"who published 14 volumes of his *Bibliotheque Grecque* in
"quarto, in which, after he had finished his account of
"*Ptolemy,* on my inquiring of him at *Hamburgh* in 1772,
"how I should find it, having long sought for it in vain
"in *England;* he sent it me out of his own library, telling me
"it was so scarce, that neither prayers nor price could pur-
"chase it. Besides, there are many of the most valuable
"*Latin* authors, and a great number of modern mathema-
"ticians, with all the three editions of *Newton,* Dr. *Wallis,*
"*Halley, &c.*"

"JAMES LOGAN."

became more destructive. Sorrow sat on every brow, and nothing was to be seen but coffins carried through the streets unattended by mourners. Indeed it was not a time to practise modes of sorrow, or adjust the funeral rites; but the multitude thought only of escaping from the pestilence that wasted at noon-day, and walked in darkness.

This was a period to reflect on the vanity of human life, and the mutability of human affairs. *Philadelphia,* which in the spring was a scene of mirth and riot, was in the summer converted to a sepulchre for the inhabitants. The courts of law were shut, and no subtile lawyer could obtain a client; the door of the tavern was closed, and the drunkard was without strength to lift the bowl to his lips: no theatre invited the idle to behold the mimic monarch strut his hour upon the stage; the dice lay neglected on the gaming-table, nor did the dancing-room re-echo with the steps of the dancer: man was now humbled! Death was whetting his arrows, and the graves were open. All jollity was fled. The hospital-cart moved slowly on where the chariot before had rolled its rapid wheels; and the coffin-makers were either nailing up the coffins of the dead, or giving dreadful note of preparation by framing others for the dying, where lately the mind at ease had poured forth its tranquility in songs; where the loud laugh had reverberated, and where the animating sound of music had stolen on the ear.—In this scene of consternation, the negroes were the only people who could be prevailed on to assist the dying, and inter those who were no more. Their motive was obvious; they plundered the dead of their effects, and adorned themselves in the spoils of the camp of the King of Terrors. It was remarked to me by a lady of *Philadelphia,* that the negroes were never so well clad as after the yellow fever.

I had been a week at *Philadelphia,* without hearing any tidings of my friend the Doctor, when walking one evening past the Franklin's-Head, I recognised him conversing with a stranger in the front room. The physician had arrived only that evening. He had staid six days at *Trenton,* leading a pleasant, convalescent life; from whence he had written me a letter, which I found afterwards at the post office. We were rejoiced to meet each other, and the better to exchange minds, I accompanied the Doctor into Arch-street, where taking possession of the porch of an abandoned dwelling, we sat conversing till a late hour. The most gloomy imagination cannot conceive a scene more dismal than the street before us: every house was deserted by those who had strength to seek a less baneful atmosphere; unless-where parental fondness prevailed over self-love. Nothing was heard but either the groans of the dying, the lamentations of the survivors, the hammers of the coffin-makers, or the howling of the domestic animals, which those who fled from the pestilence had left behind, in the precipitancy of their flight. A poor cat came to the porch where I was sitting with the Doctor, and demonstrated her joy by the caresses of fondness. An old negro-woman was passing at the same moment with some pepper-pot * on her head. With this we fed the cat that was nearly reduced to a skeleton; and prompted by a desire to know the sentiments of the old negro-woman, we asked her the news. God help us, cried the poor creature, very bad news. Buckra die in heaps. By and bye nobody live to buy pepper-pot, and old black woman die too.

I would adduce this as a proof, that calamities usually move us as they regard our interest. The negro-woman lamented the ravages of the fever, because it prevented the sale of her pepper-pot.

Finding all business suspended at *Philadelphia,* and the atmosphere becoming hourly more noisome, we judged it prudent to leave the city without delay; and finding a vessel at the wharfs ready to sail for *Charleston,* in *South Carolina,* we agreed for the passage, and put our luggage on board.

* Tripe seasoned with pepper.

Having taken leave of Monsieur *Pecquet,* whose excellent dinners had enhanced him in the opinion of the Doctor, we on the 22nd of *September,* 1798, went on board, and bade adieu to *Philadelphia,* which was become a *Golgotha.*

The vessel having hauled out into the stream, we weighed with a fair wind, and shaped our course down the serpentine, but beautiful river of the *Delaware.* Our cabin was elegant, and the fare delicious. I observed the Doctor's eyes brighten at the first dinner we made on board, who expressed to me a hope that we might be a month on the passage, as he wished to eat out the money the captain had charged him.

The first night the man at the helm fell asleep, and the tide hove the vessel into a cornfield, opposite *Wilmington;* so that when we went upon deck in the morning, we found our situation quite pastoral. We floated again with the flood-tide, and at noon let go our anchor before *Newcastle.*

It took us two days to clear the Capes. The banks of the *Delaware* had been extolled to me as the most beautiful in the world; but I thought them inferior to those of the *Thames.*

We were now at sea, bounding on the waves of the *Atlantic.* Of our passengers the most agreeable was an old *French* gentleman from *St. Domingo.* Monsieur *Lartigue,* to the most perfect good breeding joined great knowledge of mankind, and at the age of sixty had lost none of his natural gaiety. It was impossible to be dejected in the company of such a man. If any person sung on board, he would immediately begin capering; and when the rest were silent, he never failed to sing himself.

Nothing very remarkable happened in our passage, unless it be worthy of record that one morning the captain suffered his fears to get the better of his reason and mistook a *Virginian* sloop for a *French* privateer; and another day the mate having caught a dolphin, Mr. *Lartigue* exclaimed, *Il faut qu'il soit ragouti.*

After a passage of five days we came to an anchor in *Rebellion Roads,* from which we could plainly discern the spires and houses of *Charleston;* and the following day we stood towards *Fort Johnson,* which no vessels are suffered to pass without being examined.

Here the Port Physician came on board, with orders for us to perform quarantine a fortnight, to the great joy of the Doctor, who had not yet eaten half of what he wished to eat on board. Monsieur *Lartigue* had abundantly stocked himself with confitures and wine; and I doubt not but the Doctor still remembers the poignancy of his preserved cherries, and the zest of his claret.

CHAP. II.

Projects at Charleston.—Solemnity the Mask of Ignorance.—Interview with a Planter and his Lady.—The Erudition of a Professor.—A new and desirable Acquaintance.—College Toils.—A Journey on foot from Charleston to Coosohatchie.

I LANDED at *Charleston* with Doctor *De Bow,* who had clad himself in his black suit, and though a young man, wore a monstrous pair of spectacles on his nose. Adieu jollity! adieu laughter! the Doctor was without an acquaintance on a strange shore, and he had no other friend but his Solemnity to recommend him. It was to no purpose that I endeavoured to provoke him to laughter by my remarks; the Physician would not even relax his risible muscles into a smile.

The Doctor was right. In a few days he contrived to hire part of a house in Union-street; obtained credit for a considerable quantity of drugs; and only wanted a chariot to equal the best Physician in *Charleston.*

The Doctor was in possession of a voluble tongue; and I furnished him with a few *Latin* phrases, which he dealt out to his hearers with an air of profound learning. He generally concluded his speeches with *Nullius addictus jurare in verba magistri!* *

Wishing for some daily pursuit, I advertised in one of the papers for the place of Tutor in a respectable family; not omitting to observe that the advertiser was the translator of *Buonaparte's* Campaign in *Italy*. The editor of the Gazette assured me of an hundred applications; and that early the next morning I should not be without some. His predictions were verified; for the following day, on calling at the office, I found a note left from a Planter who lived a mile from the town, desiring me to visit him that afternoon at his house. I went thither accordingly. Every thing indicated opulence and ease. Mr. H—— received me with the insolence of prosperity. You are, said he, the person who advertised for the place of Tutor in a respectable family? I answered with a bow.

Planter. What, Sir, are your qualifications?

Tutor. I am competently skilled, Sir, in the *Latin* and *French* languages, not unacquainted with *Greek,* conversant with Geography, and accustomed to composition in my vernacular idiom.

Planter. But if you possess all *that there* learning, how comes it you could not get into some College, or School.

Tutor. Why, Sir, it is found even in Col-

[* Horace, *Epist*, I, 1, 14.]

leges that dunces triumph, and men of letters are disregarded by a general combination in favour of dulness.

Planter. Can you *drive* well, Sir? *

Tutor. Drive, Sir, did you say? I really do not comprehend you.

Planter. I mean, Sir, can you keep your scholars in order?

Tutor. Yes, Sir, if they are left entirely to my direction.

Planter. Ah! that would not be. Mrs. H——, who is a woman of extensive learning, (she lost a fine opportunity once of learning *French*, and only a few years ago could write the best hand of any lady in *Charleston*,) Mrs. H—— would superintend your management of the school.

Tutor. Mrs. H——, Sir, would do me honour.

Planter. Mrs. H——, Sir, is in the real sense of the word, a woman of literature; and her eldest daughter is a prodigy for her age. She could tell at nine years old whether a pudding was boiled enough; and, now, though only eleven, can repeat *Pope's* Ode on Solitude by heart. Ah! *Pope* was a *pretty* poet;

---

* The term *drive*, requires some little note explanatory to the *English* reader. No man forgets his original trade. An Overseer on a Plantation, who preserves subordination among the negroes, is said to *drive well;* and Mr. H—— *having once been an Overseer himself*, the phrase very naturally predominated in his mind.

my wife is very fond of *Pope*. You have read him, I make make no doubt, Sir. What is your opinion of his works?

Tutor. In his Rape of the Lock, Sir, he exhibits most of the *vis imaginandi* that constitutes the poet; his Essay on Criticism is scarcely inferior to *Horace's* Epistle to the Pisoes; his Satires——

Planter. But I am surprised, Sir, you bestow no praise on his Ode on Solitude. Mrs. *H*——, who is quite a critic in those matters, allows the Ode on Solitude to be his best, his noblest, his sublimest production.

Tutor. Persuaded, Sir, of the critical acuteness of Mrs. *H*——, it is not safe to depart from her in opinion;—and if Mrs. *H*—— affirms the Ode on Solitude to be the sublimest of Mr. *Pope's* productions, it would be rather painful than pleasant to undeceive her in opinion.

Planter. That is right, Sir, I like to see young men modest. What spelling-book do you use?

Tutor. What spelling-book, Sir? Indeed —really—upon my word, Sir,—any—oh! *Noah Webster's,* Sir.

Planter. Ah! I perceive you are a New England man, by giving the preference to *Noah Webster.*

Tutor. Sir, I beg your pardon; I am from Old England.

Planter. Well, no matter for that,—but Mrs. *H*——, who is an excellent speller, never makes use of any other but *Matthew Carey's* spelling-book. It is a valuable work, the copy-right is secured. But here comes Mrs. *H*—— herself.

Mrs. *H*—— now entered, followed by a negro girl, who held a peacock's feather in her hand. Mrs. *H*—— received my bow with a mutilated curtesey, and throwing herself on a sopha, called peremptorily to *Prudence* to brush the flies from her face. There was a striking contrast between the dress of the lady and her maid; the one was tricked out in all the finery of fashion; while the black skin of the other peeped through her garments.

Well, my dear, said Mr. *H*——, this young man is the person who advertised for the place of tutor in a respectable family. A little conversation with him will enable you to judge, whether he is qualified to instruct our children in the branches of a liberal education.

Mrs. H.—— Why independent of his literary attainments, it will be necessary for him to produce certificates of his conduct. I am not easily satisfied in my choice of a tutor; *a body* should be very cautious in admitting a stranger to her family. This gentleman is young, and young men are very frequently addicted to bad habits. Some are prone to late hours; some to hard drinking; and some to

Negur girls: the last propensity I could never forgive.

Mr. H. Yes, my dear, you discharged Mr. *Spondee*, our last tutor, for his intimacy with the *Negur* girls:—*Prudence* had a little one by him. *Prudence* looked reproachfully at her master; the child was in reality the offspring of Mr. H——, who fearing the inquiries of the world on the subject, fathered it upon the last tutor. But they must have been blind who could not discover that the child was sprung from Mr. H——; for it had the same vulgar forehead, the same vacant eye, and the same idiot laugh.

Mr. H. Do, my dear, examine the young man a little on literary matters. He seems to have read *Pope*.

Mrs. H. What, Sir, is your opinion of Mr. *Pope's* Ode on Solitude?

Tutor. It is a tolerable production, madam, for a child.

Mrs. H. A tolerable production for a child! Mercy on us! It is the *most sublimest* of his productions. But tastes differ. Have you read the works of Dr. *Johnson?* Which do you approve the most.

Tutor. Why, Madam, if you allude to his poems, I should, in conformity with your judgment, give a decided preference to his Epitaph on a Duck, written, if I mistake not, when he was four years old. It need scarcely fear competition with *Pope's* Ode on Solitude.

At this moment the eldest daughter of this learned lady, of this unsexed female, tripped into the room on light, fantastic toe. Come, my daughter, said the lady, let this gentleman hear you repeat the Ode on Solitude.

Excuse me, Madam, cried I, taking up my hat and bowing.

Do you hear the child, bawled Mr. *H*——.
I pray you, sir, to excuse me, rejoined I.

Mrs. H. It will not take the child ten minutes.

Tutor. Ten minutes, Madam, are the sixth part of an hour that will never return!

Mr. H. Politeness dictates it.

Tutor. Excuse me, I entreat you, Sir.

Mr. H. I cannot excuse you, I shall hire you as tutor, and I have a right to expect from you submission. I may perhaps give you the sum of fifty pounds a year.

Don't mention it, Sir, said I. There again you will have the goodness to excuse me. Madam, your most obedient. Miss, your very obsequious. Sir, your humble servant.*

My walk back to *Charleston* was along the

---

* It has been my object in this scene to soften the condition of private tutors in America, by putting up Mr. H—— *in signum terroris et memoriæ* to other purse-proud planters. I write not from personal pique, but a desire to benefit society. Happy shall I think myself should this page hold the mirror up to the inflation of pride, and the insolence of prosperity.

shore of the *Atlantic,* whose waves naturally associated the idea of a home I despaired ever again to behold. Sorrow always begets in me a disposition for poetry; and the reflexions that obtruded themselves in my lonely walk produced a little ode.

ODE ON HOME.

DEAR native soil! where once my feet
   Were wont thy flow'ry paths to roam,
And where my heart would joyful beat,
   From India's climes restor'd to home;
Ah! shall I e'er behold you more,
   And cheer again a parent's eye?
A wand'rer from thy blissful shore,
   Thro' endless troubles doomed to sigh?

Or shall I, pensive and forlorn,
   Of penury be yet the prey,
Long from thy grateful bosom torn,
   Without a friend to guide my way?
Hard is the hapless wand'rer's fate,
   Tho' blest with magic power of song;
Successive woes his steps await,
   Unheeded by the worldly throng.

It was not long before my advertisement brought me other applications. The principal of Charleston College * honoured me with a letter, whom, pursuant to his desire, I waited on at his house.

I found Mr. *Drone* in his study, consulting

[* The first Commencement was held in 1794. Ravenel, *Charleston.* New York. 1906; p. 348.]

with great solemnity the ponderous lexicon of *Schrevelius.** I could not but feel a secret veneration from the scene before me. I was admitted to the presence of a man who was not less voluminous than learned; for no book under a folio ever stood on his shelf.

How stupendous, thought I, must be the erudition of this professor, who holds in sovereign contempt a volume of ordinary dimensions! Every animal has an aliment peculiarly suited to its constitution. The ox finds nourishment only from the earth; and a professor cannot derive knowledge from any volume but a folio.

Mr. *Drone* received me with all the little decorums of dulness. He, however, talked learnedly. He lamented the degeneracy of literature in England and America; discovered that taste was on the decline; and despaired of ever beholding the spirit of that age revived when writers sought not for new combinations of imagery, but were content to compile lexicons, and restore the true punctuation to an ancient poet.

Mr. *Drone* asked me whether I was conversant with Latin; and on my replying in the affirmative, he produced a Horace in folio, and desired I would construe the Ode of *Quem tu Melpomene.*

[* One of the earliest American editions of Schrevelius was that of 1814, " Novi-Eboraci: Impensis Eastburn, Kirk et Soc. Apud Cameras Literararias, Wall-Street."]

Horace had never before assumed so formidable an aspect. In the ordinary editions he had always looked at me *placido lumine;* but he now appeared crabbed and sour, and I found his text completely buried amidst the rubbish of annotations.

By making *isthmius labor* the agent to *clarabit* * the difficulty of the inversion vanished; but when I came to analyze the construction of the ode, not having some rule for verbs construed at memory, I think it was the important one of *mo fit ui,* as *vomo vomui;*† the Professor, with a shake of his head, which doubtless put all his sagacity into motion, told me very gravely I had yet something to learn.

I ought to apologize to my reader for detaining him so long in the company of Professor *Drone;* but it is a link in the chain of my history, however rusty. To be brief, he engaged me as an Assistant to his sublime College for three months; and had the vanity to assert, that in consequence of it I should become *fama super aethera notus.*

I was about to take leave of Mr. *Drone,* when his principal Tutor entered the room,

[* *Odes,* IV, 3—

    Quem tu, Melpomene, semel
      Nascentem placido lumine videris,
    Illum non labor Isthmius
      Clarabit pugilem, non equus inpiger
    Curru ducet Achaico
      Victorem—]

† Vide *Lilly's* Grammar.

to whom he introduced me. Mr. *George* taught the *Greek* and *Latin* classics at the *College,* and was not less distinguished by his genius than his erudition.

On surveying my new acquaintance, I could not but think that he deserved a better office than that of a Gerund-grinder. Nature seemed to have set her seal on him to give the world assurance of a man.

Mr. *George* laughed obstreperously at the pedantry of the Professor. Peace, said he, to all such! Old *Duffey,* my first schoolmaster in *Roscommon,* concealed more learning under the coarseness of his brogue, than *Drone* will ever display with all his rhetoric of declamation. It is true he can talk of *Luitprandus, Bertholdus,* and *Lambertus;* but an acquaintance with these writers, however it may display reading, discovers little judgment.

Two young men, of similar pursuits, soon become acquainted. The day of my introduction to Mr. *George,* we exchanged thoughts without restraint; and during three months that I continued at *Charleston,* we were inseparable companions.

I know not whether I was qualified to fill the vacant chair of instruction at the College; but I remember, that zealous to acquit myself with dignity in my new office, I assumed the aspect of a pedagogue, and when an idle boy stared at me, I checked him with a frown. I, however, was not ambitious of this honour more than six weeks; a space of time, which, however it cannot be long, may surely be tedious. The Professor complained that I was always last in the College;* and I replied by desiring my discharge.

I was now dismissed from the College; but I was under no solicitude for my future life. A planter of the name of *Brisbane,* had politely invited me to his plantation, to partake with him and his neighbours, the diversion of hunting, during the winter; and another of the name of *Drayton,* the owner of immense forests, had applied me to live in his family, and undertake the tuition of his children. Of these proposals, the first flattered my love of ease, and the other insured me an augmentation of wealth. I was not long held in suspense which of the two to chuse; but I preferred the summons of industry to the blandishments of pleasure.

The winters of *Carolina,* however piercing to a native, who during the summer months may be said to bask rather than breathe, are mild to an *Englishman* accustomed to the frosts of his island. In the month of *November* my engagement led me to *Coosohatchie,* an insignificant village about seventy-eight miles from *Charleston;* for the plantation of Mr. *Drayton* was in the neighbouring woods.

[* " Omnibus hoc vitiumst cantoribus " ?]

The serenity of the weather invited the traveller to walk, and, at an early hour of the morning, I departed on foot from *Charleston,* having the preceding evening taken leave of Mr. *George.*

The foot-traveller need not be ashamed of his mode of journeying. To travel on foot, is to travel like *Plato* and *Pythagoras;* and to these examples may be added the not less illustrious ones of *Goldsmith* and *Rousseau.* The rambles of the ancient sages are at this distance of time uncertain; but it is well known that *Goldsmith* made the tour of *Europe* on foot, and that *Rousseau* walked from choice, through a great part of *Italy.*

An agreeable walk of ten miles, brought me to the bank of *Ashley River,* where I breakfasted in a decent public house, with the landlord and his family. That man travels to no purpose who sits down alone to his meals; for my part I love to mingle with the sons and daughters of industry; to mark the economy of their household, and compare their mode of living with that of the same class of people in my own country. The opulent of every nation are nearly the same; refinement has polished away the original stamp of character: the true estimate of manners is to be made among those in a middle rank of life.

Having crossed the ferry, I resumed my

journey through a country which might be assimilated to one continued forest. Tall trees of pine, planted by the hand of nature in regular rows, bordered the road I travelled, and I saw no other animals, but now and then a flock of deer, which, ceasing awhile to browse, looked up at me with symptoms of wonder rather than fear.

> "Along these lonely regions, here retir'd
> From little scenes of art, great Nature dwells
> In awful solitude, and naught is seen
> But the wild herds that own no master's stall." *

At three in the afternoon I reached *Jacksonborough,* the only town on the road from *Charleston* to *Coosohatchie.* Though a foot-traveller, I was received at the tavern with every demonstration of respect; the landlord ushered me into a room which afforded the largest fire I had ever seen in my travels; yet the landlord, rubbing his hands, complained

[* The author intends his quotation, in the matter of herds, to apply to deer, &c. In this region, somewhat to the northwest, was the early ranch country of the United States, and cattle 'owning no master's stall' might have been seen in the woods.

Cf. *American Husbandry,* London 1775. Vol. I, pp. 337-338.—"It is not an uncommon thing to see one man (in North Carolina) the master of from 300 to 1200, and even to 2000 cows, bulls, oxen, and young cattle; hogs also in prodigious numbers. Their management is to let them run loose in the woods all day."

Cf. also J. F. D. Smyth, *Tour in the United States of America,* London, 1784, II, p. 78 ff.; and Schoepf, *Reise,* &c. Erlangen 1788, II, 168 ff.]

it was cold, and exclaimed against his negroes for keeping so bad a fire. Here, *Syphax,* said he, " be quick and bring more wood; you have made, you rascal, a *Charleston* fire; fetch a stout back log, or I'll make a back-log of you.

The exclamations of the landlord brought his wife into the room. She curtesied, and made many eloquent apologies for the badness of the fire; but added that her waiting man, *Will,* had run away, and having whipped *Syphax* till his back was raw, she was willing to try what gentle means would do.

A dinner of venison, and a pint of Madeira, made me forget I had walked thirty miles; and it being little more than four o'clock, I proceeded forward on my journey. The vapours of a *Spanish* segar promoted cogitation, and I was lamenting the inequality of conditions in the world, when night overtook me.

I now redoubled my pace, not without the apprehension that I should have to seek my lodgings in some tree, to avoid the beasts that prowled nightly in the woods; but the moon, which rose to direct me in my path, alienated my perturbation, and in another hour I descried the blaze of a friendly fire through the casements of a log-house. Imaginary are worse than real calamities; and the apprehension of sleeping in the woods was by far more painful than the actual experience of it would have been. The same Being who sends trials can also inspire fortitude.

The place I had reached was *Asheepo,* a hamlet consisting of three or more log-houses; and the inhabitants of every sex and age had collected round a huge elephant, which was journeying with his master to *Savannah.*

Fortune had therefore brought me into unexpected company, and I could not but admire the docility of the elephant, who, in solemn majesty, received the gifts of the children with his trunk. But not so the monkey. This man of Lord *Monboddo* was inflamed with rage at the boys and girls; nor could the rebukes of his master calm the transports of his fury.*

I entered the log-house which accommodated travellers. An old negro-man had squatted himself before the fire. Well, old man. said I, why don't you go out to look at the elephant? Hie! Massa, he calf! In fact the elephant came from *Asia,* and the negro from *Africa,* where he had seen the same species of animal, but of much greater magnitude.

Traveling, says *Shakespeare,* acquaints a man with strange bed-fellows; and there

[* Want of speech may have been no disadvantage at such a juncture. Lord Monboddo, in his *Origin and Progress of Language,* 6 Vols., 1773-1792, 'maintained that the orang-outang, was a class of the human species and that its want of speech was merely accidental.']

being only one bed in the log-house, I slept that night with the elephant driver. Mr. *Owen* was a native of *Wales,* but he had been a great traveller, and carried a map of his travels in his pocket. Nothing shortens a journey more than good company on the road; so I departed after breakfast from *Asheepo,* with Mr. *Owen,* his elephant, and his monkey.

Mr. *Owen* related to me the wonders of his elephant, which at some future day, I may perhaps publish in a separate treatise; but they would be irrevalant to my present journey, which towards noon I was left to prosecute alone. The elephant, however docile, would not travel without his dinner; and Mr. *Owen* halted under a pine-tree to feed the mute companion of his toils.

For my own part, I dined at a solitary log-house in the woods, upon exquisite venison. My host was a small planter, who cultivated a little rice, and maintained a wife and four children with his rifled-barrel-gun. He had been Overseer to a Colonel *Fishborne,* and owned half a dozen negroes; but he observed to me *his property was running about at large,* for four of them had absconded.

As I proposed to make *Pocotaligo* the end of my day's journey, I walked forward at a moderate pace; but towards evening I was roused from the reveries into which my walking had plunged me by a conflagration in the woods. On either side of the road the trees were in flames, which, extending to their branches, assumed an appearance both terrific and grotesque. Through these woods, *belching flames and rolling smoke,* I had to travel nearly a mile, when the sound of the negro's axe chopping of wood, announced that I was near *Pocotaligo.*

At *Pocotaligo* I learned that the conflagration in the woods arose from the carelessness of some backwoods-men, who having neglected to extinguish their fires, the flames had extended in succession to the herbage and the trees.*

I was somewhat surprised on entering the tavern at *Pocotaligo* to behold sixteen or more chairs placed round a table which was covered with the choicest dishes; but my surprise ceased when the *Savannah* and *Charleston* stage-coaches stopped at the door, and the passengers flocked to the fire before which I was sitting. In the *Charleston* coach came a party of comedians. Of these itinerant heroes the greater part were my countrymen;

[* Naturally, the early Traveller in this country [1776-1800] often mentions forest fires. Isaac Weld gives a particularly vivid description of a fire in the pine woods,—*Travels through the States of North America,* &c. London, 1800. Vol. I, pp. 161-162. Cf. also *Travels through the Interior Parts of America* [Thomas Anburey], London, 1789. Vol. II, pp. 412-413.]

and, as I was not travelling to see *Englishmen,* but *Americans,* I was not sorry when they retired to bed.*

I was in a worse condition at *Pocotaligo* than *Asheepo;* for at *Pocotaligo* the beds were so small that they would hold only respectively one person. But I pity the traveller who takes umbrage against *America,* because its houses of entertainment cannot always accommodate him to his wishes. If he images no other happiness to himself in travelling, but what is to be obtained from repasts that minister to luxury, and beds distinguished by softness, let him confine his excursions to the cities of polished *Europe.* The Western Continent can supply the Traveller an employment more noble than a minute attention to the casualties of the road, which are afterwards to be enlarged upon with studied declamation. The world is called upon to sympathize with the sufferer; he who at home had been accustomed to the luxury of a bed, groaned the night out in *America* on the rack of a mattress; and for this the country is to be execrated, and the beautiful scenes of nature beheld with a jaundiced eye.

Finding there was no bed to be procured, I seated myself in a nook of the chimney, called

[* Two years later John Bernard, the English comedian, might have been of the company. Cf. his *Retrospections of America, 1797-1811.* New York, 1887, Chapter IX.]

for wine and segars, and either attended to the conversation of the negro girls who had spread their blankets on the floor, or entertained myself with the half-formed notions of the landlord and coachman, who had brought their chairs to the fire, and were disputing on politics. Both *Americans* and *English* are subject to loquacious imbecility. Their subjects only differ. The *American* talks of his government,* the *Englishman* of himself.

Early in the morning, I resumed my journey in the coach that was proceeding to *Savannah;* I had but a short distance more to go; for *Coosohatchie* is only ten miles from *Pocotaligo*. In journeying through *America*, the Indian names of places have always awakened in my breast a train of reflection; a single word will speak volumes to a speculative mind; and the names of *Pocotaligo*, and *Coosohatchie*, and *Occoquan*, have pictured to my fancy the havoc of time, the decay and succession of generations, together with the final extirpation of savage nations, who, unconscious of the existence of another people, dreamt not of invasions from foreign enemies, or inroads from colonists, but believed their power invincible and their race eternal.

[* Cf. Chastellux, *Travels in North America*, 1780-1782. New York, 1828, p. 276.—"This subject led us naturally to that which is the most favourite topic among the Americans, the origin and commencement of the present revolution."]

I was put down at the post office of *Coosohatchie*. The post-master was risen, expecting the mail. He invited me to partake of a fire he had just kindled, before which a negro boy was administering pap to a sickly infant, whom the man always addressed by the homeric title of My Son.

I sat with the post-master an hour, when I sought out the village tavern, where with some trouble I knocked up a miserable Negress, who, on my entrance, resumed her slumbers on an old rug spread before the embers of the kitchen fire, and snored in oblivion of all care. After all, I know not whether those whose condition wears the appearance of wretchedness, are not greater favourites of nature than the opulent. Nothing comes amiss to the slave; he will find repose on the flint, when sleep flies the eye-lids of his master on a bed of down. I seated myself in a nook of the chimney till daylight, when the landlord came down; and, not long after, a servant was announced with horses to conduct me to the house of Mr. *Drayton*.*

An hour's ride through a forest of stately pines brought me to the plantation, where I

[* It is very likely this was Thomas Drayton, of "Magnolia," on Ashley River, d. *circa* 1820, brother of Charles Drayton, of "Drayton Hall." Of this family John Drayton, Governor, etc., published a book of Travels, *Letters Written During a Tour Through the Northern and Eastern States*, 1794.]

was received with much affability by Mr. *Drayton* and his lady, and where I was doomed to pass the winter in the woods of *Carolina*.

CHAP. III.

MEMOIR OF MY LIFE

IN THE WOODS OF SOUTH CAROLINA *

Ocean Plantation.—Poetry delightful in Solitude. —Walks in the Woods.—Family of Mr. Drayton.—Midnight Lucubrations.—Sketches of Natural History.—Deer-Hunting.—Remarks on Slaves and Slavery.—Militia of Coosohatchie District.—A School Groupe.—Journey into Georgia.

Deep in the bosom of a lofty wood,
Near *Coosohatchie's* slow revolving flood,
Where the blithe Mocking-bird repeats the lay
Of all the choir that warble from the spray;
Where the soft fawn, and not less tim'rous hind,
Beset by dogs, outstrip in speed the wind;
Where the grim wolf, at silent close of day,
With hunger bold, comes near the house for prey;

[* Volney, who was in the United States at this time, partitioned the country into three cantons or forests: the Southern forest, the Middle forest, and the Northern forest—his Middle forest comprising the mountainous parts of the Carolinas and of Virginia; all Pennsylvania, Southern New York, all Kentucky, and Northern Ohio. *Climat et Sol des Etats-Unis,* &c. Paris. 1803. I, 9-11.]

> Along the road, near yonder fields of corn,
> Where the soft dove resorts at early morn,
> There would my breast with love of Nature glow,
> And oft my thoughts in tuneful numbers flow;
> While friendly *George,* by ev'ry Muse belov'd,
> Smil'd his assent, and all my lays approv'd.

ABOUT half way on the road from *Charleston* to *Savannah* is situated a little village called *Coosohatchie,* consisting of a blacksmith's shop, a court-house, and a jail. A small river rolls its stagnant water near the place, on whose dismal banks are to be found many vestiges of the *Indians* that once inhabited them; and in the immeasurable forests of the neighbourhood (comprehended within the district of *Coosohatchie*), are several scattered plantations of cotton and of rice, whose stubborn soil the poor negro moistens with his tears, and

> *Whose sore task*
> *Does not divide the Sunday from the week!*

It was on one of these plantations that I passed the Winter of 1798, and the Spring of the following year.

I lived in the family of Mr. *Drayton,* of whose children I had undertaken the tuition, and enjoyed every comfort that opulence could bestow.

To form an idea of Ocean Plantation, let the reader picture to his imagination an avenue of several miles, leading from the *Savannah* road, through a continued forest, to a wooden house, encompassed by rice-grounds, corn and cotton-fields. On the right, a kitchen and other offices; on the left, a stable and coach-house; a little further a row of negro huts, a barn and yard; the view of the eye bounded by lofty woods of pine, oak and hickory.

The solitude of the woods I found at first rather dreary; but the polite attention of an elegant family, a sparkling fire in my room every night, and a horse always at my command, reconciled me to my situation; and my impulse to sacrifice to the Muses, which had been repressed by a wandering life, was once more awakened by the scenery of the woods of *Carolina*.

I indulged in the composition of lyric poetry, and when I had produced an Ode, transmitted it to *Freneau* at *Charleston,* who published it in his Gazette.* But planters have little disposition for poetry, and the eye of the *Carolina* reader was diverted from my effusions by the more interesting advertisements for fugitive slaves. I was therefore apprehensive that my reputation would not become extended by the Muse, when at the

---

[* Peter Freneau (younger brother of Philip Freneau), Secretary of State of South Carolina, about 1795 became editor, and proprietor of the Charleston *City Gazette*. d. 1813. Cf. Duyckinck, I, 334.]

distance of fourteen hundred miles, I found an Eulogist in Mr. *Dennie*,* who conducted the only literary paper in the United States, and whose praise was the more grateful from its being voluntary and remote. " As conductors
" of the only paper on our Continent that is
" professedly literary, we consider it incum-
" bent on us to pay the tribute of praise to
" certain easy poems which have appeared in
" the *Charleston* Gazette, and which, instead
" of being dated from *Parnassus,* or *Helicon,*
" or at least from some town of our Union,
" appear to originate in an obscure hamlet,
" of the barbarous and wigwam name of
" *Coosohatchie.* Among the many pleasing
" effusions of this writer is an imitation of
" that exquisite Ode in which *Horace,* under
" the name of *Pyrrha,* depicts the wiles of a
" Courtezan. Mr. *D.,* though stunned with
" *Indian* names, and resident among *Indian*
" readers, has a mind to comprehend the
" language, and catch the spirit of a liberal
" *Roman.* There is, perhaps, no Ode of
" *Horace* more difficult to render into English
" than the Ode to *Pyrrha;* and many are the
" versions that have been attempted without
" success by writers distinguished for their

[* Joseph Dennie, 1768-1813, Editor of the *Farmer's Museum* (Walpole, New Hampshire), from 1796 to 1799, " gathered around it one of the most brilliant corps of writers ever congregated to advance the fortunes of a similar undertaking in America." Duyckinck, I, 562.]

"classical attainments, and liveliness of im-
"agination. We, therefore, rejoice to find the
"task performed with felicity on a soil *where*
"*genius sickens, and where fancy dies!*"

HORACE, *Book* i, *Ode* 5, *Imitated.*
Quis multa gracilis te puer in rosa, &c.

TO PYRRHA.

WHAT essenc'd youth, on bed of blushing roses,
   Dissolves away within they glowing arms?
Or with soft languor on thy breast reposes,
   Deeply enamor'd of thy witching charms?

For whom do now, with wantonness and care,
   Thy golden locks in graceful ringlets wave?
What swain now listens to thy vows of air?
   For whom doth now thy fragrant bosom heave?

Alas! how often shall he curse the hour,
   Who, all-confiding in thy winning wiles,
With sudden darkness views the heavens low'r,
   And finds too late the treach'ry of thy smiles.

Wretched are they, who, by thy beauty won,
   Believe thee not less amiable than kind:
No more deluded, I thy charms disown,
   And give thy vows, indignant, to the wind,

"We would recommend this writer if he
"should chuse, or be compelled to remain at
"*Coosohatchie,* or any other *American* town
"of barbarous etymology, to turn either
"Usurer, Speculator or Jew. His poetry,
"however happy, will in this country experi-
"ence only the fate of being buried among

" the rubbish of advertisements for runaway "negroes. Neither *Horace,* nor his imitator, " will be inquired after; but What's the price " of cotton? and how a yoke of bullocks? "

My ardour of literary application was increased by such spontaneous praise from a man whose writings were held in the highest estimation, and who was considered, from prescriptive veneration, the *American Arbiter Elegantiarum.* I now cultivated the lighter Ode, and felicitated myself on having sacrificed to the laurelled god in the woods of *Carolina.** The common names of common towns, of *Boston, New-York,* and *Philadelphia,* awaken no curiosity, because every Traveller has described them; but *Coosohatchie,* which has scarce ever reached the ear of an European, cannot but possess the recommendation of novelty from the *Indian* derivation of its name, and the wildness of its situation. I, therefore, rejoice at the destiny which brought me to the spot; and I envy not other Travellers the magnificence of their cities.

The country near *Coosohatchie* exhibited with the coming Spring a new and enchanting prospect. The borders of the forests were covered with the blossoms of the dog-wood,

[* The poems so produced were published in a small volume, a copy of which is in the Library of the South Carolina Historical Society—*Poems, Written at Coosohatchie in South Carolina.* Printed by T. C. Cox, N. 137 Tradd St., Charleston. 120 pp. (12°, n.d.)]

of which the white flowers caught the eye from every part; and often was to be seen the red-bud tree, which purpled the adjacent woods with its luxuriant branches; while, not infrequently, shrubs of jessamine, intertwined with the wood-bine, lined the road for several miles. The feathered choir began to warble their strains, and from every tree was heard the song of the red-bird, of which the pauses were filled by the mocking-bird, who either imitated the note with exquisite precision, or poured forth a ravishing melody of its own.

I commonly devoted my Sundays to the pleasure of exploring the country, and cheered by a serene sky, and smiling landscape, felt my breast awakened to the most rapturous sensations. I lifted my heart to that Supreme Being, whose agency is everywhere confessed; and whom I traced in the verdure of the earth, the foliage of the trees, and the water of the stream. I have ever been of the opinion that God can be as well propitiated in a field as a temple; that he is not to be conciliated by empty protestations, but grateful feelings; and that the heart can be devout when the tongue is silent. Yet there is always something wanting to sublunary felicity, and I confess I felt very sensibly the privation of those hills which so agreeably diversify the country of *Europe*. I would exclaim in the animated language of *Rousseau, Jamais pays de plaine, quelque beau qu'l fut, ne parut tel à mes yeux.—Il me faut des torrens, des rochers, des sapins, des bois noirs, des chemins raboteux a monter & a descendre, des précipices à mes cotés qui me fassent bien peur!"* *

In my walk to *Coosohatchie* I passed here and there a plantation, but to have called on its owner without a previous introduction would have been a breach of etiquette which has its source from the depravity of great cities, but has not failed to find its way into the woods of *America*. When I first beheld a fine lady drawn by four horses through the woods of *Carolina* in her coach, and a train of servants following the vehicle, clad in a magnificent livery, I looked up with sorrow at that luxury and refinement, which are hastening with rapid strides to change the pure and sylvan scenes of nature into a theatre of pride and ostentation. When *Venus* enchanted *Æneas* with her presence in the woods she was not attired in the dress of the ladies of Queen *Dido's* court; but, huntress like, had hung from her shoulders a bow, and was otherwise equipped for the toils of the chase.

On coming to *Coosohatchie,* I repaired to the post-office, which never failed to give me an epistle from my beloved and literary friend Mr. *George;* who enlightened me with his knowledge, enlivened me with his wit, and

* Confessions. Tom. 2.

consoled me with his reflections. I shall not expatiate on our genuine, disinterested friendship. He has consecrated to it a monument in his Poem of the Wanderer. What but the heart could have dictated the following passage?

"Here doom'd to pant beneath a torrid sky,
"And cast to happier climes a wishful eye;
"No friend had I my sorrows to deplore,
"With whom to pass the sympathetic hour!
"For many a stream, and many a waste divide,
"These lonely shores from *Coosohatchie's* tide!"

I remember, with lively pleasure, my residence in the woods of *South Carolina*. Enjoying health in its plentitude, yet young enough to receive new impressions; cultivating daily my taste by the study of polite literature; blest with the friendship of a *George,* and living in the bosom of a family unruffled by domestic cares; how could I be otherwise than happy, and how can I refrain from the pleasure of retrospection.

Coosohatchie! thou shalt not be unknown, if, by what eloquence nature has given me, I can call forth corresponding emotions in the breast of my reader to those which my own felt when wandering silently through thy woods.

My pupils, in the woods of *Coosohatchie,* consisted of a boy and two young ladies. *William Henry* was an interesting lad of fourteen, ingenuous of disposition, and a stranger to fear.

He was fond to excess of the chase. His heart danced with joy at the mention of a deer; and he blew his horn, called together his dogs, and hooped and hallooed in the woods with an animation that would have done honour to a veteran sportsman. O! for the Muse of an *Ovid,* to describe the dogs of this young *Actæon.* There were Sweetlips, and Ringwood, and Music, and Smoker, whose barking was enough to frighten the wood nymphs to their caves. His eldest sister, *Maria,* though not a regular beauty, was remarkable for her dark eyes and white teeth, and, what was not less captivating, an amiable temper. She was grateful to me for my instruction, and imposed silence on her brother when I invoked the Muse in school. But it was difficult to controúl her little sister *Sally,* whom in sport and wantonness they called *Tibousa.* This little girl was distinguished by the languish of her blue eyes, from which, however, she could dart fire when *William* offended her. *Sally* was a charming girl, whose beauty promised to equal that of her mother. That I passed many happy hours in watching and assisting the progress of the minds of these young people, I feel no repugnance to acknowledge. My long residence in a country where *honour and shame from no condition rise,* has placed me above the ridiculous pride of disowning the situation of a Tutor.

Though the plantation of Mr. *Drayton* was immense, his dwelling was only a log-house; a temporary fabric built to reside in during the winter. But his table was sumptuous, and an elegance of manners presided at it that might have vied with the highest circles of polished *Europe*. I make the eulogium, or rather exhibit the character of Mr. *Drayton*, in one word, by saying he was a Gentleman; for under that portraiture I comprehend whatever there is of honour. Nor can I refrain from speaking in panegyric terms of his lady, whose beauty and elegance were her least qualities; for she was a tender mother, a sincere friend, and walked humbly with her God. She was indeed deserving the solicitude of her husband who would *not suffer the winds of heaven to visit her face too roughly.*

It is usual in *Carolina* to sit an hour at table after supper; at least it was our custom in the woods of *Coosohatchie*. It was then I related my adventures to Mr. and Mrs. *Drayton,* in the eastern section of the globe, who not only endured my tales, but were elated with my successes, and depressed by my misfortunes.

About ten I withdrew to my chamber and my books, where I found a sparkling fire of wood, and where I lucubrated, smoked segars, and was lost in my own musings. The silence of the night invited meditation; but often was I to be seen at three in the morning sitting before my chamber fire, surrounded like *Magliabechi* by my papers and my books. My study was *Latin,* and my recreation the Confessions of the eloquent Citizen of *Geneva.*

But I was not without company. A merry cricket in my chimney corner never failed to cheer me with his song.—A cricket is not to be contemned. It is related by *Buffon* that they are sold publicly in the *Asiatic* markets; and it is recorded of *Scaliger* that he kept several in a box. I remember an Ode which I consecrated to my midnight companion.

ODE TO A CRICKET.

LITTLE guest, with merry throat,
  That chirpest by my taper's light,
Come, prolong thy blithsome note,
  Welcome visitant of night.

Here enjoy a calm retreat,
  In my chimney safely dwell,
No rude hand thy haunt shall beat,
  Or chase thee from thy lonely cell.

Come, recount me all thy woes,
  While around us sighs the gale;
Or rejoic'd to find repose,
  Charm me with thy merry tale.

Say that passion moves thy breast:
  Does some flame employ thy care?
Perhaps with love thou art opprest,
  A mournful victim to despair.

Shelter'd from the wintry wind,
Live and sing and banish care;
Here protection thou shalt find,
Sympathy has brought thee here.

The country in our neighbourhood consisted of lofty forests of pine, oak, and hickory. Well might I have exclaimed in the words of my poetical friend:

"Around an endless wild of forests lies,
And pines on pines forever meet the eyes!"

The land, as I have before suggested, was perfectly level. Not the smallest acclivity was visible, and therefore no valley rejoiced the sight with its verdure.

The staple commodity of the State is rice, but cotton is now eagerly cultivated where the soil is adapted to the purpose. The culture of indigo is nearly relinquished.* It attains more perfection in the *East-Indies,* which can amply supply the markets of *Europe.* It is to the crop of cotton that the Planter looks for the augmentation of his wealth. Of cotton there are two kinds; the sea-island and inland.

[* Swift and far-reaching changes brought in by Whitney's gin machine. Cf. Schoepf, *Reise durch einige der mittlern und südlichen vereinigten nordamerikanischen Staaten. Erlangen.* 1788, II, 287, 288.—" Nächst dem schon berührten Indigo, ist der Reis die vorzüglichste Stapelwaare von Südkarolina. . . . Auf Reis, Indigo, und in den hintern Gegenden auf Toback, haben die Einwohner von Karolina bisher ihre hauptsächlichste Aufmerksamkeit verwendet" (1784).]

The first is the most valuable. The ground is hoed for planting the latter part of *March;* but as frosts are not infrequent the beginning of *April,* it is judicious not to plant before that time. Cotton is of a very tender nature. A frost, or even a chilling wind, has power to destroy the rising plant, and compel the Planter to begin anew his toil.

The winds in autumn are so tempestuous that they tear up the largest trees by the roots. *Homer,* some thousand years ago, witnessed a similar scene:

> " Leaves, arms and trees aloft in air are blown,
> " The broad oaks crackle, and the sylvans groan;
> " This way and that, the rattling thicket bends,
> " And the whole forest in one crash descends."

Of the feathered race, the mocking-bird first claims my notice. It is perfectly domestic, and sings frequently for hours on the roof of a log-house. It is held sacred by the natives. Even children respect the bird whose imitative powers are so delightful.*

I heard the mocking-bird for the first time on the first day of *March.* It was warbling, close to my window, from a tree called by some the Pride of *India,* and by others the Poison-berry Tree. Its song was faint, re-

[* Cf. Castiglioni, *Viaggio negli Stati Uniti, 1785, 1786, 1787,* Milan. 1790. I, 357.—" The mocking-bird is bought at extravagant prices by the English. At Boston the price is often three to four guineas."]

sembling that of birds hailing the rising sun; but it became stronger as the spring advanced. The *premices* of this mocking songster could not but delight me; and I adressed the bird in an irregular Ode, which Mrs. *Drayton* did me the honour to approve.

ODE TO THE MOCKING-BIRD.

SWEET bird, whose imitative strain,
Of all thy race can counterfeit the note,
  And with a burthen'd heart complain,
Or to the song of joy attune the throat;

  To thee I touch the string,
While at my casement, from the neighb'ring tree,
  Thou hail'st the coming spring,
And plaintive pour'st thy voice, or mock'st with merry
      glee.

  Thou bringest to my mind
  The characters we find
Amid the motley scenes of human life;
  How very few appear
  The garb of truth to wear,
But with a borrow'd voice, conceal a heart of strife.

  Sure then, with wisdom fraught,
  Thou art by nature taught
Dissembled joy in others to describe;
  And when the mournful heart
  Assumes a sprightly part,
To note the cheat, and with thy mocking chide.

But when, with midnight song,
Thou sing'st the woods among,
And softer feelings in the heart awake;*
  Sure then thy rolling note
  Does sympathy denote,
And shews thou can'st of others' grief partake.

Pour out thy lengthen'd strain †
With woe and grief complain,
And blend thy sorrows in the mournful lay;
  Thy moving tale reveal,
  Make me soft pity feel,
I love in silent woe to pass the day.

The humming bird was often caught in the bells of flowers. It is remarkable for its variegated plumage of scarlet, green, and gold.

The whip-poor-will is heard after the last frost, when, towards night, it fills the woods with its melancholy cry of *Whip poor Will! Whip poor Will!* I remember to have seen mention made of this bird in a *Latin* poem, written by an early Colonist.

Hic Avis repetens, Whip! Whip! Will, voce jocosa,
Quæ tota verno tempore nocte canit.

The note of the red-bird is imitated with nice precision by the mocking-bird; but there

---

* Put for awak'st.

[† "And thou America's sole boast!
Pour out the joy sincere."

Pietas et Gratulatio, p. 89,—a slightly different philosophy: that of the ode is dubious. The importance of this bird, in the pages of the early traveller, is suggested by the frequent mention in Davis's book.]

is a bird called the loggerhead that will not bear passively its taunts. His cry resembles *Clink, clink, clank;* which, should the mocking-bird presume to imitate it, he flies and attacks the mimic for his insolence. But this only incurs a repetition of the offence; so true is it that among birds as well as men, anger serves only to sharpen the edge of ridicule. It is observable, that the loggerhead is known to suck the eggs of the mocking-bird and devour the young ones in the nest.

Eagles were often seen on the plantation. The rencounter between one of them and a fish-hawk is curious. When the fish-hawk has seized his prey, his object is to get above the eagle; but when unable to succeed, the king of birds darts on him fiercely, at whose approach the hawk, with a horrid cry, lets fall the fish, which the eagle catches in his beak before it descends to the ground.

The woods abound with deer, the hunting of which forms the chief diversion of the Planters. I never failed to accompany my neighbours in their parties, but I cannot say that I derived much pleasure from standing several hours behind a tree.

This mode of hunting is, perhaps, not generally known. On riding to a convenient spot in the woods, the hunters dismount, take their stands at certain distances, hitch their horses to a tree, and prepare their guns,—while a couple of negroes lead the beagles into the thickest of the forest. The barking of the dogs announces the deer are dislodged, and on whatever side they run, the sportsmen fire at them from their lurking places. The first day two bucks passed near my tree. I heard the cry of the dogs and put my gun on a whole cock. The first buck glided by me with the rapidity of lightning, but the second I wounded with my fire, as was evident from his twitching his tail between his legs in the agony of pain. I heard Colonel *Pastell* exclaim from the next tree, after discharging his piece, " By heaven, that fellow is wounded, let us " mount and follow him,—he cannot run far." I accompanied the venerable Colonel through the woods, and in a few minutes, directed by the scent of a beagle, we reached the spot where the deer had fallen. It was a noble buck, and we dined on it like kings.*

Fatal accidents sometimes attend the hunters in the woods. Two brothers a few years ago, having taken their respective stands behind a tree, the elder fired at a deer which the dogs had started; but, his shot being diverted by a fence, it flew off and lodged in the body of his brother. The deer passing on, the wounded brother discharged his gun which had been prepared, killed the animal, and staggering a

[* Cf. John Bernard, *Retrospections of America*, New York, 1887. pp. 206, 207 (South Carolina, *temp.* 1800, deer-hunting by torchlight).]

few paces, expired himself. This disaster was related to me by Colonel *Pastell* and his son, Major *Warley,* and Captain *Pelatte,* who lived on the neighbouring plantations, and composed our hunting party.

After killing half a dozen deer, we assembled by appointment at some planter's house, whither the mothers, and wives, and daughters of the hunters had got before us in their carriages. A dinner of venison, killed the preceding hunt, smoked before us; the richest Madeira sparkled in the glass, and we forgot, in our hilarity, there was any other habitation for man but that of the woods.

In this hunting party was always to be found my pupil *William Henry,* who galloped through the woods, however thick or intricate; summoned his beagles after the toil of the chase with his horn; caressed the dog that had been the most eager in pursuit of the deer, and expressed his hope there would be good weather to hunt again the following Saturday.

I did not repress this ardour in my pupil. I beheld it with satisfaction; for the man doomed to pass every winter in the woods would find his life very irksome could he not partake, with his neighbours, in the diversions they afford.

Ludere qui nescit, campestribus, abstinet armis,
Indoctusque Pilæ, Discive, Trochive quiescit,
Ne spissæ risum tollant impune Coronæ. Hor.*

[* *Epist.,* II., (*Ars Poet.*), 3, 379.]

Wolves were sometimes heard on the plantation in the night; and, when incited by hunger, would attack a calf and devour it. One night, however, some wolves endeavouring to seize on a calf, the dam defended her offspring with such determined resolution, that the hungry assailants were compelled to retreat with the tail only of the calf, which one of them had bitten off.

Wild cats are very common and mischievous in the woods. When a sow is ready to litter, she is always enclosed with a fence or rails, for, otherwise, the wild cats would devour the pigs.

I generally accompanied my pupil into the woods in his shooting excursions, determined both to make havoc among birds and beasts. of every description. Sometimes we fired in vollies at the flocks of doves that frequent the corn fields; sometimes we discharged our pieces at the wild geese, whose empty cackling betrayed them; and once we brought down some paroquets that were directing their course over our heads to *Georgia*. Nor was it an undelightful task to fire at the squirrels on the tops of the highest trees, who, however artful, could seldom elude the shot of my eager companion.

The affability and tenderness of this charming family in the bosom of the woods will be ever cherished in my breast, and long recorded, I hope, in this page. My wants were always anticipated. The family Library was transported without entreaty into my chamber; paper and the apparatus for writing were placed on my table; and once, having lamented that my stock of segars was nearly exhausted, a negro was dispatched seventy miles to *Charleston* for a supply of the best *Spanish*.

I conclude my description of this elegant family with an observation that will apply to every other that I have been domesticated in, on the Western Continent;—that cheerfulness and quiet always predominated, and that I never saw a brow clouded, or a lip opened in anger.

One diminution to the happiness of an *European* in the woods of *Carolina* is the reflection that every want is supplied him by slaves. Whatever may be urged on the subject of negroes, as the voice of millions could lend no support to falsehood, so no casuistry can justify the keeping of slaves. That negroes are human beings is confessed by their partaking with the rest of mankind the faculty of speech, and power of combination. Now no man being born a slave, but with his original rights, the supposed property of the master in the slave, is an usurpation and not a right; because no one from being a person can become a thing. From this conviction should every good citizen promote the emancipation of Negroes in *America.*

The negroes on the plantation, including house-servants and children, amounted to a hundred, of whom the average price being respectively seventy pounds, made them aggregately worth seven thousand to their possessor.

Two families lived in one hut, and such was their unconquerable propensity to steal that they pilfered from each other. I have heard masters lament this defect in their negroes. But what else can be expected from man in so degraded a condition, that among the ancients the same word implied both a slave and a thief.

Since the introduction of the culture of cotton in the State of *South Carolina,* the race of negroes has increased. Both men and women work in the field, and the labour of the rice-plantation formerly prevented the pregnant Negress from bringing forth a long-lived offspring. It may be established as a maxim that, on a plantation where there are many children, the work has been moderate.

It may be incredible to some that the children of the most distinguished families in *Carolina* are suckled by negro women. Each child has its *Momma,* whose gestures and accent it will necessarily copy, for children, we all know, are imitative beings. It is not unusual to hear an elegant lady say, *Richard always grieves when Quasheehaw is whipped, because she suckled him.* If *Rousseau* in his Emile could inveigh against the French mother, who consigned her child to a woman of her own color to suckle, how would his indignation have been raised to behold a smiling babe tugging with its roseate lips at a dug of a size and color to affright a Satyr?

Of genius in negroes many instances may be recorded. It is true that Mr. *Jefferson* has pronounced the Poems of *Phillis Whately* below the dignity of criticism,* and it is seldom safe to differ in judgment from the Author of Notes on *Virginia*. But her conceptions are often lofty, and her versification often surprises with unexpected refinement. *Ladd,* the *Carolina* poet, in enumerating the bards of his country, dwells with encomium on " *Whately's* polished verse "; nor is his praise undeserved, for often it will be found to glide in the stream of melody. Her lines

[* *Notes on Virginia*, ch. XIV.—" Among the blacks is misery enough, God knows, but no poetry. . . Religion indeed has produced a Phyllis Whately but it could not produce a poet. . . . Ignatius Sancho has approached nearer to merit in composition, yet his letters do more honor to the heart than the head." Joseph Brown Ladd of Rhode Island, lived for two years (1783-1785) in South Carolina. His poems were not published in book form until 1832. Gilbert Imlay, who described Kentucky, published in 1793, a three-volume novel, *The Emigrants,* a story of life in America.—John Gabriel Stedman's *Narrative of a Five Years' Expedition against the revolted Negroes of Surinam, in Guiana, on the wild coast of South America,* appeared in 1776.]

on Imagination have been quoted with rapture by *Imlay* of *Kentucky,* and *Steadman,* the *Guiana* Traveller; but I have ever thought her happiest production the Goliah of Gath.

Of *Ignatius Sancho,* Mr. *Jefferson* also speaks neglectingly; and remarks that he substitutes sentiment for argumentation. But I know not that argumentation is required in a familiar epistle; and *Sancho,* I believe, has only published his Correspondence.

Before I quit the woods of *Coosohatchie* it will be expected from me to fill the imagination of my reader with *the vengeful terrors of the rattle-snake* that meditates destruction to the unwary. Were I really pleased with such tales, I would not content myself with the story of the fascinating power of a rattle-snake over birds, but relate how a negro was once irresistibly charmed and devoured.*

Vegetation is singularly quick in the woods of *Carolina.* Of flowers, the jessamine and woodbine grow wild; but the former differs widely from that known by the same name in *England,* being of a straw color, and having large bells. Violets perfume the woods and roads with their fragrance.

[* The negro Cæsar, mentioned by several of the early Travellers, found a charm against rattlesnake poison: equal quantities of the juice of hore-hound and plantain, administered internally. "The assembly, or parliament of North Carolina, rewarded him with his freedom and two hundred pounds." Cf. Smyth, *Travels* &c. London 1784, I, 109.]

In bogs, and marshy situations, is found the singular plant called the fly-catcher by the natives, and, I believe, *dionæ muscipula* by botanists. Its jointed leaves are furnished with two rows of strong prickles, of which the surfaces are covered with a quantity of minute glands that secrete a sweet liquor, which allures the flies. When these parts are touched by the legs of a fly, the two lobes of the leaf immediately rise, the rows of prickles compress themselves, and squeeze the unwary insect to death. But a straw or pin introduced between the lobes will excite the same motions.

The honey of the bees in *Carolina* is exquisitely delicious, and these insects are very sagacious in chusing their retreats. They seek lodgings in the upper part of the trunk of the loftiest tree; but here their nests cannot elude the searching eyes of the negroes and children. The tree is either scaled, or cut down, the bees are tumbled from their honeyed domes, and their treasures rifled.

Sic vos non vobis mellificatis Apes!

These are the few observations that I made on the productions of nature before me; a study I have ever considered subordinate, when compared to that of life. I have used only the popular names, though without any labour I could have dignified my page with the terms of the Naturalist, for I had all the *Latin* phrases at the end of my pen.* But I return from brutes to man, though many readers may be of the opinion that in exhibiting the cruelty and wantonness of planters, over their slaves, I change not the subject.

It appears to me that in *Carolina,* the simplicity of the first colonists is obliterated, and that the present inhabitants strive to exceed each other in the vanities of life. Slight circumstances often mark the manners of a people. In the opulent families, there is always a negro placed on the look-out, to announce the coming of any visitant; and the moment a carriage, or horseman, is descried, each negro changes his every day garb for a magnificent suit of livery. As the negroes wear no shirts, this is quickly effected; and in a few moments a ragged fellow is metamorphosed into a spruce footman. And woe to them should they neglect it; for their master would think himself disgraced, and *Sambo* and *Cuffy* incur a severe flogging.

In *Carolina,* the legislative and executive powers of the house belong to the mistress, the master has little or nothing to do with the administration; he is a monument of uxoriousness and passive endurance. The negroes are

[* And probably Catesby's works were accessible. William Bartram's 'Travels through North and South Carolina, &c' was published in 1791. In 1796 Dr. Michaux had returned to France, after spending several years in South Carolina. The travellers Schoepf and Castiglioni made careful studies of the botany of the Carolinas.]

not without the discernment to perceive this; and when the husband resolves to flog them, they often throw themselves at the feet of the wife, and supplicate her mediation. But the ladies of *Carolina,* and particularly those of *Charleston,* have little tenderness for their slaves; on the contrary, they send both their men-slaves and women-slaves, for the most venial trespass, to a hellish-mansion, called the Sugar-house: here a man employs inferior agents to scourge the poor negroes: a shilling for a dozen lashes is the charge: the man, or woman, is stripped naked to the waist; a redoubtable whip at every lash flays the back of the culprit, who, agonized in every pore, rends the air with his cries.

Mrs. D—— informed me that a *lady* of *Charleston,* once observed to her, that she thought it abominably dear to pay a shilling for a dozen lashes, and, that having many slaves, she would bargain with the man at the Sugar-house to flog them by the year.

It has been observed by Mr. *Jefferson,* that negroes secreting little by the kidnies, but much by the pores, exhale a strong effluvia.* But great is the power of habit, and in the hottest day of summer, when the thermometer in the shade has risen to a hundred, I have witnessed a dinner party of ladies and gentlemen, surrounded by a tribe of lusty negro-men

* Vide Notes on *Virginia.*

and women. I leave my reader to draw the inference.

Of the understanding of negroes, the masters in *Carolina* have a very mean opinion. But it is obvious to a stranger of discernment, that the sentiments of black *Cuffy* who waits at table, are often not less just or elevated than those of his white ruler, into whose hand, Fortune, by one of her freaks, has put the whip of power. Nor is there much difference in their language; for many planters seem incapable of displaying their sovereignty, by any other mode than menaces and imprecations. Indeed, it must occur to every one, that were things to be re-organized in their natural order, the master would in many parts of the globe, exchange with his servant.

An *Englishman* cannot but draw a proud comparison between his own country and *Carolina*. He feels with a glow of enthusiasm the force of the poet's exclamation:*

> " Slaves cannot breathe in *England!*
> They touch our country, and their shackles fall;
> That's noble, and bespeaks a nation proud
> And jealous of their rights."

[* Duyckinck (Vol. I, p. 563) describes Davis's Travels as "a book of pleasant exaggerations." Throughout this book it must be remembered that the author is a novelist, and a sentimentalist. Slavery as it existed in the Southern States was a rudimentary education. If the design was to bring the black man out of Guinea into modern handicraftsmanship, it is difficult to see how the introduction could have been better effected.]

It is, indeed, grating to an *Englishman* to mingle with society in *Carolina;* for the people, however well-bred in other respects, have no delicacy before a stranger in what relates to their slaves. These wretches are execrated for every involuntary offence; but negroes endure execration without emotion, for they say, *when Mossa curse, he break no bone.* But every master does not confine himself to oaths; and I have heard a man say, By heaven, my *Negurs* talk the worst English of any in *Carolina:* that boy just now called a bason a round-something: take him to the driver! let him have a dozen!

Exposed to such wanton cruelty the negroes frequently run away; they flee into the woods, where they are wet with the rains of heaven, and embrace the rock for want of a shelter. Life must be supported; hunger incites to depredation, and the poor wretches are often shot like the beasts of prey. When taken, the men are put in irons, and the boys have their necks encircled with a " pot-hook."

The *Charleston* papers abound with advertisements for fugitive slaves. I have a curious advertisement now before me. " Stop the
" runaway. Fifty dollars reward. Whereas
" my waiting fellow, *Will,* having eloped
" from me last Saturday, *without any provo-*
" *cation,* (it being known that I am a *hu-*
" *mane master*) the above reward will be

" paid to any one who will lodge the afore-
" said *slave* in some jail or deliver him to
" me on my plantation at *Liberty Hall.*
" *Will may be known by the incisions of the*
" *whip on his back;* and I suspect has taken
" the road to *Coosohatchie,* where he has a
" wife and five children, whom I sold last
" week to Mr. *Gillespie."*

A. Levi.

Thus are the poor negroes treated in *Carolina.* Indeed, planters usually consider their slaves as beings defective in understanding; an opinion that excites only scorn from the philosopher. The human soul possesses faculties susceptible of improvement, without any regard to the color of the skin. It is education that makes the difference between the master and the slave. Shall the imperious planter say, that the swarthy sons of *Africa,* who now groan under his usurpation of their rights, would not equal him in virtue, knowledge and manners, had they been born free, and with the same advantages in the scale of society? It is to civilization that even *Europeans* owe their superiority over the savage; who knows only how to hunt and fish, to hew out a canoe from a tree, and construct a wretched hut; and but for this, the inhabitants of *Britain* had still bent the bow, still clothed themselves in skins, and still traversed the woods.

No climate can be hotter than that of *South Carolina* and *Georgia*. In the piazza of a house at *Charleston,* when a breeze has prevailed, and there has been no other building near to reflect the heat of the sun, I have known the mercury in *Fahrenheit's* thermometer to stand at 101. In the night it did not sink below 89.

Animal heat I ascertained to be less than the heat of the weather. By confining the thermometer to the hottest part of my body, I found the mercury subside from 101 to 96. In fact I never could raise the thermometer higher than 96 by animal heat.*

In a voyage to the *East Indies,* I kept a regular account of the height of the thermometer, both in the sun and shade. My journal is now before me. At eight in the morning, when our ship was on the Equator, the thermometer in the shade was only 77 degrees; and the same day in the sun at noon it was 99.†

It may be advanced that the pavements of *Charleston,* and the situation of *Savannah,* which is built on a sandy eminence, may augment the heat of the weather; but be that as

---

* *Boerhave* fixed the vital heat at only 92 degrees; but both *Sir Isaac Newton* and *Fahrenheit* have made it 96.

† I have found since making these observations, that from nearly 4000 experiments made at *Madras,* the medium height of the thermometer was 80,9. The general greatest height, 87,1; and the least, 75,5. The extreme difference 11,$\frac{1}{4}$.

it may, it is, I think, incontrovertible, that no two places on the earth are hotter than *Savannah* and *Charleston*. I do not remember that the thermometer in the shade at *Batavia* exceeded 101.

But if the heat of the weather in the southernmost States be excessive,* not less sudden are its changes. In fact, so variable is the weather, that one day not infrequently exhibits the vicissitudes of the four seasons. The remark of an early colonist is more than poetically true.

> *Hic adeo inconstans est, et variable cælum,*
> *Una ut non raro est æstus hiemsque die.*

I have known one day the mercury to stand at 85; and the next it has sunk to 39.

But it is from the middle of *June* to the middle of *September*, that the excessive heats prevail. It is then the debilitating quality of the weather consigns the languid lady to her sopha, who, if she lets fall her pocket handkerchief, has not strength to pick it up, but calls to one of her black girls, who is all life and vigour. Hence there is a proportion of

[* A letter from Georgia is given in *American Husbandry*, London, 1775 (II, 7). The writer says, " In the observations I have made on the climate's being uncommonly hot, I confine myself entirely to the hottest part of the summer, July, August, and part of September, and perhaps, but not always, a week the latter end of June. As to the rest of the year, you have no idea of the charms of this climate at a distance from the sea."]

good and evil in every condition; for a negro-girl is not more a slave to her mistress, than her mistress to a sopha; and the one riots in health, while the other has every faculty enervated.

Negroes are remarkably tolerant of heat. A negro in the hottest month will court a fire.

From the black there is an easy transition to the white man. Society in *Carolina* exhibits not that unrestrained intercourse which characterises *English* manners. And this remark will apply throughout the States of the Union. The *English* have been called reserved; and an *American* who forms his notions of their manners from *Addison* and *Steele*, entertains a contemptible opinion of the cheerfulness that prevails in the *nook-shotten isle of Albion*.

But let the cheerfulness of both countries be fairly weighed, and I believe the scale will preponderate in favour of the *English*. That quality termed humour is not indigenous to *America*. The pleasantries of a droll would not relax the risible muscles of a party of *Americans,* however disposed to be merry; the wag would feel no encouragement from the surrounding countenances to exert his laughter-moving powers; but like the tyrant in the tragedy, he would be compelled to swallow the poison that was prepared for another.

Cotton in *Carolina,* and horse-racing in

Virginia, are the prevailing topics of conversation: these reduce every understanding to a level, and to these *Americans* return from the ebullitions of the humourist, as the eye weary of contemplating the sun, rejoices to behold the verdure.

Captain *Pelotte,* who, I have observed, composed one of our hunting party, having invited me to the review of the Militia of *Coosohatchie* district, I rode with him to the muster-field near *Bee's-Creek,* where his troop was assembled. It was a pleasant spot of thirty acres, belonging to a school-master, who educated the children of the families in the neighbourhood.

There is scarcely any contemplation more pleasing than the sight of a flock of boys and girls just let loose from school. Those whom nature designed for an active, enterprising life, will contend for being the foremost to cross the threshold of the school-door; while others of a more wary temper keep remote from the strife.

A throng of boys and girls was just released from the confinement of the school, as I reached *Bee's Creek* with Captain *Pelotte.* Our horses and they were mutually acquainted. The beasts pricked up their ears, and some of the children saluted them by name; while some, regardless of both the horses and their riders, were earnestly pursuing butterflies; some stooping to gather flowers; some chaunting songs; and all taking the road that led to the muster-field. If ever I felt the nature that breathes through *Shenstone's* School poem, it was on beholding this band of little men and little women.

"*And now Dan Phœbus gains the middle skie,*
  And Liberty unbars her prison-door,
 And like a rushing torrent, out they fly,
  And now the grassy cirque is cover'd o'er
 With boist'rous revel-rout and wild uproar;
  A thousand ways in wanton rings they run.
 Heav'n shield their short-liv'd pastimes, I implore!
  For well may Freedom, erst so dearly won,
 Be to Columbia's sons more gladsome than the sun." *

Captain *Pelotte* having reviewed his soldiers, marched them triumphantly round a huge oak that grew in the centre of the parade, animated by the sound of the spirit-stirring drum; and afterwards laid siege to a dinner of venison in the open air, to which I gave my assistance. It was a republican meal. Captain, Lieutenants, and Privates, all sat down together at table, and mingled in familiar converse. But the troop devoured such an enormous quantity of rice, that I was more than once inclined to believe they had emigrated from *China*.

On the 7th of *April* 1799, I accepted the invitation of a Mr. *Wilson*, who was visiting

[* *The Schoolmistress*, St. 30.]

the family at *Ocean,* to accompany him to *Savannah;* glad with the opportunity to extend my travels into *Georgia,* and not less happy to cultivate his acquaintance.

We left *Ocean* plantation at eight in the morning. Mr. *Wilson* drove himself in a sulky, and I rode on horseback, followed by a servant on another.

Our journey offered nothing to view but an uncultivated tract, or one continued pine barren; for *Priesburg* * is a village composed of only three houses, and *Barnazoba* can boast only the same number of plantations.

Having refreshed ourselves in the house of Mrs. *Hayward's* Overseer, (the lady was gone to *Charleston*) we waded from *Barnazoba,* through mud and mire to the mouth of a creek, where we embarked with a couple of negroes in a canoe, and were paddled into a small river that empties itself into that of *Savannah.* Again we landed, and walked about a mile to another plantation, of which the white people were absent, but the negroes remained. *Jee Chri!* exclaimed a negro-wench, *too much buckra come here today, for true!* Here we launched a large canoe, and were rowed to my companion's plantation; dining on the water in our passage thither. The negroes of the plantation beheld the coming of Mr. *Wilson* with joy; old and young of both sexes came to the landing place to

[* Purysburg.]

welcome his approach. The canoe was in a moment run high and dry upon the beach, and the air resounded with acclamations.

We left the plantation in a four-oared canoe, and were rowed with velocity up the beautiful river of *Savannah*. Quantities of alligators were basking in the sun on both shores. They brought to my recollection the happy description of *Ariosto*.

> *Vive sub lito è dentro a la Riviera,*
> *Ei corpi umane son le sue vivande,*
> *De le persone misere è incaute,*
> *Di Viandanti è d'infelice naute.**

This animal (says the poet) lives on the river and its banks; preying on human flesh: the bodies of unwary travellers, of passengers, and of sailors.

We landed at *Yamacraw,* the name given by the *Indians* to the spot on which part of *Savannah* is built; and after ploughing through one or two streets of sand, we reached *Dillon's* boarding-house, where we were obligingly received, and comfortably accommodated. There was a large party at supper composed principally of cotton manufacturers from *Manchester,* whose conversation operated on me like a dose of opium. Cotton!

[* E grande a maraviglia questa fiera;
    Vive molto, e vivendo sempre cresce:
    Sta ora in terra, ed or nella riviera.
                    Berni: *Orlando*, III, 3, 6.]

Cotton! Cotton! Cotton! was their never-ceasing topic. Oh! how many Travellers would have devoured up their discourse; for my part I fell asleep, and nodded till a negro offered to light me to my room.*

Savannah is built on a sandy eminence. Let the *English* reader picture to himself a town erected on the cliffs of Dover, and he will behold *Savannah*. But the streets are so insupportably sandy, that every inhabitant wears goggles over his eyes, which give the people an appearance of being in masquerade. When the wind is violent *Savannah* is a desärt scene.

Having purchased a little edition of Mrs. *Smith's* sonnets,† my delight was to ascend the eminence which commands the view of the river, and read my book undisturbed. With my pencil I wrote on my tablets the following sonnet to the author.

SONNET TO CHARLOTTE SMITH.

BLEST Poetess! who tell'st so soft thy woe,
   I love to ponder o'er thy mournful lay,
In climes remote, where wan, forlorn and slow,
   To the wash'd strand I bend my listless way.

[* Historically the visit of these manufacturers is very interesting. De Quincey, who was a Manchester man, says somewhere that of all talk the purely literary is the worst, and that the talk of merchants is apt to be the wisest and the best.]

[† Charlotte Smith, 1749-1806. *Elegiac Sonnets and Other Poems.* 1797.]

Now, on *Savannah's* cliffs, I wayward read,
  In joy of grief, thy pity-moving strain,
While smiles afar the variegated mead,
  And not a wave disturbs the tranquil main.

Like thee, the Muse has from my infant hours,
  With smiles alluring won me to the grove;
Snatch'd, in a playful mood, some scatter'd flow'rs
  To deck my head, gay emblems of her love:

But mine of light, deceitful hues are made,
While thine of bloom perennial ne'er will fade.

The 11th of *April,* I returned with Mr. *Wilson* to the woods of *Coosohatchie,* which, I found Mr. *Drayton* and family, about to leave to their original tenants of racoons, squirrels, and opossums.

My table was covered with letters that were truly Ciceronian, from my elegant friend. Mr. *George* had left the sublime College of *Charleston,* for a seminary less famous, but more profitable, at *George-town,* at the confluence of the rivers *Winyaw* and *Waccamaw.* There, in concert with his uncle, an Episcopal Minister, he enjoyed an elegant society, and indulged in his favourite studies.

CHAP. IV.

Picture of a Family travelling through the Woods, —Terror Inspired by two Snakes, and the gallantry of an American boy.—Residence at Ashley River.—Removal to Sullivan's Island.—Literary Projects.—Anecdotes of Goldsmith.—A Journey on Foot from Charleston to Georgetown.—Elegy over the Grave of a Stranger in the Woods of Owendaw.—Reception at Georgetown.—Death of General Washington.—Journey back to Charleston.—Embark for New York.—Incidents of the Voyage.

IT was in the month of *May,* 1799, that Mr. *Drayton* and his family exchanged the savage woods of *Coosohatchie,* for the politer residence of their mansion on *Ashley River.* In our migration we formed quite a procession. Mr. *Drayton* occupied the coach with his lady and youngest daughter, and I advanced next with my fair pupil in a chair, followed by *William Henry* on a prancing nag, and half a dozen negro fellows, indifferently mounted, but wearing the laced livery of an opulent master. Thus hemmed in by the coach before, a troop of horsemen behind, and impenetrable woods on both sides, I could not refrain from whispering in the ear of my companion, that her friends had put it out of my power to run away with her that day.

About three in the afternoon, our journey being suspended by the heat of the weather, we stopped to eat a cold dinner, in a kind of lodge that had been erected by some hunters on the roadside, and which now hospitably accommodated a family travelling through the woods.

Here we took possession of the benches round the table to enjoy our repast: turning the horses loose to seek the shade; and cooling our wine in a spring that murmured near the spot. *William Henry,* having snatched a morsel, got ready his fowling-piece, to penetrate the woods in search of wild turkies; and while we were rallying him on his passion for hunting, the cry from a negro of a rattlesnake! disturbed our tranquillity. The snake was soon visible to every eye, dragging its slow length along the root of a large tree, and directing its attention to a bird, which chattered and fluttered from above, and seemed irresistibly disposed to fall into his distended jaws. *London,* a negro-servant, had snatched up a log, and was advancing to strike the monster a blow in the head, when a black snake, hastening furiously to the spot, immediately gave battle to the rattlesnake, and suspended, by his unexpected appearance, the power of the negro's arm. We now thought we had got into a nest of snakes, and the girls were screaming with fright, when, *William Henry,* taking an unerring aim with his gun, shot the rattlesnake, in the act of repulsing his enemy. The black snake, without a moment's procrastination, returned into the woods, and profiting by his example, we all pursued our journey, except *William Henry,* who stopped with a negro to take out the rattles of the monster he had killed. My pupil presented me with these rattles, which I carried for three years in my pocket, and finally gave them to the son of a Mr. *Andrews,* of *Warminster,* who had emigrated to *Baltimore,* and had been to me singularly obliging.*

We stopped a few days at *Stono,* where we

---

* Much has been said by Travellers of the fascinating power of snakes in *America. Credat Judæus Apella, non Ego!* Things are best illustrated by comparison. It is known to almost every man who has not passed his days in the smoke of *London, Salisbury,* or *Bristol,* but incited by the desire of knowledge, has made a *Tour* into the country; I maintain it could not escape the observation of such a *Tourist,* that birds will flatten their wings, and exhibit the utmost agitation, at the approach of a fox near a tree on which they are perched. Filled with the same dread, a bird in *America* cannot refrain from fluttering over a snake; and the *American* snakes, however inferior in cunning to the *English* foxes, being endowed with more perseverance; fear deprives the bird of motion, and it falls into his jaws. It is by thus tracing effects to their causes that truth is promulgated; and hence I am enabled to detect and expose the fallaciousness of the opinion, that there is any charm, or fascination in the eye of a snake.

were kindly received by Mr. *Wilson*, my late travelling companion into *Georgia*. I expected that *William Henry* would receive the applauses of his friends for the presence of mind he had displayed in killing the rattlesnake; but when the youngest sister recited the story to the family; they heard her without emotion, and only smiled at it as a trifling incident.

In the venerable mansion at *Ashley River*,* I again directed the intellectual progress of my interesting pupils, and, enlarged the imagination of *William*, by putting *Pope's* version of the Odyssey into his hands, which I found among other books that composed the family library. He had before read the Iliad; but neither *Patroclus* slain by *Hector*, nor *Hector* falling beneath the avenging arm of *Achilles*, imparted half the rapture which *Ulysses* inspired with his companions in the cave of *Polyphemus*. I am of the opinion of *Warton*,† that the great variety of events and scenes exhibited in the *Odyssey*, cannot fail to excite a more lively interest than the martial uniformity of the *Iliad*.

The garden of Mr. *Drayton's* mansion led to the banks of *Ashley River*, which after a rapid course of twenty miles, discharged it-

[* "Magnolia," now the famous Magnolia Gardens.]
[† Joseph Warton, *Essay on Pope*, Vol. I, 1757; Vol. II, 1782.]

self into the *Atlantic*. The river was not wanting in picturesqueness, and, once, while stretched at my ease on its banks, I meditated an Ode.

ODE ON ASHLEY RIVER.*

ON gentle *Ashley's* winding flood,
    Enjoying philosophic rest;
I court the calm, umbrageous wood,
    No more with baleful care opprest.

Or, on its banks supinely laid,
    The distant mead and field survey,
Where branching laurels form a shade
    To keep me from the solar ray.

While flows the limpid stream along,
    With quick meanders through the grove,
And from each bird is heard the song
    Of careless gaiety and love.

And when the moon, with lustre bright,
    Around me throws her silver beam,
I catch new transport from the sight,
    And view her shadow in the stream.

While *Whip-poor-will* repeats his tale,
    That echoes from the boundless plain;
And blithsome to the passing gale,
    The Mocking-bird pours out his strain.

Hence with a calm, contented mind,
    Sweet pleasure comes without alloy;
Our own felicity we find—
    'Tis from the heart springs genuine joy.

[* Later, Hayne made verses on Ashley River.]

An elder brother of Mr. *Drayton* was our neighbour on the river; he occupied, perhaps, the largest house and gardens in the United States of America.* Indeed I was now breathing the politest atmosphere in *America;* for our constant visitors were the highest people in the State, and possessed of more house-servants than there are inhabitants in *Occoquan.* These people never moved but in a carriage, lolled on sophas instead of sitting on chairs, and were always attended by their negroes to fan them with a peacock's feather. Such manners were ill suited to an Englishman [who] loved his ease; and who, whenever their carriages were announced, I always took my gun, and went into the woods. Oh! for a freedom from the restraint imposed by well-bred inanity.

From *Ashley River,* after a short residence, we removed to *Charleston,* which was full of visitors from the woods, and exhibited a motley scene. *Here* was to be perceived a *Coachee,* without a glass to exclude the dust, driven by a black fellow, not less proud of the livery of luxury, than the people within the vehicle were of a suit made in the fashion. *There* was to be discovered a *Carolinian* buck, who had left off essences and powder, and, in what related to his hair, resembled an ancient *Roman;* but in the distribution of his dress,

[* Charles Drayton, of "Drayton Hall," on Ashley River.]

was just introducing that fashion in *Charleston*, which was giving way in succession to another in *London*. But he had an advantage over his transatlantic rival; he not only owned the horse he rode, but the servant who followed. To be brief, such is the pride of the people of *Charleston,* that no person is seen on foot unless it be a mechanic, or some mechanical Tutor. He who is without horses and slaves incurs always contempt. The consideration of property has such an empire over the mind, that poverty and riches are contemplated through the medium of infamy and virtue. Even negroes are infected with this idea; and *Cuffey* shall be heard to exclaim, *He great blackguard that—he got no negur. Where his horse? He alway walk.*

I found my friend Doctor *De Bow* in high repute at *Charleston,* and not without the hope that he should soon keep his carriage. *Scribimus docti indoctique.* He was busy in writing a piece for the Medical Repository at *New-York;* that is, he was communicating his thoughts in a letter to the great Doctor *Mitchel.** His object was to undermine the fame of the *Charleston* Physicians, by exposing the impropriety of their treatment of the *Croup;* a complaint uncommonly prevalent in the Southern States of the Union. " This

[* Samuel Latham Mitchill, 1764-1831, " Nestor of American Science."]

"treatise, whispered the Doctor, will make me be called in to children, and if I once get the child for a patient, I shall soon have the parents. Oh! that I could only express my thoughts on paper! I would carry every thing before me. But writing and talking require very different qualifications. Impudence will make an orator; but to write well requires reading digested by reflection."

The Doctor entreated I would lend him my assistance to write his Essay on the Croup. I begged to be excused by professing my utter unacquaintance with the mode of treating the disease.

"No matter, said the Doctor. How to treat the disease no man knows better than I; but treating it, and writing a treatise on it are things widely different. Come, let me dictate to you the heads of the discourse, and do you *lengthify* and ramify them *secundum artem* into a treatise. Quote a good deal of *Latin,* and dignify your style with all the hard words you can remember. But let the title be powerful; let it smite the eye of the reader with irresistible force. For the Medical Repository! New, but unanswerable, objections against the present mode of treating the Croup by the Physicians of *Charleston;* communicated in a letter to Dr. *Mitchel,* by *W. De Bow,* M.D.— *Nullius addictus jurare in verba magistri!*"

Bravo, cried I. And now, Doctor, for a few words of introduction to the philippic.

That, sir, you shall have; I never could endure a play without a prologue. Why, say (but write the first word in capitals), " PHYSICIANS, however they may be es-" tablished and in vogue, are yet liable to be " mistaken in their prognostics and diagnos-" tics. *Humanum est errare!*"

The Doctor was here interrupted by a negro boy, who called him to attend his master in the last stage of the yellow fever. The Doctor immediately slipped on a black coat, put his enormous spectacles on his nose, and snatching up his gold-headed cane, followed the negro down stairs.

The Doctor being gone, it was not possible to do justice to the Treatise on the Croup; but finding myself disposed to write something, I addressed my friend in an Ode. The Doctor was about to embark for the *Havannah* as Surgeon of a ship; and his approaching voyage furnished me with a hint.

ODE TO WILLIAM DE BOW, M.D.

SINCE on the ocean's boundless deep,
  Once more impelled by fate you go,
The Muse the trembling wire would sweep,
  And soft invoke each gale to blow.

Long has it been our doom to roam,
  With hearts by friendship's cement bound,

(The world at large our only home)
  O'er many a wide expanse of ground.

At PHILADELPHIA's sad confine,
  Where death stalk'd round with aspect wild,
We saw the widow vainly pine,
  And heard the mother mourn her child:

While desolation mark'd the scene,
  And groans of dying fill'd each gale,
Where dance no more rejoic'd the green,
  Nor song re-echo'd from the dale.

May no such griefs again demand
  The sigh of pity from thy breast,
But jocund pleasure's mirthful band,
  Sooth ev'ry baleful care to rest.

Then festive let thy moments flow,
  While round thee roars the briny flood;
May ev'ry breeze auspicious blow,
  And nought provoke the wat'ry god.

Having leisure for some literary undertaking, I issued a prospectus for the publication of two Voyages to the *East Indies*. The work was to be comprised in an octavo volume, and delivered to subscribers for two dollars. Mr. *Drayton*, without hesitation, subscribed for ten copies; and in a few weeks I could boast a long list of subscribers from the circles of fashion.

Shortly after, the Farmers' Museum, published in *New Hampshire*, was found to contain a curious notice on the subject; "The

"Translator of *Buonaparte's* Campaign,
"whose poetry we have praised in a former
"Museum, has issued a subscription-paper,
"for the publication of *Two Voyages to the
"East Indies.* From the genius of this Gen-
"tleman, we have the strongest reason to con-
"clude, that his work will be a pleasing pro-
"duction. But these are coster-monger times
"for his book, and ere the date of fresh liter-
"ary disappointment begin, he should remem-
"ber that if in any of the peddling streets of
"*Charleston, Philadelphia, Boston,* or *New-
"York,* he were to expose for sale a single
"bale of *Gurrahs,* or *Hummum,* it would ad-
"vance his fortune and reputation more than
"by writing volumes of instructive or amus-
"ing narrative. We wish this writer success;
"to ensure it, let him direct his bookseller to
"make a shipment to *England* of the whole
"impression." *

It is difficult to say, whether this encomium of Mr. *Dennie* promoted or retarded the subscription to the volume; but it was of little consequence, for notwithstanding my friend *George* wrote a poetical epistle for the work, I contented myself with abridging it for my own amusement.

[* Warrant for the Edinburgh Reviewer's celebrated questions, posed twenty years later: 'Who reads an American book? who drinks out of American glasses? or eats from American plates? or wears American coats or gowns? or sleeps in American blankets?' *Edinburgh Review,* No. 65.]

To avoid the fever which every summer commits its ravages at *Charleston*, Mr. *Drayton* removed with his family in *July* to a convenient house on *Sullivan's Island*. The front windows commanded a view of the *Atlantic*, whose waves broke with fury not a hundred yards from the door. It is almost superfluous to observe, that *Sullivan's Island* lies opposite to *Charleston*, at the distance of eight miles.

In the garden on our premises, I took possession of a neat little box, which served me for a seminary, and house of repose. Here I was gratified with the company of Mr. *George*, who came to visit me from *Georgetown*. Not more joyous was the meeting of *Flaccus* and *Maro* at the Appian Way:

O! qui complexus, et gaudia quanta fuerunt! *

He was received with every elegance of urbanity by Mr. and Mrs. *Drayton;* but he compared our situation to *Æneas* among the *Greeks; vadimus immixti Danais haud numine nostro.* So natural is it for a wit to ridicule his host.

Passage-boats are always to be procured from *Sullivan's Island* to *Charleston*, and I was introduced by my friend to an Irish Clergyman, of the name of Best, who was attached to Mr. *George*, partly from his being

[* Hor. *Sat.*, I, 5, 43.]

an Irishman, and partly from esteem for his attainments.

Mr. *Best* communicated to me a few anecdotes relative to *Goldsmith*, which I minuted down in his presence.

" The Deserted Village, said he, relates to
" scenes in which *Goldsmith* was an actor.
" *Auburn* is a poetical name for the village
" of *Lissoy*, in the county of *Westmeath*
" *Barony, Kilkenny West*. The name of the
" schoolmaster was *Paddy Burns*. I remem-
" ber him well. He was indeed a man severe
" to view. A woman called *Walsey Cruse*,
" kept the ale house."

> " Imagination fondly stoops to trace
> The parlour-splendors of the festive place."

" I have often been in the house.
" The hawthorn bush was remarkably large,
" and stood opposite the alehouse. I was once
" riding with *Brady*, titular Bishop of *Ar-*
" *dagh*, when he observed to me, Ma foy,
" *Best*, this huge, overgrown bush, is mightily
" in the way; I will order it to be cut down.
" What, Sir, said I, cut down *Goldsmith's*
" Hawthorn-Bush, that supplies so beautiful
" an image in the Deserted Village! Ma foy!
" exclaimed the Bishop, is that the hawthorn-
" bush! Then ever let it be sacred to the edge
" of the axe, and evil to him that would cut
" from it a branch."

Mr. *Best* also related to me some anecdotes that would serve to illustrate the Traveller, which I regret are not preserved, for the Traveller is a poem that is ever read with new rapture. The mind can scarcely refrain from picturing *Goldsmith* in the capacity of an Adventurer; travelling with an expansion to his mental powers, and feeling the impulse of his poetical genius; observing with a philosophic eye the mingled scenes before him, and framing from their diversity the subject of his poem.

The stone of *Sisyphus* calling my friend back to *George-town,* I was once more left to the tuition of *William Henry,* and his sisters. My pupil was not, I believe, content with his insular situation, but sighed for the woods, his dogs, and his gun. Man laughs at the sports of children; but even their most trifling pastimes form his most serious occupations; and their drums, and rattles, and hobbyhorses, are but the emblems and mockery of the business of mature age.

No families are more migratory than those of *Carolina.* From *Sullivan's Island* we went again to the mansion on *Ashley River,* where I had invitations to hunt, to feast and to dance. But nothing could sooth the despondency I felt on the approaching return of Mr. *Drayton* to the woods of *Coosohatchie.* He guessed the cause of my woe-begone looks, and, rather than be deprived of my services, politely offered to pass the winter on the banks of *Ashley River:* Nay, he even proposed to send his son, when the war terminated, to make with me the tour of the Continent of *Europe.* There are few men that in my situation would have resisted such allurements; but I dreaded the tainted atmosphere that had despatched so many of my countrymen to the house appointed for all living; and, filled with apprehension, I left this charming family in whose bosom I had been so kindly cherished, to seek another climate, and brave again the rigours of adversity.*

* The mortality among foreigners during the summer months, at *Charleston,* is incredibly great. Few Europeans escape that plague of plagues the yellow fever. The attack is always sudden, and lays hold of the strongest. He whose veins glowed but yesterday with health shall to-day be undergoing the agonies of the damned. The temporal arteries of the wretched victim are ready to burst; black vomiting ensues; the skin turns yellow; the man so lately rioting in lustihood is without the strength of a child; and his tongue lolling out, he dies delirious.

"What now avail
The strong-built sinewy limbs, and well-spread shoulders?
See how he tugs for life, and lays about him,
Mad with his pain! The sight how hideous!
Oh! how his eyes stand out, and stare full ghastly!
While the distemper's rank and deadly venom
Shoots like a burning arrow cross his bowels,
And drinks his marrow up. Heard you that groan?
'Twas his last. See how the great Goliah,
Just like a child that crawl'd itself to rest,
Lies still."

[The author's footnote is one of alarm. The mortality

The fifteenth of *December,* 1799, I rode from *Ashley River* to *Charleston,* with the design of proceeding to *George-town,* and visiting the academic bowers of my friend. I had again determined to travel on foot, and enjoy the meditations produced from walking and smoking amidst the awful solitude of the woods. Having provided myself with a pouch of *Havannah* segars, and put a poem into my pocket, which Mr. *George* had composed over the grave of a stranger on the road, I crossed the ferry at *Cooper's River,* and began my journey from a spot that retains the aboriginal name of *Hobcaw.*

In travelling through an endless tract of pines, a man can find few objects to describe, but he may have some reflections to deliver. I was journeying through endless forests, that, once inhabited by numerous races of *Indians,* were now without any individual of their original possessors; for the diseases and luxuries introduced by the Colonist had exterminated the greater number, and the few wretches that survived, had sought a new country beyond the rivers and mountains.*

from yellow fever among strangers in Charleston at that time was undoubtedly high. See, Dr. David Ramsay's Charleston Medical Register for 1802, reviewed in *Medical Repository,* VI, 308 ff. Dr. Ramsay gives an interesting account of an attempt, during the hot season, to rob the Charleston Bank. The operator, a Kentucky man, was ninety days underground: the hypothesis is that desire of gain rendered him immune.]

[* Not very distant. The country between Knoxville and

For the last fifteen miles of my journey I encountered no human being but a way-faring German; and heard no sound but that of the wood-pecker,* and the noise of the negroe's axe felling trees. There was no other object to employ the sight, and no other noise to disturb the repose of the desert.

I supped and slept at a solitary tavern kept by young Mr. *Dubusk,* whose three sisters might have sat to a painter for the Graces. Delicate were their shapes, transparent their skins, and the fire of their eyes drove the traveller to madness. Finding my young landlord companionable, I asked him why he did not pull down the sign of General *Washington,* that was over his door, and put up the portrait of his youngest sister. That, said he, would be a want of modesty: and, besides, if *Jemima* is really handsome, she can want no effigy; for good wine, as we landlords say, needs no bush.

Mr. *Dubusk* was a mighty great dancer.

Nashville, Tennessee, was Indian Territory then, and the Creeks and Chickasaws lay to the south. In 1796 and 1797 Francis Baily, later President of the Royal Astronomical Society, travelled through that region. Cf. his *Journal of a Tour in Unsettled Parts of North America.* London, 1856, pp. 346 ff.]

* The wood-pecker of Carolina, in striking his beak against a tree, makes a quick, sharp noise, which he keeps up for some time by repetition. An emigrant planter on first hearing it, was terrified beyond measure; and ran pale and quaking to his house, calling out, a rattlesnake! oh! a rattlesnake!

Indeed, he would frequently fall a capering, unconscious of being observed. But he swore he would dance no more in the day-time, because it was ungenteel. We drew our chairs near the fire after supper, when Mr. *Dubusk* did his utmost to entertain me. He related that, only a few nights before, some sparks had put a black-pudding into his bed, which, by the moon-light through his window, his apprehension magnified into a black snake, and made him roar out murder!

What, cried I, can you, who are a native of *Carolina,* be afraid of a snake? Not, said he, if I meet him on the road, or in the woods. I wish I had as many acres of land as I have killed rattlesnakes in this country. My plantation would be a wide one.—Mr. *Dubusk* was somewhat a wag. Being called on after supper to sing the patriotic song of *Hail Columbia;* he parodied it with much drollery.

> Hail Columbia! happy land!
> Full of pines, and burning sand!

At this I was surprised; for *Hail Columbia* exacts not less reverence in *America,* than the Marselloise Hymn in *France,* and Rule Britannia in *England.*

Before I quit the subject of Mr. *Dubusk,* I will mention a delicacy of conduct which I could not but remark in him; and which I record for the imitation of *American* Planters. Having thoughtlessly chastised a negro-boy in the room, he apologized for doing it before me; a circumstance which verified the observation that good breeding is the natural result of good sense.

The next morning, Mr. *Dubusk* walked with me a few miles on my road; but my companion having business at a plantation in the woods, I was soon left to pursue my journey alone through the sand. My sight was still bounded by the same prospect as ever. I could only distinguish before me a road that seemed endless, and mossy forests on each border of it. An *European* gazes with wonder at the long and beautiful moss, that spreading itself from the branches of one tree to those of another, extends through whole forests.*

It was now eight in the morning; the weather was mild, and I walked vigorously forward, *chewing the cud of sweet and bitter fancy.*

At *Darr's* tavern, I found nobody but a negro-woman, who was suckling her child, and quieting its clamours by appropriating, instead of a common rattle, the rattles of a snake. I would have much rather heard her

---

* This moss when it becomes *dead* serves many useful purposes. The negroes carry it to *Charleston*, where it is bought to stuff mattrasses, and chair bottoms. The hunters always use it for wadding to their guns.

jingle the keys of the cupboard in the child's ears; but, unfortunately for me, Mr. *Darr* was gone out, and had taken the keys with him.

I was, therefore, glad to obtain a plate of *Mush,** which having eaten *sans* milk, *sans* sugar, and even *sans* molasses, I gave the good woman a piece of silver, and again pursued my journey.

Beshrew the Traveller who would let fall a reflection over the dinner I here made. Though plain, it was wholesome; and instead of wishing it was better, I thanked God it was not worse.

A walk of eight more miles brought me to *Owendaw* bridge, and, taking a small path that led into the woods, I sought for the grave of a stranger, of whom tradition has preserved no remembrance; and whose narrow house I at length discovered under a large and stately pine. I suppress the reflections which filled my breast on beholding it. Mr. *George* had anticipated me in a poem, which I meditated over the grave in all the luxury of melancholy.

ELEGY OVER THE GRAVE OF AN UNKNOWN, IN THE WOODS OF OWENDAW.

NOW while the sun in ocean rolls the day,
Pensive I view where yonder trees display
The lonely heap of earth, where here unmourn'd,
Beneath the pine the stranger lies inurn'd.

* Indian meal boiled.

Near these green reeds, that shade the passing wave,
The grass proclaims the long neglected grave,
Where dark and drear the mossy forests rise,
And nature hides her form from mortal eyes;
Where never print of human step is found,
Nor ever sun-beam cheers the gloomy ground,
But towering pines the light of heaven preclude,
And cedars wave in endless solitude;
Where stretch'd amid the leaves, the branching hind
Hears the tall cypress murmur to the wind.
All now unknown, if here this space of dust
Enclose the ashes of the base or just;
Nor wept by friendship, nor enroll'd by fame,
Without a tomb, and e'en without a name.
So rests amid these over-arching woods,
Some hapless corse, regardless of the floods,
Which oft around with angry deluge sweep,
And roll the wrecks of ages to the deep.
Those warring passions struggling to be free,
Those eyes that once the blaze of heaven could see;
That hand from which, perhaps, the brave retir'd;
That heart which once the breath of life inspir'd,
Now shut forever from the face of day,
Claim but at last this narrow spot of clay.
Unhappy dust, no memory remains
Of what of thee once trod these gloomy plains,
Whether some wish, that fires the human breast,
Of glory, or of wealth, was here supprest;
Or great, or humble, was thy former lot,*
To all unknown, by all the world forgot!

[* In the old churchyard at Cheraw, South Carolina, there is a stone with this inscription—

"My name—my country—what are they to thee?
What—whether high or low my pedigree?
Perhaps I far surpassed all other men.
Perhaps I fell below them all—what then?

But what is friendship or exalted fame,
Which time may wound, or Envy's eye may blame?
Alike the lofty and the low must lie,
Alike the hero and the slave must die;
A few short years their names from earth shall sweep,
Unfelt as drops when mingling with the deep.
For thee no tomb arrests the passing eye,
No muse implores the tributary sigh,
Nor weeping sire shall hither press to mourn,
Nor frantic spouse invoke thee from thine urn;
But here unwept, beneath this gloomy pine,
Eternal nights of solitude are thine.
So when conflicting clouds, in thunder driven,
Shake to its base the firmament of heaven,
Prone on the earth the lofty cedar lies,
Unseen, and in an unknown valley dies:
So falls the towering pride of mortal state,
So perish all the glories of the great.
In vain with hope to distant realms we run,
Some bliss to share, or misery to shun.
In vain the man of narrow bosom flies,
Where meanness triumphs, and where honour dies;
And fills the sable bark with sordid ore,
To swell the pomps that curse a guilty shore;
Pursu'd by fate through every realm and sea,
He falls at last unwept, unknown, like thee.

Pursuing my journey, in somewhat a dejected mood, I crossed over *Owendaw* Bridge, and walked forward at a moderate rate. In fact I regulated my pace by the sun,

Suffice it, stranger, that thou see'st a tomb.
Thou know'st its use; it hides no matter whom."

Cf. *Idle Comments.* By Erwin Avery. Charlotte, N..C., 1905.]

which was descending behind me in the woods, and at which I occasionally looked back.

About night-fall I reached Mr. *Mac Gregor's* tavern, of which the proximity was announced by the axe of the negro chopping wood. No sound can be more delightful than this to the foot-traveller in *America,* when night has cast its shadows over the face of the country. It not only informs him that he is near some human habitation; but associates the welcome image of a warm fire-side, and an invigorating supper.

The house of Mr. *Mac Gregor* was agreeably situated on the *River Santee.* But it was filled with the Planters and young women from the neighbouring woods, who had assembled to celebrate their *Christmas* festival; for, it was, I discovered, the anniversary of the day that gave birth to our Redeemer. Strange! that I should regard time so little, as not to know that its inaudible and noiseless feet had stolen through another year.

The party was, however, taking time by the forelock. They had formed a dance! but could not begin it for want of their musician, whom they expected with impatience.

Curse that *Orpheus!* exclaimed one of the young men, who held by the hand a little girl of true virginal beauty, with fair hair floating over her shoulders; curse that *Orpheus!*

said he: I'll lay you,* he has got drunk again, and has lost himself in the woods! *Mac Gregor,* do lend me your horn; I'll go a little way, and blow to him.

Do *Jack,* said the landlord. I hope some bear or panther has not got him fast by the nape of the neck. The old sinner is down three shillings on the score.

Keep yourself cool, replied *Jack.* If I find the *Musicianer* dead, I'll lodge an execution against his fiddle for the benefit of his creditors.

Jack snatched up the horn, and slipping on his great coat, was about to sally into the woods to seek for the lost *Orpheus,* when the little girl, whose hand he had let go, anticipating his design, clung fondly round him, and burst into a violent flood of tears.

Why! what ails you, *Barbara,* cried *Jack.*

You are go—go—going in the woods! sobbed the afflicted girl. You'll meet with a—a—a panther!

Woman! all conquering woman! thou art every where the same; and thy empire over man is every where confest. Whether in the polished cities of *Europe,* or among the rude forests of *America,* thou canst practice the same arts, and inspire the same tenderness!

* Phrase of frequent occurrence among the southern *Americans.* [' My fortunes against any lay worth naming.' *Othello,* 2, 3, 330.]

The ferocity of *Jack* was softened by the mournful distraction of *Barbara*. It was a ludicrous spectacle. *Jack* in the towering height and breadth of his body, could scarcely, I think, be inferior to *Sampson;* he would have slain with his nervous arm a whole host of enemies. Yet here he was killed himself by only one glance from a virgin eye, that was brimful of tears; for some minutes his speech was suspended, and the giant could only look and sigh unutterable things. Oh! for the chisel of a *Praxiteles,* to represent this tender damsel; the most seducing object that love could employ to extend the limits of his empire. Insensibility itself would have fallen at the feet of so sweet a creature.

At length *Jack* recovered the use of his faculties. He laid down the horn; and catching *Barbara* in his arms, smacked her lips with such ardour, that he seemed to be tearing up kisses by the roots.

The girls in company blushed, or held down their heads; but the men fell into a roar of such loud and obstinate laughter, that, like the peal of *Homer's* gods, I thought it inextinguishable.

Mr. *Mac Gregor* now took the horn, and, going to the door, began to blow it with vehemence, and then to exclaim *Orpheus!* Yo ho! *Orpheus!* Must I come and look for my old snowball?

At length a voice was heard to reply, Who call *Orpheus?* That *Mossa Mac Gregee?* Here *Orpheus* come! Here he come himself!

It was not long before *Orpheus* made his appearance in the shape of an old *Guinea Negro,* scraping discord on a fiddle, reeling about from side to side, and grinning in the pride of his heart.

Each man now seized his partner, *Orpheus* struck up a jig, and down the dance went *Jack* and *Barbara,* with light, though untutored steps. Not being for any of their ambling, and finding that amidst such riot no sleep was to be had, I summoned a negro, and was paddled in a canoe, through *Push-and-go Creek,* to the opposite bank of *Santee River.* The *Whip-poor-will,* on my landing, was heard from the woods; and in prosecuting my walk, I meditated a sonnet to the bird.

SONNET TO THE WHIP-POOR-WILL.

POOR, plaintive bird! whose melancholy lay
   Suits the despondence of my troubled breast,
I hail thy coming at the close of day,
   When all thy tribe are hush'd in balmy rest.

Wisely thou shunn'st the gay, tumultuous throng,
   Whose mingled voices empty joys denote,
And for the sober night reserv'st thy song,
   When echo from the woods repeats thy note

Pensive, at silent night, I love to roam,
  Where elves and fairies tread the dewy green,
While the clear moon, beneath the azure dome,
  Sheds a soft lustre o'er the sylvan scene,

And hear thee tell thy moving tale of woe,
To the bright Empress of the Silver Bow.

I had now not to walk through woods, but over ground that had been cleared by the industry of the husbandman. But I had scarce proceeded half a mile when a party of horsemen, and girls double-mounted, came ambling over the plain; and all seemed to ask, with one voice, if the boat was at the ferry. I informed them that I had crossed *Santee River* in a canoe, which, I believed, was at the ferry, but that, far from embarking their party, it would not hold a third of them.

Then you came, said one of the men, through *Push-and-go Creek?*

I replied in the affirmative.

The devil take *Mac Gregor,* cried he. There are no snakes in *South Carolina* if I am not up to him for this. I hope *Orpheus* has not been able to find his way through the woods!

I assured the gentleman, that, if by *Orpheus* he meant a drunken negro, who scraped upon the fiddle,—he had not only reached the house, but put all the company in motion.

And is *Jack Douglas* there? said the horseman. He is a great, *lengthy* * fellow.

I answered in the affirmative.

And is he dancing, rejoined he, with a little girl; a black-eyed girl, with rather *lightish* hair, a pretty turn-up nose, and a dimple in one of her cheeks?

Sir, said I, the dimple in the young lady's cheek is particularly visible when she smiles.

'Tis she! 'Tis *Barbara!* exclaimed the fellow. Oh! all the devils! I'll not wait for the boat; I'll swim my beast across the river.

The company endeavoured to dissuade this *Leander* from his enterprize; but love was not to be cheated of its right; and putting his spurs into the horse's sides, he galloped towards *Santee*.

And now, my friends, said I, having satisfied your interrogations, let me ask you if there be any house on the road where I shall be likely to obtain a lodging?

Are you for *George-town?* said one of the men.

I replied in the affirmative.

Then, rejoined he, it is hard saying; for there is no house in the main-road between this and the *Run;* † and the *Run* is so high

* *Lengthy* is the *American* for *long*. It is frequently used by the *classical* writers of the New World.

† A stream that crosses a road is called a *Run* in the southern States. After a heavy rain, the *freshes* (floods) render these Runs for some time impassable. [Nice distinction be-

from the freshes, that you will not be able to ford it. We did not cross the *Run;* we live this side of it—away there (pointing with his hand), among the back-woods.

Old Billy, said another, would give the gentleman a lodging.

Old Billy! replied his companion. Do you think a white man would bemean himself to take up his quarters with a *negur?* Come, let us jog on.

Nothing can give more poignancy to the misfortunes of a Traveller, than for him to repine at them. I therefore walked forward with a decisive step, and whistled a merry tune as I brushed the dew with my feet.

In about half an hour, I reached a mud-hut, which stood adjoining to a wood. A little smoke arose from the chimney, but not a mouse was stirring near the dwelling. But from the woods was heard the cry of the Whip-poor-will, and the croaking of the bull-frogs.

I peeped through a chink in the wall of this lonely hut. I soon discovered it was the habitation of *Old Billy* and *Billy's* old wife. I could distinguish an old negro-man and negro-woman, huddled together, like *Darby*

tween 'stream crossing a road,' as against 'road crossing a stream.' Then, as now, the smaller stream was often called 'branch.' 'Run' is a term particularly of the Piedmont country.]

and *Joan,* before the embers of an expiring fire, and passing from one to another the stump of an old pipe. I tapped at the door. Please God Almighty! said the old woman; who knock at our door this time of night? Why I thought nobody was awake but Whippoor-will!

Open the door, said the old man, very calmly. 'Tis mayhap some negur-man that has run away, and is now come out of the woods to beg a hoe-cake, or a bit of hominy.

Lack-a-day! you don't say so, replied the old woman. Some poor runaway without a bit of victuals to keep life and soul together. Well! there's a whole hoe-cake in the platter. That's lucky, for true!

The old woman came to the door, but, starting back on beholding me, exclaimed, Hie! this not negur! This one gentleman!

Let my page record the hospitality of this poor black woman and her husband. They proffered me their provisions, and helped me to the sweetest draught of water I ever remember to have drunk. They proposed to spread a blanket for me before the fire, and supply me out of their garments with a pillow for my head. In a word, though their faces were black, their hearts were not insensible.*

[* In his book, *The American Mariners* &c. Salisbury, 1822, the author gives his Greek version of a negro song, (p. 236)—

I could not overcome my prejudices. I felt the fulness of their humanity, but, my heart harboured that pride, which courted the rigours of the night rather than descend to become the guest of an *African* slave. I declined their offer with acknowledgments, and prosecuted my walk into the woods.

I had walked about three miles, lighted forward by the moon, and admonished of the lateness of the hour by the appearance of the Morning Star, when the barking of dogs, and the voices of men at a distance, filled me with the hope that I was approaching some village. My heart caught new pleasure, and I redoubled my pace; but in a few minutes, instead of entering a village, I found myself among a croud of waggons and waggoners, who, having their journey suspended by a run of water which had overflowed its banks, were preparing to encamp on the side of the road. Of these some were backing their waggons, some unharnessing their cattle, and some kindling a fire.

On coming to the bank of the stream, I asked a man who was splitting wood, whether there was any canoe to carry Travellers across the Run.

Indeed, I don't know, said he.

> " The winds roared, and the rains fell
> " The poor white man, faint and weary,
> " Came and sat under our tree &c."]

How is that? cried another waggoner, approaching the spot. If the stranger is willing to go to the expence of a canoe, I'll hew him one out of the stump of a tree in less than half an hour. I have tools in my waggon.

Sir, replied I, I think it will be more adviseable to tarry here till the floods are subsided. But is there no tavern near here?

There is not a grog-shop, said the man, between this and *George-town*. But if you chuse to drink some whiskey, I have got a demi-john in my waggon. Come, don't make yourself strange because I drive a waggon.

Sir, said I, it was my anxiety to obtain a lodging that made me ask for a tavern; I did not want liquor. But as you are polite enough to welcome me to your jorum of whiskey, I shall be happy to pledge you.

The fellow now went to his waggon, and, taking out a small demi-john of whiskey, returned to the place where I stood, followed by the whole of his fraternity. Come, said he, here's a good market for our tobacco! * And after taking a long draught, which called a profound sigh from his lungs, he handed me the demi-john, of which having drunk, I passed it in succession to my neighbour.

[* Cf. La Rochefoucauld, *Travels through the United States of North America*, London, 1799, Vol. I, p. 627: 'First six months of 1796, amount of tobacco exports, port of Charleston, 1,991 hogsheads.']

No man is more tenacious of etiquette than I. For two persons to become acquainted, the laws of good breeding exact the introduction of a third. This third personage I had now found in the demi-john of whiskey, and so without any further ceremony, I accompanied the gentlemen waggoners to their fire, and squatted myself before the blaze.

The man whom I had pledged, I very soon discovered to be the chief of the gang; for his mien was more lofty, and his speech more imperious than that of the rest. Halloa! *Ralph Noggin!* cried he, Turn the horses out loose with their bells on, that we may find them again in the woods. And do you hear. Get the pig out of the hay waggon, that we may barbacue him while there's a slow fire.

This motion of the waggoner was I thought not a bad one; my hunger seconded it in secret; and I began to entertain a higher opinion of the company I had got into.

Having barbacued the pig, each man drew forth his knife, and helped himself to a portion. I was invited to do the same, but when I had laid hands on a savoury morsel, it was difficult to retain it, for a dog, that accompanied the waggons, placed himself before me in a menacing attitude, and every time I put a piece of meat into my mouth, the cur gnashed his teeth, and rebuked me with an angry bark. At length, I was relieved from the importunities of the dog, by the politeness of a waggoner, who snatching up his whip, cracked it over the dog's back with such violence, that the animal slunk his tail between his hind legs, and ran howling into the woods with a most tragical tone; a tone that suspended for some minutes the bellowing of the bull-frogs, and the cry of the Whip-poor-will.

My companions having satisfied their hunger, they soon fell asleep; and it was not very long before I followed the example. My bed was composed of leaves, and I had no other canopy but the skies; but, in two watchful voyages to the *East Indies,* I had often snored on the hard deck, and my repose in the open air was a thing I had been used to.

About sun-rise I awoke, refreshed beyond measure with three hours sound sleep. Some of my companions were awake, but others were yet snoring. At length, they all rose and shook themselves, and the chief of the party had expressed it to be his opinion, that the Run would not go down before noon, when a chariot came up to the spot, followed by a horseman.

In the carriage were two elderly ladies, who, it was easy to discover, were Quakers. Of these one put her head out of the window, and calling to the horseman, said, *" Obadiah,* " inquire, I beseech thee, of these honest peo-

"ple, whether the Run be passable, or "whether we had not better go back to our "plantation, and tarry there till to-morrow?"

The Quaker rode up to our fire, around which we were all sitting, Waggoners, said "the Quaker, is the Run fordable yet for a "horse? Do you think, friends, it would be "safe for mother and aunt to venture across? "Is the water above the horses' knees?"

There is no danger, master, at all, said the chief of the party. Two young women and a negur-boy, crossed over an hour ago. The water, then, did not come up to the horses' knees, and now it is much lower. Friend, said the Quaker, I thank thee. And he then rode to the window of the carriage, where he imparted the intelligence to his mother and aunt.

I verily, said the old lady, have an apprehension that some accident will befal us.

Why, mother, said the Quaker, thy fears overcome thy reason. Two damsels and a man-servant have crossed over this morning already.

The postilion now whipped his cattle, and plunged into the stream, accompanied by the man on horseback. In a few minutes the beasts were up to their necks in water, and the women within the carriage were overwhelmed with the torrent. The horse of the man, who had gone higher up, was evidently obliged to swim for it; and now the woods echoed with the cries of the women in distress, and the groans of *Obadiah,* who gave himself up for lost. I cannot but acknowledge that the cries of the women knocked against my heart; I ran to the bank, and vociferated to the postilion not to spare his horses, but flog them over to the other side. The fellow profited by my injunctions, and presently the carriage, together with *Obadiah,* got in safety to the opposite bank; the women not remitting their screams, *Obadiah* still pouring forth his ejaculations, and the cattle shaking their manes.

In this scene of consternation, I could not be wholly inattentive to the waggoners. These gentlemen had thrown themselves on their backs, and were keeping up a peal of the loudest laughter I ever remember to have heard.*

About noon the water went down, and my companions, who had previously harnessed their cattle, crossed without any obstacle to the opposite bank. I followed on a led-horse, which they did not judge prudent to fasten to a waggon, and which took me over in safety. I then dismounted, and, having shaken each of the party by the hand, pursued my journey

[* Castiglioni had a very similar adventure in 1786, recorded in his book of Travels, (*Viaggio* &c. Milan. 1790), Vol. I, pp. 358-359. The ford is no less treacherous to-day, but the alternative is not so imperative. Cf. also Dr. Thomas Coke's *Journals of Five Visits to America.* London. 1793. pp. 26-28.]

on foot. The sun, which in the early part of the morning had been obscured, now gladdened the plains; and, as I journeyed onward, I sent forth in concert with the creation a prayer to that Universal Lord, at whose altar of praise and thanksgiving, all religions, though by different paths assemble; and ultimately unite in one centre of adoration.

A walk of ten miles brought me within sight of *George-town,* which exhibited an agreeable *coup d'œil,* as I approached the back of *Sampit* river. The opening of *Waccamaw* bay, at the confluence of *Sampit, Black,* and *Pedee* rivers, brought to my mind the happy description which my friend Mr. *George* had given the world of it; who is not less exact than felicitous in the combination of his images.

" Here as you enter from the winding wood,
" The wand'ring eye beholds the confluent flood,
" Where the wide waves of *Waccamaw* o'erflow,
" And gloomy wilds an endless prospect shew:
" Where roll the placid streams from *Sampit's* source,
" And *Winyaws* waves with slow meanders course,
" Through many a tainted marsh and gloomy wood,
" The dark abodes of dreary solitude."

I felt no little exultation in reflecting that it was the Author of this description, whom I was about to visit; that he expected with solicitude my coming, and that I should be received by him with transports. I crossed the river *Sampit* in the ferry-boat, and rejoiced to find myself in the company of my friend. But I did not find him at his studies. Mr. *George* was neither composing Mœonian Verse, the plaintive Elegy, nor soothing Sonnet. In profane prose, he was at dinner, and such was the unclassical condition of my appetite from a walk of fourteen miles, that a welcome to turkey and chine was greater music in my ear, than the softest verses my friend could have produced from his invocations of the morning.

It is only those whose breasts have been distended with friendship, that can form a just estimate of the happiness I enjoyed in the company of Mr. *George*. In a public party he was somewhat reserved; but in the unrestrained interchange of his mind with a friend, no man could be more pleasant. That the conversation of Mr. *George* was not coveted by the inhabitants of *George-town,* is not the least extraordinary. Pride is the same in all; and there is none who would not rather be amused than instructed.

There is a vivacity in the *Irish* character, which an *Englishman* cannot but envy. It is not indeed of a uniform tenour in either; both have their moments of depression, and exclamations of sorrow. But the *Irishman* seldom flies to a rope, or a phial, for an oblivion of his woes, and, taking it in his hand, cries,

This shall end them! His soul is sanguine; his grief evanescent; the clouds that darkened the horizon of life, give way in succession to sun-shine and a clear sky; his mind recovers its elasticity, and finally it triumphs.

The old lady at the boarding-house, informed me that she hardly knew what to make of Mr. *George;* sometimes he would be sociable, and chat round the parlour fire with the rest of her boarders; but that oftener he shut himself in his chamber, and pored over an outlandish book; or, wandering alone in the woods, was overheard talking to himself. Alas! for the simplicity of the woman! She little knew the enjoyments of a cultivated mind, or the delight a poet felt in courting the silence of solitude, and muttering his wayward fancies as he roved through the fields.

It, however, appeared to me, that Mr. *George* was not so enamoured of the Muses, but that he had an eye for a fair creature, who lived within a few doors of his lodgings. He manifested, I thought, strong symptoms of being in love. He delighted in the perusal of the Sorrows of *Werter,* perfumed his handkerchief with lavender, brushed his hat of a morning, and went every Sunday to church.

Mr. *George* had a supreme contempt for *American* genius and *American* literature. In a sportive mood, he would ask me whether I did not think that it was some physical cause in the air, which denied existence to a poet on *American* ground. No snake, said he, exists in *Ireland,* and no poet can be found in *America.**

You are too severe, said I, in your strictures. This country, as a native author observes, can furnish her quota of poets.

Name, will you, one?

Is not *Dwight,* a candidate for the epic crown? Is he, Sir, not a poet?

I think not. He wants imagination, and he also wants judgment; Sir, he makes the shield of *Joshua* to mock the rising sun.

Is not *Barlow* a poet? Is not his Vision of *Columbus* a fine poem?

The opening is elevated; the rest is read without emotion.

What think you of *Freneau?*

Freneau has one good ode: *Happy the Man who safe on shore!* But he is voluminous; and this ode may be likened to *the grain in the bushel of chaff.*

[* Dr. Schoepf, a very discriminating traveller and a man of high accomplishments, remarks, Vol. I, p. 128,—" Amerika hat seine Genies, so gut wie die alte Welt; in seiner bisherigen Lage und Verfassung aber, da Handel und Ackerbau ein leichteres und reichlicheres Auskommen gewährten, blieben sie unerkannt und unentwickelt." Vol. II, p. 332, " Der nun eben geendigte Krieg hat bereits verschiedene Männer von Wichtigkeit, und von so entschiedenen Talenten, in Thätigkeit gesezet dass America gewissermassen auch von der Seite der Gelehrsamkeit gewonnen hat." Vol. II, p. 336, " Genies sind in Amerika so gut zu Hause, als in der alten Welt, und sie werden mit der Zeit sich gegen jene messen."]

What is your opinion of *Trumbull?*

He can only claim the merit of being a skilful imitator.

Well, what think you of *Humphreys?*

Sir, his mind is neither ductile to sentiment, nor is his ear susceptible to harmony.

What opinion do you entertain of *Honeywood?* *

I have read some of his wretched rhymes, The bees, as is fabled of *Pindar,* never sucked honey from his lips.

Of the existence of an *American* poet, I perceive, Sir, your mind is rather skeptical. But, I hope, you will allow that *America* abounds with good prose.

Yes, sir; but, then, mind me, it is imported from the shores of *Great Britain.*

Oh! monstrous! Is not *Dennie* a good prose-writer?

Sir, the pleasure that otherwise I should find in *Dennie,* is soon accompanied with satiety by his unexampled quaintness.

Of *Brown,* Sir, what is your opinion?

The style of *Brown,* Sir, is chastised, and he is scrupulously pure. But nature has utterly disqualified him for subjects of humour. Whenever he endeavours to bring forth hu-

[* The poets by the classicist dismissed are,—President Dwight (1752-1817), Joel Barlow (1755-1812), Philip Freneau, (1752-1832), Col. David Humphreys, (1753-1818), St. John Honeywood (1764-1798); notices of whose work are to be found in the first volume of Duyckinck's *Cyclopædia.*]

mour, the offspring of his throes are weakness and deformity. Whenever he attempts humour, he inspires the benevolent with pity, and fills the morose with indignation.

What think you of the style of *Johnson,* the Reviewer?

It is not *English* that he writes, Sir; it is *American.* His periods are accompanied by a yell, that is scarcely less dismal than the war-hoop of a *Mohawk.*

George-Town is built on the South bank of *Sampit* river; the houses are handsome, and the little streets intersect each other at right angles. But so lovely are the women, that, had this place existed in an age of antiquity, it would not have been said that *Venus* fixed her abode at *Cytherea.*

The academy at *George-Town* is under the direction of Mr. *Spierin,* an *Irish* clergyman of the episcopal persuasion; a man profoundly versed in the languages of *Greece* and *Rome,* not unconversant with the delicacies of the *English,* and a powerful preacher.

I was delighted with Mr. *Spierin's* eldest boy. This little fellow, always followed his cousin (Mr. *George*) to his room, and took more pleasure in hearing the bard repeat to him his compositions than in listening to the talk of the boarders, whose topic was either horse-racing, cock-fighting, or gunning.

I make the same use of this boy, said Mr.

George to me, that *Moliere* did of his old house-keeper. His feelings are not perverted by the subtilties of criticism; his mind so tender, has acquired no fastidiousness from cultivation; and what charms the boy will charm also the multitude.

I wish, cousin, said the boy, you would read me that poem again about Papa and Doctor ——, who went over to *Waccamaw* to a ball, and, when they got there, found they could not dance.

What, *George,* said I, have you been satirizing your uncle! the most learned of the Professors! and has not Doctor —— escaped your lash; the man who instituted and supports your academy!

Sir, said my friend, whatever may be their attributes, they ruined our dance; nor could the laughter they provoked atone for the time they made us lose.

Do, cousin, said the boy, let me read the poem to this gentleman. It is so funny!—My friend put his manuscript into the boy's hand, who read it aloud.

THE DANCING PHILOSOPHERS.

WHAT dire events from trivial causes rise,
Mirth to the gay, but satire to the wise.
I sing, two chiefs, who lately pass'd the floods,
To *Waccamaw's* wide wastes and piney woods;
Invited to partake the soft delight
Of festive dance, and hymeneal rite;

The one a sage disciple of the gown,
The other much renown'd throughout the town,
For bolus, nostrum, Esculapian skill,
The rich to fleece, the lingering to kill.
These in a galley, with their sable train.
Press'd to the shore that bounds the distant main;
There in the Sylvan shades the youths around,
With laughter-loving nymphs in silk were found;
The bridal beauty in the midst appear'd,
And next the bridegroom, but without a beard;
For not as yet for wisdom was he famed,
Nor had his chin his manhood yet proclaim'd.

   Soon as the Priest had joined them hand in hand,
At signal giv'n arose the tuneful band;
Musicians skill'd the tambourine to ring,
And fiddlers numberless to swell the string.
Then shine the train, in two collected rows,
The left a range of belles, the right of beaux;
Of these the forms in figur'd muslin veil'd,
Of those the legs in silken hose conceal'd.
Now all at once two swift for sight they rise,
With nimble footsteps, and with glowing eyes;
So the round wheels in giddy circles roll,
And bear along the fix'd spectator's soul.
Seiz'd with the scene, the solemn Priest lays down
His band, his bible, and his sable gown;
For when Divinity to mirth's inclin'd,
No text intrusive enters in the mind.
The Doctor too, forgetful that his heels,
As lead were heavy, through the circle wheels;
This way and that he stumbles as he goes,
And oft results upon his neighbor's toes.

   And now the merry violin resounds,
And now the DOCTOR, now the PARSON bounds.

All gravity was lost; the solemn air,
The frowning eye-brow, the adjusted hair,
No more so venerably met the view,
To damp the ardour of the dancing crew.

The PARSON now, revolving from his place,
As down the ring he ran his godly race,
His partner leaving in the midst to chance,
Casts off behind and leads alone the dance.
His Nymph with eager eye displays her hand,
To call his Reverence to his proper stand;
But not for hands or nods he car'd at all,
This way and that he whirls around the hall;
One calls aloud, one stops his rapid flight,
Both nymphs and youths contend to set him right;
" This way! this way! you turn; lead out of sides,
" That lady's hand you take! and next the bride's";
But while the merry violins resound,
The ready Parson ceases not to bound.
And now through right and left, across they go,
And now the Priest, as in a solemn show,
Stands in the midst and knows not what to do.
As when some brisly boar the swains surround,
To drive him through some gate, or sylvan ground,
In vain—the stubborn savage glaring stands,
Immoveable, and braves the rustic bands.
The PARSON thus, oft push'd, repulsive stood,
With leaden legs, and with a head of wood;
Till shame and wrath compell'd him to retire,
His visage glowing, and his eyes on fire.

The DOCTOR too no better fate obtain'd,
Soon as in dance his giant limbs he strained,
His step, subverted by an almond shell,
Upheav'd his central poise, and down he fell.

Like some huge whale when dash'd against a rock,
So groan'd the Doctor! and so loud the shock,
Then bursts of universal laughter rise,
Shake the high dome, and fill the starry skies.
The nymph assists her partner from the ground,
Again the laughter and the jest resound.
Scarce could the Chief, when rais'd amidst the throng,
Drag his slow length of ponderous limbs along;
Groaning he moves; supported by a staff,
Like Polypheme!—what Stoic would not laugh?
A crowd of slaves with solemn mien, draw near,
And slowly through the dome the body bear.
Then on a bed they softly lay the sage,
And strive the dorsal torrent to assuage;
Loud from his room, the man of mighty bone,
All dancing curs'd, and heav'd a piteous groan;
And now, lest any say, this noble throng,
Have danc'd too heavily, or danc'd too long;
Here shall the Muse her mournful story close,
And let the DOCTOR and the PRIEST repose.

Mr. *Spierin* will forgive my insertion of this poem. No person respects him more than I; and nothing but real esteem for a man, would induce me to make serious mention of him in this volume. That Traveller has little acquaintance with the policy of literature, and estimates but lightly the power of his page, who speaks indiscriminately of every individual with whom he has eaten a meal, or caroused over a bowl. I have been feasted and caressed by many of my friends, both at *New-York,* and *Philadelphia,* and *Baltimore,* and *Washington;* who, knowing that I contemplated to publish a narrative, did me the honour to desire a niche in my work. But of such characters what could I record? It surely could give the reader no satisfaction to be told, that, Mr. ——, having imported a turtle from *Jamaica,* guttled down for nearly three hours the callipash and callipee; or that the constant practice of Mr. ——, was to smoke his pipe every day after dinner. The epitaph-maker will do all that can be done for such characters; for it can only be recorded of them that they were born, and that they died.

During my visit at *George-town,* the melancholy tidings were brought of the death of General *Washington.* The inhabitants of the town were crouding to the ball-room, at the moment the courier arrived with the dispatch. But the death of so great a man converted their hilarity into sorrow; the eye of many a female, which, but a moment before had sparkled with pleasure, was now brimful of tears; and they all cast off their garments of gladness, and clothed themselves with sackcloth.

The following Sunday, the men, women, and children, testified their veneration for the Father of their Country, by walking in procession to the church, where Mr. *Spierin* delivered a funeral oration. Never was there a discourse more moving. Tears flowed from every eye; and lamentations burst from every lip.

Nor were the orators of *America* silent at the death of their hero. They called all their tropes and metaphors together; collected all the soldiers and statesmen of history, and made them cast their garlands at the feet of his statue.

I look back both with pleasure and satisfaction on the time I passed with my friend, at the confluence of the rivers *Waccamaw* and *Winyaw*. Our conversation was commonly on the writers of the *Augustan* Age, and I corrected many errors I had imbibed by solitary study. The taste of Mr. *George* had been formed on the polished models of antiquity; to these he always recurred as to the standards of elegant composition. It is recorded, I believe, of *Euler,* that he could repeat the whole of the Æneid by heart; but the memory of Mr. *George* had not only digested the Eneid, but also the Georgics and Eclogues.

But the moment was approaching that called me to another climate. I found a schooner lying at the wharfs of *George-Town,* that was bound to *New-York,* and thither I had formed the resolution of going. To this resolution I was particularly determined by the projects of Mr. *George;* who, disgusted with the society at *George-town,*—the eternal discourse of the inhabitants about their negroes and cotton-fields; and the innovations of the Trustees on his mode of tuition, had come to the determination of seeking another people, and opening a school of his own.

When I, therefore, waved my hand on board the vessel to my friend, who stood on the wharf with the calm inhabitants of *Waccamaw,* my heart was rather elated with joy at the expectation of soon meeting him at *New York,* than depressed with sorrowful emotions to separate from him at *George-town.*

Heaven prosper you, my dear fellow, said Mr. *George.* But your impending gales of wind, and rolling of the vessel, will excite little sympathy, because I shall reflect you are again in your own element. Yet shall I never cease exclaiming, *Sic te diva potens Cypri, &c.,* till you give me a missive that acquaints me with your safe landing. Adieu! I will soon shake you by the hand again in a region less unhealthy, less inhospitable, and less unclassical.

The sails of the vessel were now distended by a breeze that was both favourable and fresh. We shaped our course out of the harbour; the waves roared around the bark; and in half an hour she appeared to the eye of the beholder from land a white speck only on the ocean.

Our passengers were composed of a *Georgian* saddle-maker, a Quaker, and three vagrants from *New England.** Of these the *Georgian* was an original character. His very figure was the title-page of a joke, for never before did I behold such *a bed-presser, such a horseback-breaker, such a huge hill of flesh.* He exulted in his bulk, and informed us, that on first coming on board he weighed two hundred and seventy-five pounds.

The wind changed off *Cape Hatteras* to the North East, from which quarter it blew a tremendous gale. We lay-to in a most miserable condition, wet, sick, and unable to cook any food. I now sighed for *Coosohatchie,* the company of my pupils, and my walks in the woods; but my ambition of travel struggled over my weakness, and I sought refuge in jollity with my portly companion.

What, Sir, said he, is your opinion of this wind? It is only, answered I, a top-gallant-breeze. Only a top-gallant-breeze! exclaimed the Captain, it is enough to blow the devil's horns off!—A few minutes after a sea struck the vessel in the stern, and, staving in the dead lights, nearly overwhelmed the sadler, who was reposing in the aftermost berth; but, how-

[* Cf. Schoepf, *Reise* &c. 1788, II, 196,—" Dass sie [New Englanders] aber mit den Einwohnern von Nordkarolina einen, wie es scheint, etwas stärkern Verkehr treiben, mochte ausser den für beyde Theile entspringenden Vortheilen und Bequemlichkeiten, auch noch diese besondere Veranlassung haben, dass sehr viele Neuengländische Emigranten sich in Nordkarolina niedergelassen haben."]

ever incommoded by his trunk of humours, he carried himself most nimbly towards the cabin-door; running and roaring, and roaring and running, till he got upon deck.

The next morning the sun shone down the sky light into the cabin. We were all in our beds, and a silence had prevailed several hours, when Mr. *Waters,* charmed with its rays, exclaimed, " Great luminary of the world! welcome to my sight! No more shall I wonder that thou art worshipped by the heathen."

The gale having abated, we prosecuted our voyage, and on the morning of the 5th of *February,* 1800, saw the high land of the *Jerseys.* As the day advanced we could distinguish the light-house on *Sandy-Hook,* and with a pleasant breeze were wafted to the wharves of *New-York.*

CHAP. V.

Engagements at New-York.—An American Author.—Mr. George arrives at New-York.—Epistolary Correspondence.—A Visit to Long Island.—The Classical Elegance of the New-York Reviewers exhibited.—Journey to the City of Washington.

MY first care on returning to *New-York* was to deliver a letter I had been favoured with from Mr. *Spierin,* to his friend Bishop *Moore.* I waited on the Bishop most opportunely, for the preceding day he had been applied to by an opulent merchant to procure a Tutor for his children, and I was a Tutor by trade.

The Bishop introduced me to Mr. *Ludlow* and his lady, who received me with formality; but whose conversation I thought interesting, because they offered me a handsome salary to educate their children. In the woods of *Carolina,* I had received eighty guineas a year; but Mr. *Ludlow* proposed a hundred.

I therefore exchanged my lodgings with Major *Howe* for an elegant structure in *Broadway,** and took possession of a chamber that was worthy to lodge a Prince.

[* Cf. Barber and Howe's *Historical Collections,* p. 315—
" The fashionable part of the city, or *west end of the town,* was [1800] in Wall and Pine streets, between Broadway and Pearl, Pearl from Hanover Square to John-Street, along

My pupils were few for the salary I enjoyed. I had only three boys, *Robert, Ferdinand,* and *Edward,* (I delight to give their names *) who possessed much suavity of manners, and volubility of tongue. They learned very well when disposed to learn their books; for, as I was restricted to practice only blandishments, their application was never imposed.

The author of *Arthur Mervyn,* living at *New-York,* I sought acquaintance with a man who had acquired so much intellectual renown. I found Mr. *Brown* quite in the *costume* of an author,† embodying virtue in a new novel, and making his pen fly before him.

Mr. *Brown* occupied a dismal room in a dismal street. I asked him whether a view of nature would not be more propitious to composition; or whether he should not write with more facility were his window to command the prospect of the Lake of *Geneva.*—Sir, said he, good pens, thick paper, and ink well diluted, would facilitate my composition more

State-Street and a part of Broadway, below Wall-Street." Population, 1798, about 50,000.

The situation of the house identifies Mr. Ludlow—either Thomas Ludlow or Daniel Ludlow. Cf. Wilson, *Memorial History of New York,* Vol. III, p. 151. The most famous of the various Ludlow houses at that time was the Carey Ludlow house, State Street, facing the Battery, No. 9.]

[* Cf. *Vicar of Wakefield,* ch. XI.]

† By the costume of an author I imply a great coat and shoes down at heel.

than the prospect of the broadest expanse of water, or mountains rising above the clouds.*

I pass over common occurrences to embrace again Mr. *George,* who had left the Academy at *George-town,* and, like a true poet, was without a settled habitation. I procured him lodging under the roof of Major *Howe;* and, the better to enjoy a freedom from interruption, I took my friend to *King's* little tavern, near the Presbyterian Church,—where we drank, and smoked, and chatted, and laughed till midnight.

I introduced Mr. *George* to Colonel *Burr,* whom I had not neglected; and I also presented him to Bishop *Moore,* who had procured me a salary of a hundred guineas. I have ever felt the highest veneration for the dignified office of Prelate. There are many different feelings. But as the *English* soldier detested a *Frenchman* because he wore wooden shoes; so many cannot endure a Bishop because he wears lawn to his sleeves.

* When I mentioned this reply of Mr. *Brown* to one of the most distinguished literary characters now living.—Sir, said he, this *American* Author cannot, I think, be a man of much fancy. [Cf. Bernard, *Retrospections of America,* pp. 250-252—"One of the most agreeable acquaintances I formed was with Charles Brockden Brown, the first, and for many years the only, novelist America had produced. Few men have united talent and worth in a larger proportion. 'Edgar Huntly' appears to me to be one of his most pleasing productions. 'Arthur Mervyn' contains the most powerful descriptions (the ravages of the Plague, etc.), but 'Wieland' taken on all points, must be considered his chef d'œuvre."]

It was the custom of Mr. *Ludlow* every summer to exchange the tumult of the city for the quiet of his rural retreat; or, in other words, to remove his family from *New-York* to a place called *West Chester*. But knowing that Mr. *George* was in some solicitude for his future support, and being myself engaged by *Caritat,* on liberal terms, to compile a volume of modern Poetry,* I presented my friend to the family, extolled the multiplicity of his attainments, and resigned to him my place. In truth I was weary of setting boys their copies, and I wanted some remission to my fatigue.

Mr. *George* a few days after followed the family into their retreat, which he has described, together with the state of his own feelings, in a familiar epistle.

" No prospect can be more enchanting than
" that from our mansion. Two tufted islands
" at a distance, leave a vista between them,
" through which gleam the turrets of *New-*
" *York,* rising like a new creation from the
" sea. But my time rolls heavily along. Let

---

* This volume of modern Poetry was to be a royal octavo, of one thousand pages. It was to contain all the poems of all the modern Poets. *Caritat* made a voyage to *England* with no other purpose than to collect all their works. He bought up all the modern poetry that *London* could furnish; and when I say this, I need not observe that the ship which contained his cargo drew a great depth of water. The pumps were kept constantly going.

" casuists reason as they will; a vigorous mind
" can derive no satisfaction from retirement.
" It is only on the great theatre of the world
" that we can be sensible of the pleasures of
" existence. The solitary mind is its own
" sepulchre; and where variety is unknown,
" or the passions are suppressed, the noblest
" energies are lost for want of pleasures to
" sooth, or ambition to excite them. I have
" one consolation; the delight of your corre-
" spondence; which will alone sooth my mind
" to tranquillity in these regions of solitude.
" Really friendship includes something in its
" essence that is divine; and I begin to per-
" suade myself ours is not of that frail struc-
" ture whose fabric may be overthrown by
" the collision of interest, or the competition
" of vanity.

" I have again read over your epistles from
" *Coosohatchie,* and am now travelling with
" you through the swamps of *Pocotaligo,* and
" the woods of *Asheepoo.* There is certainly
" a pleasure in retracing our former footsteps,
" and pursuing our adventures through the
" wilds of *Carolina.* I can now behold you
" sitting with the driver in the front seat,
" and smoking your segar, while the soli-
" tary vehicle rolls slowly through the
" forests.

" I return to domestic occurrences. Yes-
" terday we had the breakfast table placed in

"the piazza, and a number of ladies from "*New-York,* formed a circle around it. None "were remarkable for taste, but all for *Tea-* "*table-talkativeness* (a long word to spell), "and I overheard a fair damsel say to another, "that the Tutor was a *keen* young fellow. "Had I been a Prince instead of a Tutor, I "would have told her, as *Hamlet* did *Ophelia,* "that it would have cost her a groaning to "take off my edge.

"Women know not what to be at. In the "evening they were contending who should "first take the telescope to look at the full "moon, which arose from the distant hills "with unusual beauty. The telescope was "brought,—and I shewed each lady in regular "succession, the Polar Hemisphere, together "with the constellations of *Arcturus* and "*Orion;* repeating at the same time their de- "scription from the eighteenth Iliad.

"I went down to the Sound to swim awhile "ago, and, during my stay in the water, some "fellow threw in my shirt; so I came up like "one of *Falstaff's* men. This lamentable ac- "cident brought the servants about me; and "the gardener's wife made no scruple to lend "me one of her husband's shirts.

"I knew not when I entered on the office of "Tutor in this family, that one part of my "duty would be to teach my pupils to swim. "Is not this a work of supererogation? How-

"ever, I never fail to duck most fervently
"these enemies to silence and reflection.

"Apropos of my pupils. This morning I
"was roused from slumber (for I sometimes
"teach school before breakfast in bed), by
"the vociferation of the eldest boy, who,
"laughable to relate, construed *raucæ palum-*
"*bes,** into *roasted wood-pigeons.* Risum
"teneas Amice?

"After dismissing these lads, I walked to
"the water-side, and sat down under a spread-
"ing tree, not as *Tityrus,* to play on my pas-
"toral reed, but as a miserable Tutor; tired
"with the *ennui* of a solitary life, and en-
"deavouring to sooth a restless imagination
"by the objects of nature.

"You enjoy many advantages over me. I
"presume you have access to the libraries of
"*Caritat,* and of the city, and wander through
"the shelves of literature with *poetica licentia.*

"I fear this letter will be tedious; but only
"writing to you, dear fellow, can make my
"situation supportable. How shall I escape
"from this cursed obscurity? I have been
"here three days, of which every minute has
"been passed in brooding over my misfor-
"tunes!"

My readers will, perhaps, be ready to exclaim, as the inhabitants of the subterranean
abode did to *Gil Blas,* that Mr. *George* was

* Vide Virgil, Eclogue I.

an inveterate enemy to the stillness of solitude; but it was ever the fate of genius to be impatient of restraint, and the carol of the birds, the bloom of the meads, and the vernal softness of the breeze, lost all impression on a vigorous mind reduced to dependance.

Some symptoms of the yellow fever appearing in *New-York,* spread universal consternation; and the subscribers to the volume of modern Poetry not coming in crouds with their subscription-money, the compilation of it was postponed. Being now without any determined employment, I had nothing to detain me in the town; and transporting my books and baggage over to *Long Island,* I was fortunate enough to procure lodgings at *Newtown,* under the roof of the Episcopal Minister, Mr. *Vandyke.* He was a garrulous valetudinary old creature, who would have been excellent company for the Elders that viewed the *Grecian* forces from the battlements of *Troy.*

The parsonage-house was not unpleasantly situated. The porch was shaded by a couple of huge locust-trees, and accommodated with a long bench. Here I often sat with my host, who, like Parson *Adams,* always wore his cassoc; but he did not read *Eschylus.* Alas! the old gentleman was not descended from the family of the Medici; nor would learning have been ever indebted to him for its revival.

Mr. *Vandyke* was at least sixty; yet if a colt, a pig, or any other quadruped entered his paddock, he sprang from his seat with more than youthful agility, and vociferously chased the intruder from his domain. I could not but smile to behold the parson running after a pig, and mingling his cries with those of the animal!

It would be ungrateful were I not to enumerate the friends I found on *Long Island*. —Mr. *Titus,* who lived on a creek that communicated with the Sound, both feasted and caressed me; he was a worthy old gentleman; and at his house, as in the days before the flood, they were eating and drinking, marrying and giving in marriage.

Farmer *Moore*, brother to Bishop *Moore*, of *New-York*,* (I love to give their names, and kindred), always entertained me with a hearty welcome. Every one acknowledged his daughter was charming:

> *A maiden never bold;*
> *Of spirit so still and quiet, that her motion*
> *Blush'd at itself.*

Indeed the manners of the whole family were worthy of the Golden Age.

Mr. *Remsen,* who lived with more magnificence on the river-side, opposite *Flushing*,

[* Benjamin Moore, 2nd Bishop of that Diocese, (1748-1816), b. at Newtown.]

gave me sumptuous dinners, and Madeira after each repast. His lady was not without elegance; but his two daughters were lovely.

Nor in enumerating the Belles of Newtown, ought I omit Mrs. *Dungan,* and Miss *Townshend,* who dressed with splendour, and moved with grace.

From Mr. Remsen's dwelling, on the waterside, the mansion of Mr. *Ludlow* could be clearly distinguished, lifting its proud turrets above the shore of *West Chester.* I had been invited, both by the family and my friend to visit the " new house;" and having, on a serene day, dined with Mr. *Remsen,* I was paddled in a canoe from his landing place to the opposite shore.

The little boys shouted with joy as the canoe approached their wharf and, *George,* abandoning an epic poem that he was composing, flew to my embrace.

I was ushered into the parlour. Every thing breathed splendour. A *Turkey* carpet covered the floor, and the richest sophas invited repose. Negus was served in a golden cup, by a servant clad in a magnificent livery; and every fruit of the season was placed on the sideboard. The room was soon filled by the family, all eager to receive me, and do the honours of the house.

I could not but be delighted with the joy expressed by the children; they either clung round my knees, or ran to bring the letters I had written them, that I might perceive with what care they had preserved my epistles.

These boys had certainly made unusual progress under the tuition of Mr. *George;* for each could repeat with every justness of quantity the first Eclogue of Virgil, and if I might judge from their emotions, feel the spirit of the Poet.—*Et jam summa procul*—exclaimed one, pointing through the window to some cottages smoking at a distance:

> *Et jam summa procul villarum culmina fumant,*
> *Majoresque cadunt altis de montibus umbræ.*

I found afterwards that these children had read *Virgil* to some purpose; for each could dilate on the enviable tranquillity of *Tityrus,* the adversity of *Melibæus,* and the perils of the pious hero.

After continuing three days with my friend, he accompanied me from *West Chester,* in a passage-boat to *New-York.* It is almost superfluous to observe, that we passed through *Hell-Gate.*

At *New-York* we experienced an oblivion of care at *King's* little tavern, next to the *Presbyterian* church; * which, from the jollity

[* The old First Presbyterian Church was in Wall Street. At this time the Brick Church (Presbyterian) was at Nassau and Beekman; the Scotch Presbyterian Church was on Cedar Street, near Broadway. Cf. Disosway's *Earliest Churches of New York.*]

that resounded in every room on a Sunday, brought to recollection the proverb, that *the nearer to church, the further from heaven.* Here, however, we drank porter, smoked segars, and forgot we were Tutors.

The following day, I prevailed on Mr. *George* to visit *Newtown,* and I introduced him to my friends. We dined with Mr. *Remsen,* from whose house he departed for *West Chester* in a canoe. I awaited in the piazza the return of the canoe, chatting most delectably with Miss *Eliza Remsen,* over a cup of tea administered by her fair hands. The canoe returned, and brought me a note from my friend.

" I (thank God) found none of the family " at home on my arrival; so I can walk about " the house without feeling my dependence."

Mr. *George* only remained with Mr. *Ludlow* till his quarter expired, when it was concerted by every party, that I should resume the place. But he was not long unemployed; for the inhabitants of *Newtown,* being in want of a teacher, converted a spare dwelling into a school, and engaged my friend on liberal terms to educate their children.

From the tenour of Mr. *George's* letters, it required but little penetration to discover that his situation was not agreeable. He was one of those men who could not appease pride by seeming submission; and who would not descend to live with a prince but on terms of equality. The verse he most admired in his own productions, was the image of his mind.

And scorn to bow before the sons of pride!

For my part, I thought differently on this subject. I thought a few sacrifices might be made for every elegance of accommodation, and a hundred guineas a year; and I was glad to resume the place, because my salary was a good one. Nor could I perceive that my friend had any real cause for complaint; on the contrary, I was of opinion that he had been disgusted without offence, and alienated without enmity.

Mr. *George* was now on *Long Island,* and I had received a very polite letter from Mrs. *Ludlow,* who entreated me to hasten my return to her family. For my part, I obeyed her orders with alacrity, for I was weary of the cant and carping of Parson *Vandyke,* who so overflowed with scripture, that he cudgelled his men-servants and maid-servants with the Bible.

I therefore drove Mr. *George* in a chair to the water-side, and at the house of Mr. *Berian,* hired a canoe to cross the Sound. But first, I smoked a segar with my friend in the porch, and left him weeping and laughing; weeping to lose his company, and laughing at his absence; for, *nescio quid meditans* *nugarum,* he forgot I had not paid for the chair, which he would unavoidably have to do.*

[* '*Nulla mihi,*' inquam '*Religiost.* Hor: Sat., I, 9; v. 2, v. 70.]

After an hour's rowing, the boatmen reached *West Chester,* and landed me at Mr. *Ludlow's.* Of the family the children were only at home, who received me with every demonstration of joy; but not long after Mrs. *Ludlow* returned in her chariot, whose elegant and conciliating manners soon reconciled me to my situation.

I sent my friend his trunks by the return of the canoe, and a short note produced from the impulse of the moment. In a few days I was favoured with an epistle from Mr. *George.*

"After your departure from *Berian's* in
" the canoe, I resumed my station with the
" old fellow on the porch; here I awaited with
" impatience the return of the boat with my
" trunk. *Berian* I found to be a plain, honest,
" sensible, old navigator, and I drank tea with
" him.

"At night-fall the boat returned with my
" trunk and a letter from my beloved com-
" panion in adversity; it is only by the absence
" of persons who are dear to us, that we can
" estimate truly their value; and I now began
" sensibly to feel the privation of your com-

"pany. I left *Berian's* at seven; the night "was very dark, and the moon (though con- "siderably above the horizon) was entirely "obscured by clouds. I was in no small "danger of breaking my neck over the rocks "which obstructed my passage, but my horse "not being of a disposition to run away with "his burden, I escaped the danger of an over- "throw. After opening and shutting several "gates that impeded my journey, and passing "over many rocky hills, I descended to the "shore, of which the waves were covered by "a thick mist, that obscured their agitation, "and rendered their fury more awful; the "tide had usurped much of the road, and the "left wheel of the chair rolled through the "water. Hence, after travelling along the "*beached verge of the salt flood,* I ascended "a high hill, and turning into a different road "from that through which you were my com- "panion, I drove into a thick spreading wood "of oak: here I was fearful of entirely losing "my way through the trees; but the clouds "dispersed, and the moon arose to light me "on my journey. At nine I reached the par- "son's, where I found the family peaceably "occupied with their needles; they received "me with kindness, but the rustic silence "which prevailed among them, and the "tedious reverberations of the clock, com- "pelled me to retire to my room, where I

" indulged myself in uninterrupted reflection,
" and in pondering over your curious epistle."

During my abode at *West Chester,* I wrote a little Novel entitled, The Farmer of *New Jersey;* the publication of which inflamed the wrath of the *Mohawk* Reviewers. In my preface I had disdained to deprecate the severity of their censure, and they besieged me from their attic stories with the javelins of criticism. What these fathers of *American* criticism chiefly objected to, was the style of the book, in which I had been purposely unambitious of ornament. That they could spy a mote in the eye of their neighbour, and not perceive the beam in their own, the following passage from the *Mohawk* Review will, I am of opinion, evince. " The slightest acquaintance with the history *of* literature is sufficient to convince the most ardent admirer *of* simplicity and *of* unadorned truth *of* the necessity *of* a good style, and *of* the advantages *of* an occasional use *of* its highest ornaments." *

Americans! rejoice! the *Augustan* age of your country cannot surely be remote, when you possess such Reviewers!

I turn from the unpleasing sounds of the

---

* *New-York* Review, Vol. I, page 16.
[This may have been a very short-lived monthly magazine. There was no such periodical, and no monthly magazine, in New York in 1805. See, citation of Longworth's Directory for that year, in *Old New York*, Vol. I, No. 3, p. 159. The title *New York Review* was revived in 1825.]

warhoop of these *Mohawks,* to the mild strain of friendship exhibited in the graceful negligence of the epistles of Mr. *George.* The following letter will not be without its use. It will exemplify, that tranquillity depends not in change of place, but must have its source in the mind; and that a man, by crossing in a boat from one shore to another, cannot leave his cares and vexations behind him.

"In this out-of-the-world village, I live
"neither pleasing, nor pleased; for a rustic
"cannot receive much gratification from the
"society of a man of letters; and surely the
"man of letters cannot derive any pleasure
"from the company of a rustic. It is only
"by a collision of minds of the same tendency,
"that inquietude can be soothed and the in-
"tellect invigorated.

"My condition, is, however, more tolerable
"than it was. Here I have no mincing, im-
"peratrix to say to me, "Mr. *George,* my
"children do nothing, I must insist, Sir, you
"will be more attentive to *Bobby* and *Neddy.*"
"Deo Gratias! O thou eater of broken
"meats! Thou lilly-livered, super-servicea-
"ble rogue of a Tutor! Avaunt!

"I was lately at *New-York.* But I went
"not to pay my respects to Members of Con-
"gress, but with the hope of encountering the
"friend of my heart, and the companion of
"my adversity.

"I slept at *Howe's,* and during the night
"was perpetually annoyed with the cry of
"fire! fire! As the noise increased, I arose
"with not less trepidation than Eneas, when
"he ascended to the top of old *Anchises'*
"palace:

> "*Et jam proximus ardet*
> "*Ucalegon.*"

"But here, as in all modern conflagrations,
"(whether real or poetic), there was more
"smoke than fire, and more consternation
"than danger; so I sunk again to slumber,
"from which not even the ghost of *Hector*
"could have awakened me.

"Shall you exchange soon the dull walks
"of *West Chester,* for the animated streets
"of *New York?* Come over, I beseech you,
"and enable me once more to exclaim with
"rapture Vixi!"

With the first frost the family of Mr. *Ludlow* removed from the solitude of *West Chester,* to the gaieties of *New York;* and I again took possession of a room boasting every convenience of accommodation, where I could prosecute, without disturbance, my lucubrations till a late hour. The library of *Caritat* supplied me with every book in the *French* and my own idiom; and before a cheerful fire, I could pass nights of rapture in the acquisition of elegant and useful knowledge. The emoluments I had derived from the publication of my little Novel, induced me to undertake another, which I was resolved to make more voluminous; for *Americans* expect quantity in a book not less eagerly than in other merchandise, and the maxim of the old *Greek* is not yet established in the New World.*

After revolving many schemes, I was determined to continue my former narrative, by writing the adventures of its principal character; for, in the Farmer of *New Jersey,* they are only partially related, and *William* (the hero of the tale), I discovered to be a favourite among the ladies.

Having finished my tale, my next care was to find a publisher; for which purpose I addressed a letter to the Editor of the Port Folio. In a few days the letter-bag was distended with petitions from the *Philadelphia* booksellers, who lavished every allurement of eloquence on the convenience of their presses, and the skill of their workmen; but none offered to buy the manuscript, and it was never my intention to give it away. However, my prospects were soon after brightened by a letter in a different strain from a copyright-purchasing patron, of the name of *Dickins;* to whom I dispatched my manuscript, together

* Μέγα Βιβλίον, μέγα Κακὸν.

with a letter written in a state of mind that generated the ΕΠΕΑ ΠΤΕΡΟΕΝΤΑ.*

About this period the attention of the public was turned towards the City of *Washington,* where the Members of both Houses of Congress had assembled to decide on the nomination of a President for the United States.

In the year 1789, General *Washington* was chosen President over the new system of confederated Government, and in the year 1793, when the term of his Presidentship had expired, he was reelected in the office. He therefore continued four years more invested with the executive power of the Government; but at the second termination of the time stipulated by the Constitution for a new election to be made, desirous of retiring from public business, he resigned his important office. This was in 1797, when Mr. *Adams* was

[* The MS so dispatched was that of *The Wanderings of William*. Philadelphia, 1801. The purchaser of the copyright was doubtless Asbury Dickins who was associated with Joseph Dennie in founding the *Port Folio* at Philadelphia, and later was secretary of the United States Senate, from 1836 to 1861.

Duyckinck, (Vol. I, p. 563), remarks on this transaction: " A very clever resident English author in the country, John Davis, writer of a lively book of travels in the United States, which he dedicated to Jefferson, offered by an advertisement, in 1801, two novels, fruits of his winter labors, to any bookseller in the country who would publish them—on the condition of receiving fifty copies. The booksellers of New York, where he lived, could not, he said, undertake them, for they were dead of the fever."]

elected into the Presidentship, and Mr. *Jefferson* was chosen Vice-President. For three years the party of Mr. *Adams* lost none of its influence; but in the fourth the contending party acquired a visible ascendancy, and it was the predominant opinion, that Mr. *Jefferson* would be chosen President in the next election. The event justified the expectation; Mr. *Jefferson* obtained the suffrages of the majority; he was elected into the office of first Magistrate of the nation, and Mr. *Adams,* who still had kept at *Washington,* and still indulged in hope, till the very moment that fixed his doom, now felt himself become again a private citizen, and departed the same night, in the stage-coach, for his paternal abode. It was by ballot that Mr. *Jefferson's* right to the office was decided; for in the nomination of the different States, Mr. *Burr* had an equal number of votes; but a ballot assigned the office to Mr. *Jefferson,* and it consequently followed that Mr. *Burr* became Vice-President.

The election of a new President of the United States could not but engage the feelings of the public. It raised the expectations of some, and damped the hopes of others; or, more properly speaking, all regarded the event as it related to their interest.

The City of *Washington* was now the centre of attraction to the nation. Multitudes flocked to it, in different directions, to hear the inaugural speech of Mr. *Jefferson.*

Of this general enthusiasm I was not without my share. Mr. *Jefferson's* notes on *Virginia* was the book that first taught me to think; and my heart now beat with the desire to hear the accents of wisdom fall from the tongue of that man, whose pen had engrafted much truth on my mind. I therefore departed for the city of *Washington,* passing through, in my way to it, *Philadelphia* and *Baltimore.*

CHAP. VI.

Emotions on entering the City of Washington. The Plan of the Place. The inaugural Speech of Mr. Jefferson to both Houses of Congress assembled at the Capitol.

"In this City may that piety and virtue, that wisdom and
"magnanimity, that constancy and self-government, which
"adorned the great character whose name it bears, be for
"ever held in veneration! Here, and throughout *America,*
"may simple manners, pure morals, and true religion,
"flourish for ever!"

THE mind of the Traveller must be abstracted from all local emotion, who can enter unmoved the city at the confluence of the *Potomac,* and *Eastern Branch.* He witnesses the triumph of freedom over oppression, and religious tolerance over superstition. It is the capital of the United States that fills his imagination! It is the country of *Jefferson* and *Burr* that he beholds! It is the rising mistress of the world that he contemplates!

The tract chosen for the City of *Washington* is situated at the junction of the *Potomac* river, and *Eastern Branch;* extending about four miles along their respective shores. This territory, which is called *Columbia,* lies partly in the State of *Virginia,* and partly in the State of *Maryland;* and was ceded, as every body knows, by those two States, to the United States of *America;* by which it was established the seat of Government, after the year of 1800.

The City of *Washington* is to be divided into squares, or grand divisions, by streets running due North and South, and East and West, which form the ground-work of the plan. But from the Capitol, the President's house, and some of the important areas, are to be diagonal streets, which will prevent the monotony that characterises *Philadelphia.*

We here perceive the superiority of taste in a travelled *Frenchman,* over a homebred *Englishman.* Penn was the founder of *Philadelphia;* the plan of *Washington* was formed by Major *L'Enfant.*

The great leading streets are to be one hundred and sixty feet wide, including a pavement of ten feet, and a gravel walk of thirty feet, planted with trees on each side; which will leave eighty feet of paved street for carriages: the rest of the streets will, in general, be one hundred and ten feet wide, with a few only ninety feet, except North, South, and East Capitol streets, which are to be one hundred and sixty feet in breadth. The diagonal streets are to be named after the respective States composing the Union; while those which run North and South, are, from the Capitol eastward, to be called, East first street, East second street, &c., and those West of it, are, in the same manner, to be named West first street, West second street, &c.

The streets running East and West are, from the Capitol northward, to be called, North A street, North B street, &c., and those South of it are to be named, South A street, South B street, &c. There is not much taste, I think, displayed in thus naming the streets; Generals and Statesmen might have lent their names, and helped in their graves to keep patriotism alive.—A wag would infer that the North and South streets received their names from a pilot, and the East and West ones from an Alphabetical teacher.

The squares, or divisions of the city, will amount to eleven hundred and fifty. The rectangular squares, will, generally, contain from three to six acres, and be divided into lots of from forty to eighty feet in front, and from forty to three hundred feet in depth, according to the size of the squares. The irregular divisions produced by the diagonal streets are partly small, but commonly in valuable situations: their acute points are without distinction to be cut off at forty feet, inasmuch that no house in the city will have an acute corner: all the houses will be of stone or brick.

In a southern direction from the President's house, and a western one from the Capitol are to run two great pleasure parks, or malls, which will intersect and terminate upon the banks of the *Potomac;* and they are to be ornamented at the sides by a variety of elegant buildings, and houses for foreign Ministers.

Interspersed through the city, where the principal streets cross each other, is to be a number of open areas formed of various figures: fifteen of these areas are to be appropriated to the different States composing the Union; and, while they bear their respective names be consecrated to the erecting of statues, obelisks, or columns, to the memory of their departed Heroes, Statesmen, and Poets. Upon a small eminence, where a line drawn due West from the Capitol, and another due South from the President's house, would intersect, is to be placed an Equestrian Statue of General *Washington.*

The Navy-yard and Marine-barracks are partly constructed. The Navy-yard is formed by the projection of a wharf into the *Eastern Branch,* from which a dock will be produced of great capaciousness; and the Marine-barracks are designed to form a mass of brick buildings two stories high.

A road is making from the Capitol to *Georgetown,* and another on the *New Jersey* avenue, between the Capitol and *Eastern Branch:* in effecting the last object, the declivity of the abrupt hill to the South of the Capitol has been effectually removed.

Of the public edifices, the Capitol and President's house are the most magnificent. They are built of freestone (resembling the white and red *Portland*), which is dug from inexhaustible quarries on the banks of the Potomac. To the builder of the President's house might be applied the epitaph of *Vanbrugh.*

> *Lie heavy on him, Earth;—for he*
> *Has laid a heavy load on thee!*

The Treasury and War-office are constructed with brick. Some have objected, that the public offices are so remote from each other, as to obstruct the business of State. A shallow, gothic remark! The symmetry of the city would have been destroyed, had these buildings been more contiguous.

The Capitol is admirably situated on an ascent called *Capitol Hill.* The name of

Capitol associates the noblest ideas in the mind. It has a *Roman* sound! In our enthusiasm we behold *Virtue* and *Freedom*, which alas! have been so long extinct, again descending from heaven, and fixing their abode in the western world.*

Between the Capitol and the President's house, there has been dug a well, which suddenly overflowed, continues to overflow, and will probably for ever overflow. The proprietor of the well informed me, that having dug it about eleven feet deep, and five and a half in diameter, the water rose with impetuosity, and increased the diameter to ten feet. He afterwards sounded with a plummet, and found it had sunk another foot. It had continued to overflow without remission, and runs into the woods across the road before the house.—This wonder-working well brought the idle in crouds to behold it; and though it had been scarcely dug a month, the man who shewed it to the gazing multitude, made

[* Descriptions of Washington before the year 1801 are to be found in: (1) Wansey, *Journal of an Excursion to the United States of North America.* Salisbury, 1796, pp. 219-226. (2) Twining, *Travels in India a hundred years ago, with a visit* (1795) *to the United States.* London, 1903, pp. 403-407. (3) Weld, *Travels* &c. 1795, 1796, and 1797. 3rd Ed. London, 1800, Vol. I, pp. 72-89. (4) Baily, *Journal of a Tour in Unsettled Parts of North America in* 1796 and 1797. London, 1856, pp. 124-129. (5) Duke of La Rochefoucauld-Liancourt, *Travels* &c. *in the years* 1795, 1796, and 1797. London, 1799, Vol. II, pp. 311-336. (6) Parkinson, *Tour in America,* &c. London, 1805, Vol. I, p. 58 ff.]

no scruple to affirm, that it was not only the astonishment of *America,* but also of *Europe!*

Of the noble river *Potomac,* on whose banks, and those of its Branch, the proud structures of *Washington* are to lift their heads, it may not be unimproving to give some account.

The *Potomac* rises in the *Allegany* mountains, and after a serpentine, but majestic course of four hundred miles, it falls into the Bay of *Chesapeak,* which is beyond all rivalry, or competition, the largest bay in the known world. At its junction with the bay it is full seven miles in breadth; which gradually decreasing, it is found to be a mile broad at *Alexandria* and *Washington.* The navigation of the *Potomac,* from its junction with the *Chesapeak,* to the city of *Washington,* is incontrovertibly tedious. It is nearly a hundred and fifty miles; and in a severe winter, the river, in the vicinity of *Washington* and *Alexandria,* being entirely frozen, an insurmountable barrier is opposed to the skill of the mariner. But the *Eastern Branch,* it must be confessed, is a commodious harbour for shipping; it is deep, and not being subject to freshes, the ice is without any mischievous effect.

The *Eastern Branch* of the *Potomac* is a tributary stream to it; and nature by their confluence invites the building of a city. The *Eastern Branch,* at its junction with the *Potomac,* vies with it in breadth; but in tracing it to its source, this mighty mouth diminishes; and, at *Bladensburgh,* to cross its rustic bridge, the wheels of a carriage have not many revolutions to undergo. The *Eastern Branch* extends about thirty miles from its discharge to its source.

It has been asserted by a late Traveller,* that the *Tiber,* which supplies the city of *Washington* with water, received that name either from the *Indians,* or the first locaters of the land; and hence is prophesied the magnificence of the city, which at some future day is to be a second *Rome.*

Of the erroneousness of this observation, accident one day convinced me. Having breakfasted at *George-town,* (it was at *Mac Glaughflin's* hotel), with a lively young *Frenchman,* I proposed a walk to the Capitol. In our progress though the houseless streets of the Imperial city, the excessive heat of the sun provoked thirst, and to allay it we retired into the woods, and seated ourselves by the *Tiber.* The Capitol was within view. *Voila,* said my companion, pointing to the edifice—*Voila un Capitol sans Ciceron; et voici* (turning his finger towards the stream) *voici le Tibre sans Rome.*†)

Are you sure, *Monsieur,* said I, that you call

[* Isaac Weld, Vol. I, p. 83.]

† Behold a *Capitol* without a *Cicero;* and a *Tiber* without a *Rome.*

this stream by its right name? Is there not some other for it?

My companion shrugged his shoulders, and said he could not tell.

At this juncture a groupe of negro boys and girls came to the stream, and filled their pitchers and pails.

I addressed them severally.

How you call this little river, my fine fellow?

You stranger, Mossa?

Yes.

Goose-Creek, Mossa.

Where's the *Tiber,* my good boy?

Where de *Tiber,* Mossa ask. Me never hear of the *Tiber;* me never see such a ting.*

After this let us hear no more far-fetched stories about the *Tiber;* but be content with the simple truth, that the first settlers of the contiguous lands conferred on it the name of *Goose-Creek.*†

* Of this I have the further testimony of Mr. *Ellicott,* who helped to project the city. [It was not Andrew Ellicott in whose family the author was Tutor.]

[† Moore, in his 'Lines to Thomas Hume, M.D., from the City of Washington,' makes use of this Tiber Creek. In his footnote he cites Weld, but is plainly inspired of Davis, since Weld does not mention Goose Creek. The lines are,

"In fancy now, beneath the twilight gloom,
Come, let me lead thee o'er this 'second Rome'
Where tribunes rule, where dusky Davi bow,
And what was Goose Creek once is Tiber now."

Thomas Moore, Riverside Ed., Houghton, Mifflin & Co., Vol. II, p. 83.

Of *Goose-Creek,* (or, more magnificently, the *Tiber*), the water is excellent; and it is in contemplation to collect it in a grand reservoir, near the Capitol, and supply the houses with it by the means of pipes; while the superfluous water will form a variety of fanciful cascades, delighting the eye and refreshing the air.

It appears to me, that the President's salary is not adequate to his house. The one is very circumscribed; the other of vast dimensions. It is a shallow policy in a government which makes money the chief good.

The salary allowed the President is only twenty-five thousand dollars a-year; that is, about £5,300 sterling; a sum that may enable him to ask a friend to dine with him *pic nic,* but will not qualify him to impress a foreign Ambassador with much veneration for the first executive office of *America.*

It may be advanced, that it is not expected from a Republican Magistrate to regale his guests out of a gold cup. But for the manners of a Republican Chief to be absolutely characteristical, he ought, like *Fabricius,* to pare his own turnips, and boil them himself.

To *Franklin* must we look for the source of this sordid œconomy. It was he who, by diffusing the maxims of poor *Richard,* made the

Cf. Warden, *Chorographical and Statistical Description of the District of Columbia.* Paris, 1816, p. 32.]

government of the United States a miserly body-politic; tenacious of a farthing, or, in popular language, a nation penny wise, and pound foolish. *Franklin,* when a child, delighted to hawk ballads for a halfpenny; and when he became a man, to save the expence of an errand-boy, he trundled his wheelbarrow through the streets.

Notwithstanding the vaunted philosophy of *Franklin,* and his discoveries in electricity, he is certainly at best but an ambiguous character. His dereliction of religion has already done more injury to the rising generation in *America,* than his maxims will do good. Where *Franklin* has made one man frugal, he has converted a hundred men to Deism. I heard the infidel *Palmer* at *New-York,* enjoin his hearers no longer to suffer passively the flagrant impositions of the Scripture, but catch a portion of the spirit of a *Franklin,* and avow themselves disciples of Natural Religion. And, I doubt not, but this argument of this preacher succeeded; for where a man has one vice of his own, he gets twenty by adoption.

Let me now come to the object of my journey to *Washington.* The politeness of a member from *Virginia,* procured me a convenient seat in the Capitol; and an hour after, Mr. *Jefferson* entered the House, when the august assembly of *American* Senators rose to receive him. He came, however, to the House without ostentation. His dress was of plain cloth, and he rode on horseback to the Capitol without a single guard, or even servant in his train, dismounted without assistance, and hitched the bridle of his horse to the palisades.*

Never did the Capitol wear a more animated appearance than on the fourth day of *March,* 1801. The Senate-Chamber was filled with citizens from the remotest places of the Union. The planter, the farmer, the mechanic and merchant, all seemed to catch one common transport of enthusiasm, and welcome the approach of the Man to the chair of Sovereign Authority, who had before served his country in various offices of dignity; who had sat in the famous Congress that produced the Revolution, acted as Governor to his native State, and been Minister Plenipotentiary to a foreign nation.

Mr. *Jefferson,* having taken the oaths to the Constitution, with a dignified mien, addressed the august assembly of Senators and Representatives.

[* The author was a novelist. It may be asked whether he was present at this inauguration. Randall (II, 630), and Parton (p. 587) give the story as told by Davis and on his authority. Forman, (*Life and Writings of Thomas Jefferson.* Indianapolis, 1900, p. 85) and Spofford, (*Centennial Celebration &c. of the District of Columbia,* p. 236) say that the story is without foundation. Forman quotes a dispatch of Mr. Thornton, then chargé of the British Legation, to the effect that Jefferson walked to the Capitol, attended,—" he came from his own lodgings to the house where the Congress convenes, and which goes by the name of the Capitol, on foot."]

"*Friends and Fellow-Citizens,*

" Called upon to undertake the duties of the
" first executive office of our country, I avail
" myself of the presence of that portion of my
" fellow-citizens, which is here assembled, to
" express my grateful thanks for the favour
" with which they have been pleased to look
" towards me, to declare a sincere conscious-
" ness that the task is above my talents, and
" that I approach it with those anxious and
" awful presentiments, which the greatness of
" the charge, and the weakness of my powers
" so justly inspire. A rising nation, spread
" over a wide and fruitful land, traversing all
" the seas with the rich productions of their
" industry; engaged in commerce with nations
" who feel power and forget right, advancing
" rapidly to destinies beyond the reach of mor-
" tal eye; when I contemplate these transcend-
" ant objects, and see the honour, the happi-
" ness, and the hopes of this beloved country
" committed to the issue and the auspices of
" this day, I shrink from the contemplation,
" and humble myself before the magnitude of
" the undertaking. Utterly, indeed, should I
" despair, did not the presence of many whom
" I here see remind me, that in the other high
" authorities provided by our Constitution, I
" shall here find resources of wisdom, of vir-
" tue, and of zeal, on which to rely under all
" difficulties. To you, then, gentlemen, who

" are charged with the sovereign functions of
" legislation, and to those associated with you,
" I look with encouragement for that guidance
" and support, which may enable us to steer
" with safety the vessel in which all are em-
" barked, amidst the conflicting elements of a
" troubled world.

" During the contest of opinion through
" which we have passed, the animation of dis-
" cussions and exertions has sometimes worn
" an aspect which might impose on strangers
" unused to think freely, and to speak and to
" write what they think; but this being now
" decided by the voice of the nation, an-
" nounced according to the rules of the Con-
" stitution, all will of course arrange them-
" selves under the will of the law, and unite
" in one common effort for the common good.
" All too will bear in mind this sacred prin-
" ciple, that, though the will of the majority is
" in all cases to prevail, that will to be right-
" ful must be reasonable; that the minority
" possess their equal rights, which equal laws
" must protect; and to violate would be op-
" pression. Let us, then, fellow-citizens, unite
" with one heart and one mind; let us restore
" to social intercourse that harmony and affec-
" tion, without which liberty, and even life
" itself, are but dreary things; and let us re-
" flect, that having banished from our land
" that religious intolerance under which man-

" kind so long bled and suffered, we have yet
" gained little if we countenance a political
" intolerance, as despotic, as wicked, as ca-
" pable of as bitter and bloody persecutions.
" During the throes and convulsions of the
" ancient world, during the agonizing spasms
" of infuriated man, seeking through blood
" and slaughter his long lost liberty, it was not
" wonderful that the agitation of the billows,
" should reach even this distant and peaceful
" shore,—that this should be more felt, and
" feared by some and less by others, and should
" divide opinions, as to measures of safety;
" but every difference of opinion is not a dif-
" ference of principle. We have called by
" different names brethren of the same prin-
" ciple. We are all republicans, all federal-
" ists. If there be any among us who would
" wish to dissolve this union, or to change its
" republican form, let them stand undisturbed
" as monuments of the safety, with which error
" of opinion may be tolerated, where reason is
" left free to combat it. I know, indeed, that
" some honest men fear that a Republican
" Government cannot be strong,—that this
" Government is not strong enough. But
" would the honest, in the full tide of success-
" ful experiment, abandon a Government,
" which has so far kept us free and firm, in the
" theoretic and visionary fear, that this Gov-
" ernment, the world's best hope, may, by pos-

" sibility, want energy to preserve itself? I
" trust not; I believe this, on the contrary, the
" strongest Government on earth. I believe it
" the only one, where every man at the call of
" the law, would fly to the standard of the law,
" and would meet invasions of the public
" order, as his own personal concern. Let
" us then, with courage and confidence pursue
" our own federal and republican principles;
" our attachment to union and representative
" government. Kindly separated by nature and
" a wide ocean, from the exterminating havoc
" of one quarter of the globe, too high-minded
" to endure the degradations of the others;
" possessing a chosen country, with room
" enough for descendants to the thousandth and
" ten thousandth generation; entertaining a
" due sense of our equal right to the use of our
" own faculties, to the acquisition of our own
" industry, to honour and confidence from our
" fellow-citizens, resulting not from birth, but
" from our actions; and their sense of them en-
" lightened by a benign religion,—professed
" indeed, and practised in various forms, yet
" all of them inculcating honesty, truth, tem-
" perance, gratitude, and the love of man—
" acknowledging and adoring an over-ruling
" Providence, which by all its dispensations,
" proves that it delights in the happiness of
" man here, and his greater happiness here-
" after; with all these blessings, what more is

" necessary to make us a happy and prosperous
" people? Still one thing more, fellow-citi-
" zens; a wise and frugal Government, which
" shall restrain men from injuring one an-
" other, shall leave them otherwise free to
" regulate their own pursuits and improve-
" ment, and shall not take from the mouth of
" labour the bread it has earned. This is the
" sum of good government, and this is neces-
" sary to close the circle of our felicities.

"About to enter, fellow-citizens, on the
" exercise of duties which comprehend every
" thing dear and valuable to you, it is proper
" you should understand what I deem the es-
" sential principles of our Government, and
" consequently those which ought to shape its
" administration. I will compress them within
" the narrowest compass they will bear; stat-
" ing the general principle, but not all its
" limitations:—Equal and exact justice to all
" men, of whatever state or persuasion, reli-
" gious or political; peace, commerce, and hon-
" est friendship with all nations; entangling
" alliances with none; the support of State
" Governments in all their rights, as the most
" competent administration for our domestic
" concerns, and the surest bulwarks against
" anti-republican tendencies; the preservation
" of the general Government in its whole
" constitutional vigour, as the sheet-anchor of
" our peace at home and safety abroad; a

" jealous care of the right of election by the
" people; a mild and safe corrective of abuses,
" which are lopped by the sword of revolu-
" tion, where peaceable remedies are unpro-
" vided; absolute acquiescence in the decisions
" of the majority, the vital principle of Re-
" publics, from which is no appeal but to force,
" the vital principle and immediate parent of
" despotism; a well-disciplined militia—our
" best reliance in peace, and for the first mo-
" ments of war, till regulars may relieve them;
" the supremacy of the civil over the military
" authority; œconomy in the public expence,
" that labour may be lightly burthened; the
" honest payment of our debts, and sacred
" preservation of the public faith; encourage-
" ment of agriculture, and commerce as its
" handmaid; the diffusion of information, and
" arraignment of all abuses at the bar of the
" public reason; freedom of religion, free-
" dom of the press, and the freedom of the
" person, under protection of the habeas-
" corpus: and trial by juries impartially
" selected. These principles form the bright
" constellation which has gone before us,
" and guided our steps through an age of
" revolution and reformation. The wisdom of
" all our sages, and blood of our heroes, have
" been devoted to their attainment: they should
" be the creed of our political faith, the text
" of civic instruction, the touchstone by which

"to try the services of those whom we trust;
"and, should we wander from them in mo-
"ments of error or of alarm, let us hasten
"to retrace our steps, and regain the road
"which alone leads to peace, liberty, and
"safety.

"I repair, then, fellow-citizens to the post
"you have assigned me. With experience
"enough in subordinate offices to have seen the
"difficulty of this, the greatest of all, I have
"learned to expect that it will rarely fall to
"the lot of imperfect man, to retire from this
"station with the reputation and the favour
"which bring him into it. Without preten-
"sions to that high confidence you reposed in
"your first and great revolutionary character,
"whose pre-eminent services had entitled him
"to the first place in his country's love, and
"destined for him the fairest page in the
"volume of faithful history, I ask so much
"confidence only, as may give firmness and
"effect to the legal administration of your
"affairs. I shall often go wrong through de-
"fect of judgment: when right, I shall often
"be thought wrong by those whose positions
"will not command a view of the whole
"ground. I ask your indulgence for my own
"errors, which will never be intentional; and
"your support against the errors of others,
"who may condemn what they would not if
"seen in all its parts. The approbation im-

" plied by your suffrage, is a great consolation
" to me for the past; and my future solicitude
" will be to retain the good opinion of those
" who have bestowed it in advance; to con-
" ciliate that of others, by doing them all the
" good in my power; and to be instrumental
" to the freedom and happiness of all.

" Relying, then, on the patronage of your
" good-will, I advance with obedience to the
" work, ready to retire from it whenever you
" become sensible how many better choices it
" is in your power to make; and may that in-
" finite Power which rules the destinies of the
" Universe, lead our councils to what is best,
" and give them a favourable issue for your
" peace and prosperity." *

[* Randall remarks on this speech, Vol. II, p. 633,—" The number of its phrases which have passed into popular axioms— which are constantly reproduced in political newspapers and addresses, as at the same time the most authoritative and most felicitous expressions of the ideas they embody—is astonishing."]

CHAP. VII.

Return to New-York.—Literary Pursuits.—Magnificent Promises from a great Man.—The Horizon of Life brightens.—I no longer feed on the Vapours of a School, but depart for the City of Washington, with a Heart dancing to the Song of Expectation—I mingle at Philadelphia with the Votaries of Taste; and am elbowed by Poets and Prose-Writers, Critics and Philosophers.—I Proceed to Washington.—Interview with the Secretary of the Treasury.—All my Hopes blasted.—I travel into Virginia, by the Way of Alexandria.—A Quaker opens his Door to receive me, and I exchange with him lasting Knowledge for perishable Coin.

WHEN I had heard the speech of Mr. *Jefferson,* there was nothing more to detain me among the scattered buildings of the desert. On my return to *New-York,* I became seriously busied in directing the tastes and cultivating the imaginations of the three sons of Mr. *Ludlow.* The mother had already polished their manners into elegance, and they never entered the room without respectively making me a low bow, not the shuffling bow of a plough boy, but a bow taught them by a dancing-master, and softened into ease by an intercourse with good company. This put me upon bowing myself, and I reciprocated bows with them till *Ferdinand,* who agonized under the slightest invasion of his sensibility, discovered my bow was ironical, and expressed his hope that I would not make a jest of him. But not so the youngest. *Edward,* who had been just trussed out in pantaloons and boots, would writhe his jolly form, and kick about his legs till both his brothers were speechless with laughter.

Indolence is more painful than labour to a mind that delights in employment; and there was no abatement of my vigour in my literary vocation. The first impression of the *Farmer of New Jersey* was nearly exhausted; a second edition was in the press; and, animated by its success, *Caritat* * published my poems in a

* I would place the bust of *Caritat* among those of the *Sosii* of *Horace,* and the *Centryphon* of *Quintillian.* He was my only friend at *New-York,* when the energies of my mind were depressed by the chilling prospects of poverty. His talents were not meanly cultivated by letters; he could tell a good book from a bad one, which few modern Librarians can do. But *place aux dames* was his maxim, and all the ladies of *New-York* declared that the Library of Mr. *Caritat* was charming. Its shelves could scarcely sustain the weight of *Female Frailty,* the *Posthumous Daughter,* and the *Cavern of Woe;* they required the aid of the carpenter to support the burden of the *Cottage-on-the-Moor,* the *House of Tynian,* and the *Castles of Athlin and Dunbayne;* or they groaned under the multiplied editions of the *Devil in Love, More Ghosts,* and *Rinaldo Rinaldini.* Novels were called for by the young and the old; from the tender virgin of thirteen, whose little heart went pit-a-pat at the approach of a beau; to the experienced matron of three score, who could not read without spectacles.

small volume, which I dedicated to my friend Mr. *Burr,* who had recently been elected Vice-President of the United States.

My book, however small, did not escape the *Mohawk* Reviewers. The criticism is the production of an Attorney, named *Beckman;* he writes the Christmas Carols, and furnishes the news-carriers with addresses to their subscribers.

"Those who are sometimes disposed to
" amuse their idle moments with ' trifles light
" as air,' may find some entertainment in this
" little volume of poems. Their chief quali-
" ties are harmony of numbers, and vivacity of
" expression. Not laden with a weight of
" sentiment, the verses move easily and lightly
" along; and though too short to be tedious,
" their brevity is not the vehicle of wit.

"The Author appears to possess a capacity
" for poetical composition, and we should be
" pleased to see his ready talents exerted on
" topics more dignified or interesting. We
" observe several instances of good taste, and
" pretty description."

[Several of these titles are to be traced, a hundred years after. *Female Fraïlty or the History of Miss Wroughton* appeared at London in 1772; there was a *Cavern of Death* published at London in 1794 and at Baltimore in 1795; *Castles of Athlin and Dunbayne,* 1789, was Mrs. Ann Radcliffe's first novel; the *Devil in Love,* translation, 1793, of Cazotte's *Diable Amoureux.* Rinaldo (cf. Lewes, *Life of Goethe,* II, 86) has been for centuries a romantic name. *More Ghosts* is a modern title.]

But the time was approaching, when I had every reason to flatter my expectation with exchanging the Muses' bower for the garden of the Hesperides. Colonel *Burr* had been elected to the place of Vice-President of the United States, and Colonel *Burr* was my friend. He had just returned from the city of *Washington,* and with the most condescending urbanity, did me the honour to call on me at Mr. *Ludlow's.* Colonel *Burr* observed, that " Mr. *Gallattin* having expressed a desire to " procure a Secretary who was skilled in com-" position, he had recommended me as a per-" son qualified to undertake the office, and was " happy to have it in his power to acknowl-" edge by any service, the sensible pleasure " he had received from my literary produc-" tions."

There is something in the professions of a great man which never fails to impart delight; our hopes become multiplied; the phantoms of imagination arise in succession, and either point to paths of pleasure, or bowers of repose. I heard " the glorious sounds," with no small emotions of joy, and looked forward with anxiety to the hour that was to exalt me from the obscurity of a pedagogue to the magnificence of a Secretary's office. It happened that when the Vice-President proposed to me a place at *Washington,* the term of my engagement with Mr. *Ludlow,* had just expired; and I was compelled to be decisive in the plan of my future operations; I was under the necessity either of resigning the situation, or no longer indulge the visions my fancy had created, from the magnificent promises held out by the Vice-President; hope triumphed over prudence, and I abandoned a salary of a hundred guineas paid me quarterly in advance, for an exaltation that was remote, and at the same time uncertain.

My pupils could be hardly persuaded I was about to leave them, till I bade them farewell; they shed many tears; but their grief, however violent, was of transient duration; for before I had walked half way down the street, I beheld them return to their ball-playing with more alacrity than ever. It is thus with men; grief is ever a short-lived passion, and no person is of sufficient consequence to interrupt by his absence the pursuits of his friends.

In my way to the Stage-office, in Courtland street, I called at the Post-office, where, to my unspeakable joy, I found a copious epistle from my friend at *Long Island*. *Letters,* says the illustrious *Bacon, come more home to men's bosoms than either annals or lives;* and, as by this time, every thing that relates to Mr. *George* will interest the Poet, the Scholar, and the Wit, I shall engraft without apology his letter upon my Memoirs.

"*Long Island, June* 12, 1801.

"While devouring Newtown-pippins, and
"drinking cider to the health of your Bard-
"ship in my heart, the stage-driver brought
"me your welcome epistles. At first, the fel-
"low pretended there was no letter for me (I
"tolerate these liberties, because the *Jehu* has
"a pretty wife) but in a few minutes, he de-
"livered me the packet. *Jucundius est legere
"quam libere,* so I left the old parson, and
"his wife, and his daughter, (her nose is like
"the tower of *Lebanon* looking towards *Da-
"mascus)* and I opened, O Devil! thy budget
"of Satire. This has revived me, and I now
"walk about with your epistles in my hand,
"which, however, I am obliged to put down
"every five minutes, to hold both my sides
"while I laugh it out.

"By Saint *Patrick,* I swear, thou art above
"all men dear to me. I love thee with more
"than brotherly love. I hope we shall never
"part. In the vast deserts of the world, I
"never could have found such another friend
"as thyself; and (to speak in the language
"of classic antiquity) I think *Apollo* himself
"must have brought us acquainted.

"I thank you kindly for the book. It was
"a mercy you did not fill it with your letters.
"I could wish, however, they had been longer;
"for never did you write with more grace,
"and less appearance of study.

"This is a beautiful day, and I purpose to
"devote it entirely to my blank volume; not
"in adding one, two, three, nor in balancing
"the preponderance of Debtor to Creditor;
"but in filling it with new energies of thought,
"and new combinations of diction. This
"book is really an acquisition. It is scarcely
"less formidable, than the mighty one with
"which *Johnson* repressed the insolence of
"his book-seller, or to speak in a more heroic
"strain, that which *Cadmus* of old threw
"wrathful at the dragon.

"Tell me if you are about publishing your
"poems? Do not go far for a title; nothing
"appears so stiff and pedantic as a little book
"with a magnificent title. Remember that
"*Horace* gives his odes no other name than
"*Carmina;* though, he might have accumu-
"lated a thousand imposing epithets, to deco-
"rate his title-page. It is rumoured you in-
"tend dedicating your effusions to *Burr.*
"Avert it literature. Dedicate not the book
"to an *American.* Can *Burr,* or *Maddison,*
"or *Adams,* or even *Jefferson,* add to the
"reputation of him who aspires to be read on
"the banks of the *Thames?*

"Was there ever so stupid a Priest as this?
"I wonder not that you hated him. Do you
"recollect when we were sitting by the fire,
"how you used to hem, and I to laugh at his
"tiresome monotony. The old grasshopper

"asked me very solemnly to-day, which I
"thought the better translation of *Virgil;*
"*Dryden's* or *Davidson's!!!* * After such an
"interrogation, can any reasonable man ex-
"pect that I will ever go again to his church;
"or is he not enough to make any man
"of letters *Parcus deorum cultor et infre-*
"*quens?*"

"The girls in this village are mad after
"literature; they know not what to be at.
"Miss T——, a young lady of easy deport-
"ment, elegant conversation, and bold counte-
"nance, has bought *Tasso's Gierusaleme,* and
"digs in a dictionary for his meaning. She
"asked me my opinion of *Tasso* and the
"*Italian* language. Madam, said I, the lan-
"guage of *Tasso* is not the language of heroes,
"but the sing-song of fidlers, and guitar-
"players. The *Italian* possesses neither the
"heroic grandeur of the *Greek,* the majesty
"of the *Roman,* nor the strength of the *Eng-*
"*lish* language.

"Then, cried she, you would advise me to
"study *English.* By all means, Madam, said
"I. And, Sir, rejoined the nymph, what
"book do you think is best suited to a female?
"*Glasse's* Cookery, Madam, said I.

* *Pope* pronounced *Dryden's* translation of *Virgil,* the noblest version ever produced by one Poet of another; *Davidson's* translation is in limping, hobbling, shuffling prose; the solace of Dunces; the clandestine refuge of schoolboys.

"I have passed three hours under an oak-tree by the way-side, in reading the Iliad.

"*Blair*, in his Lectures, says of *Homer*, that in description he is concise. The descriptions of *Homer*, on the contrary, are full and expanded paintings of nature. Of the *Homeric* poetry, copiousness is the characteristic; of the *Virgilian*, metaphorical inversion.

"There are few metaphorical inflexions of phrase in *Homer;* in *Virgil* they overflow. *Virgil* says, in the fifth book of his *Æneis*, 'Thus he spoke weeping, and *gave the reins to his fleet.*' *Homer* would have expressed it more simply. Thus in the twelfth *Odyssey* he says, 'Now they leave the inhospitable shores of the *Cyclops*, and *sail through the ocean.*' This marks strongly the distinction between the *Homeric* and *Virgilian* poetry.

"I sometimes amuse myself by translating from *Homer* into *English* verse. I will confront a brick of my house with a brick of *Pope's*.

"BY ALEXANDER POPE

"There in the forum swarm a num'rous train,
"The subject of debate a townsman slain;
"One pleads the fine discharg'd, which one denied,
"And bade the public, and the laws decide.
"The witnesses appear on either hand,
"For this or that the partial people stand;

"The appointed heralds still the noisy bands,
"And form a ring with sceptres in their hands."

"BY LUCAS GEORGE

" In noisy crouds the populace appear,
" Rise in debate, and urge the wordy war,
" Two in contention rose, &c., &c.
" This pleads his juster cause, attests the skies,
" That juster still, the seeming fact denies.
" The witnesses produc'd, the fickle croud
" To either cause divide, and shout aloud!
" Confusion fills the air; the heralds stand,
" Extend the sceptre, and the peace command."

"Pray, in the justice of criticism, do you
" not think mine the more spirited translation?
" Is not my versification also more regular,
" harmonious and natural? Answer this, I
" say.* The four last lines of *Pope* are mo-
" notonous; the pauses fall too late to be lively.
" *Sum Pius Æneas!* &c. &c.

"Have you ever seen *Mambrun's* epic poem
" in *Latin,* of *Idolatry Overthrown?* No.
" You see, Sir, how little you know of *French*
" authors.† This poem I have glanced over
" (no matter where), and can inform you that
" it is below criticism.

"News. *Townshend,* the schoolmaster, has
" fled. Finding his garrison no longer ten-

* Answer. NO. † Is not this a bull?
[Pierre Mambrun, 1600-1661, of Clermont-Ferrand, but author of *Constantinus sive Idolatria debellata*.]

"able, he wisely evacuated it, and has em-
"barked himself, and his system of book-keep-
"ing, for the island of *Bermudas.* Had this
"descendant from *Orbilius Flagosus* known
"*Latin,* he would, doubtless, have found a
"valedictory quotation in *Virgil,* and ad-
"dressed me with it at parting.

"Nos patriæ fines et dulcia linquimus arva,
"Nos patriam fugimus; tu, Tityre, lentus in umbra,
"Formosam resonare doces Amaryllida sylvas." *

"The trustees have increased my salary to
"a hundred and twenty pounds a-year, with
"boarding; so, I believe, I shall continue to
"vegetate and eat grass among the *Newtown*
"farmers, till I shall be enabled to look on
"the frowns of fortune with a more magnan-
"imous countenance.

"You say you are writing a Novel. There
"was a man in *Babylon! toll de roll!*

"*June* 18, 1801.

"I again resume my conversation with you.
"Our right reverend Parson has the predict-
"ing spirit of *Achilles'* horse, for he told me
"last night we should have fair weather, and
"I perceive the sky is without a cloud.

"The people here are become more atten-
"tive to me of late, than they formerly were;
"and though I cannot hope for intellectual

[* Virgil, *Ecloga I*, 2.]

"felicity, yet I may expect such tranquillity
"as (though inglorious) will at least be in-
"dulgent to my literary indolence.

"I dined yesterday with Mrs. ——, and her
"daughter. The old lady told me a story
"about you. She said, that instead of de-
"livering *Heloise* the novel which I sent her
"by you from *West Chester,* you lent it to
"her youngest daughter, and palmed upon
"*Heloise* an old history of *Rome.*—I again
"repeat, women know not what to be at.
"Mrs. —— acquainted me in a whisper, that
"she was preparing a critique on your fugi-
"tive poems, which she should sign *Artimesia,*
"and publish it in the Commercial Adver-
"tiser. Knowing you to be one of the *genus
"irritabile vatum,* and having the dignity of
"your character at heart, I enjoin you not to
"reply to this *Amazon* with anger, but gibbet
"her without ceremony to a gallows already
"made to your hands.

  "*When Artimesia talks by fits,*
  "*Of councils, classics, fathers, wits,*
   "*Reads Malbranche, Boyle and Locke;*
  "*Yet in some things methinks she fails,*
  "*' Twere well if she would pare her nails,*
   "*And wear a cleaner smock!*"

          Pope. *

"Having this gallows in contemplation, I
"advised Mrs. —— to publish her stricture;

[* *Imitations of English Poets*: Earl of Dorset.]

" complimenting her on her penetration, her
" acuteness, and her wit. She ought to be
" punished for her temerity. A woman has
" no business with a pen in her hand, unless
" it be to compute the expences of her house-
" keeping. When a woman is ambitious of
" literary distinction, she becomes distracted.
" Look at Mrs. *Wolstancroft's* (I may be for-
" given for not spelling the name right) *Per-
" version of Women.** It is a volume of in-
" sanity.

" It may be asked, Is a woman then to be
" debarred access to all books? I say no. If
" she discovers an avidity of reading, put
" a bible into her hands. Let a bible be
" her manual; let her lisp the scriptures
" in her childhood, and digest them in her
" youth.

" I was at *New-York* thrice last week. The
" last time I wished much to see you, and I
" called twice at the little tavern for that
" purpose; but you were too indolent to stir
" out; so I left you to meditate in your cham-
" ber, and prosecute your lucubrations, while
" I walked solitarily round the battery, and
" lamented the instability of friendship.

" *Heloise* has just sent me my stockings and
" cravats (delicately mended) by her brother.
" She is an amiable little devil, and I often

[* Mary Wollstonecraft's *Wrongs of Women or Maria*, two volumes, appeared in 1798.]

"go to see her, *mea sola voluptas!* But rather
"than be in love, I would change my human-
"ity with a baboon.

"I am sorry you are occupied in writing a
"Novel, because the world has reason to ex-
"pect something better. The mind of a young
"man of genius resembles a little stream,
"which, according to the direction that chance
"may give it, is either lost by mixing with
"other channels, or, preserving its course,
"enlarges at last its waters, and flows
"with the magnificence of the *Nile,* or the
"*Ganges.*

"I have sent *Lang* another essay to insert
"in his Gazette. It is the story of an *Indian*
"warrior; a mere cram; but no matter; any-
"thing is good enough for these calm *Amer-
"icans—fruges consumere nati.*

"Do you not think *Lang* a silly fellow, to
"place *Franklin's* head over his shop? How
"the people of *New-York* would roar with
"laughter were such a paragraph as this to
"appear in an opposition paper. *Yesterday
"Franklin's head fell upon John Lang, Esq.
"the printer, as he was opening his shop-door,
"and crushed him to cinders. Alas! poor
"Yorick!*

"Or the following, which would perhaps
"be more true. *Yesterday the bust of Dr.
"Franklin fell on Mr. Lang, the printer, as
"he was opening his shop-door, but, fortu-*

"*nately striking him in the head, he escaped
"unhurt.*

"Did you ever read the life of the illustri-
"ous *Franklin?* And did you ever read the
"memoirs of a Parish Clerk? I, P. P. Clerk
"of this parish, writeth this history, Amen!"

"*June* 23, 1801.

"I am just returned from *New-York,* and
"I sit down to relate to thee my eventful
"journey. At nine the stage-waggon called
"for me at the parson's, and, after travelling
"about a mile, we took up a middle-aged
"woman, of pleasing circumference, who kept
"a small pin-shop on the road. She was a
"notable matron, who disdained not brachial
"nor genual caresses, and who paid my
"ferriage at *Brooklyn.* Would not this be a
"favourable opportunity to quote *Ledyard's*
"Praise of Women? And to add, if, in hav-
"ing to cross the waters of the western con-
"tinent, I was without coin to pay my ferriage,
"I never applied to a woman but she put her
"hand into her pocket, and pulled out three
"farthings!

"On coming to town, my first care was to
"discharge a bill I had incurred at *Swords',*†

[* John Lang was at this time printer and publisher of the New York *Gazette and General Advertiser.*]

† Eminent printers and booksellers at *New York.* [T. & J. Swords, 160 Pearl Street. Printers to the Faculty of Physic of Columbia College.]

"for magazines and reviews. Here I encoun-
"tered the great Doctor *Phlogiston*,* a gentle-
"man of easy address, good habit of body,
"and a countenance that indicated the stoicism
"of a chymist.

"I crossed the *East River* again to *Brook-
"lyn*, with Mrs. *Dungan*, a lady of polished
"manners, and voluble elocution. Seeing a
"dirty fellow carrying a portrait of *Washing-
"ton*,—Madam, said I to my fair companion,
"General *Washington* is, I think, in bad
"hands.

"I forgot to tell you—at *Swords'* I had time
"to look into *Gibbon's* Memoirs, which were
"lying on the counter. His insertion of the
"Ode and Sonnet was puerile. And what he
"says of *Dryden* is not less injudicious. My
"choler rises when *Dryden* is depreciated.
"*Pope* could not describe the rising or setting
"of the sun without resorting to *Dryden*.

"The most beautiful triplet in all poetry
"is to be found in *Dryden's* version of the
"seventh *Æneis*.

   "From land a gentle breeze arose by night,
   "Serenely shone the stars, the moon was bright,
   "And the sea trembled with her silver light."

"Which, in my opinion, is infinitely superior
"to the original.

[* Dr. Priestley, who came to the United States in 1794. See his 'Reply to his Antiphlogistian Opponents.' *Medical Repository*, Vol. III (1801), p. 116 ff.]

" Aspirant auræ in noctem, nec candida cursus
" Luna negat—splendet tremulo sub lumine pontus."

" But this is travelling out of my road.——
" At *Brooklyn* I was accosted by a *quondam*
" acquaintance of *George-town*, to whom I
" was indebted about twenty-five dollars. *Vidi*
" *et obstupui!* I would rather have met the
" great devil. But *sic fata tulerunt*. After I
" had shaken hands with him, the barber of
" *Brooklyn,* to whom in a former expedition
" to *New-York,* I owed one or two shillings
" for cutting my hair, came up with a serious
" face and demanded his money also. Here
" were the devil and barber to pay! Leave,
" Sir, said I to the barber, your damnable
" countenance, and you shall have your money.

" From the first invader of my purse I es-
" caped as well as I could, and, handing Mrs.
" *Dungan* into the stage, I got in after her
" myself.

" By these unexpected asperities, my tran-
" quillity was disturbed, and I sought an ob-
" livion of reflexion in the company of *Heloise.*

"What essenc'd youth on bed of blushing roses!"

" I could get no sleep the whole night. I
" know not whether it was love or conscience
" kept me awake; but sleep I could not. I
" cannot think I was a victim to the anointed
" sovereign of sighs and groans; for I repeat,
" that sooner than be in love I would change

" my humanity with a baboon. It was, per-
" haps, the Muse who kept me wakeful, for
" on my midnight pillow I paraphrased the
" description of the War-horse in *Job*.

" Proud in his strength, behold the warlike horse
" Paw the green valley, and demand the course.
" With stately step he treads the dusty fields
" Glist'ning with groves of spears and moony shields.
" First with retorted eye he hears th' alarms
" Of rushing multitudes and clashing arms.
" Impatient to be free, he tears the plain,
" And tosses in his rage, his thunder-waving mane.
" In vain the javelin glitters in his eyes,
" He scorns the quiver, and the lance defies.
" Clouds of thick smoke his fiery nostrils roll,
" And all the battle rushes on his soul.
" He sees the moving phalanx rise around,
" He hears the trumpet, and the shouts resound.
" He starts! and fir'd by glory bears afar
" His trembling rider through the ranks of war."

" I had something of importance to observe
" to you. I perceive, with undissembled sor-
" row, that you admit words into your vocab-
" ulary, for which there is no authority in
" the undefiled writers of *English*. *Appreci-*
" *ate* and *meliorate* are bad words; so are
" *novel* and *derange*. Of modern writers
" none are more ridiculous coiners of words
" than the *Scotch* and *Welch Tourists*. Of
" these one introduces to *desiderate,* and tor-
" tures it through all its inflexions; and an-
" other in descanting upon ruins, says very

"gravely, they were *castleated!* The infer-
"ence to be deduced from the page in which
"words of this kind appear is, that the taste
"of the writer has been abominably vitiated.
"The *English* language is not written with
"purity in *America.** The structure of Mr.
"*Jefferson's* sentences is, I think, *French;* and
"he uses words unintelligible to an *English-
"man.* Where the d—l did he get the word
"*lengthy? Breadthy* and *depthy* would be
"equally admissible. I can overlook his word
"*belittle;* it is introduced in wantonness; but
"he has no right, that I know, to out-adverb
"all other writers, and improve *ill* into *illy.*
"Does not his description of the junction of
"the *Shenandoah* with the *Potomac,* discover
"an elevated imagination? But was one of
"my countrymen to describe the *Natural
"Bridge* (a huge mass of rock) "*springing as
"it were, up to heaven,*" would it not be said,
"that *Paddy* had made a bull.†

* If any work can transmit the *English* language uncorrupted to future generations on the banks of the *Potomac*, and
Mississippi it will be our matchless version of the Bible.
While religion exists in *America*, there will be a perpetual
standard for the *English* language.

[† Davis endorsed the fanciful construction. Cf. his *American Mariners* &c. *A Poem.* Salisbury, 1822, p. 235—The Natural Bridge: An Ode.

> When Fancy left her native skies,
> To visit earth, before unseen,
> She bade the swelling fabric rise
> In this sequester'd sylvan scene.

"Come over, will you, to my potatoe-
"ground next Saturday, and bring with you
"your Adventures of Captain *Bobadil*. You
"can pass your Sunday with me—not in an
"affectation of holiness, or hypocritical groans
"of contrition; but in study and meditation
"that lift the soul from its clay-confines, and
"transport it to the world of spirits. Vale!"

I journeyed delightfully from *New-York*
to *Philadelphia*. My finances were good, and
I was going to a place where I had only to
extend my arms and catch the golden shower.
Let the gloomy moralist insist on the position,
that life is rather to be endured than enjoyed;
but hope itself is happiness, and he who has
the knack of practising it, cannot be long a
victim to melancholy, though he find himself
cheated daily by new disappointments.

At *Philadelphia* I found Mr. *Brown*, who
felt no remission of his literary diligence, by
a change of abode. He was ingratiating himself into the favour of the ladies by writing a
new novel, and rivalling *Lopez de Vega* by
the multitude of his works. Mr. *Brown* introduced me to Mr. *Dickins*, and Mr. *Dickins*
to Mr. *Dennie;* Mr. *Dennie* presented me to

>And here perhaps the Indian stood,
>With hands upheld, and eye amaz'd,
>As, sudden, from the devious wood,
>He first upon the fabric gaz'd &c.]

Mr. *Wilkins,* and Mr. *Wilkins* to the Rev. Mr. *Abercrombie;* a constellation of *American* genius, in whose blaze I was almost consumed.*

Mr. *Dennie* was remarkable for his facility of expression; he could not only draw for thousands, but had always ready-money in his pocket; and few men excelled more in colloquial fluency than he. The Rev. Mr. *Abercrombie* was impatient of every conversation that did not relate to Dr. *Johnson,* of whom he could detail every anecdote from the time he trod on a duck, till he purchased an oak stick to repulse *Macpherson.* He was a canister tied to the tail of a canister. Mr. *Brown* said little, but seemed lost in meditation; his creative fancy was perhaps, conjuring up scenes to spin out the thread of his new novel.

Mr. *Dennie* now conducts, at *Philadelphia,* a literary paper, called the *Port Folio.* He first distinguished himself by the essays he contributed to the *"Farmer's Museum,"* under the title of the *Lay-Preacher.* He afterwards became editor of the paper, when its name was changed from the *Farmer's Museum* to that of the *Lay-Preacher's Gazette.* The essays of the *Lay-Preacher* were afterwards collected in a volume, which is, I be-

♦

[* James Abercrombe of Philadelphia, 1758-1841; and possibly the Rev. Isaac Wilkins, of St. Peter's Church, Westchester County, New York.]

lieve, the most popular work on the *American* continent.* I am of opinion, that the sermons of the *Lay-Preacher* have rather injured than assisted the cause of religion; to appropriate the remark made by *Gray* on *Yorick,* the *Lay-Preacher,* after exhorting his congregation to righteousness, throws his periwig at their heads.

The editor of the *Aurora* calls the *Port Folio,* the *Portable Foolery;* and his facetiousness is applauded by one party, and scorned by the other. But a better quibble on the word would be, I think, to name it the *Court Olio;* for it mingles the dresses at *St. James,* with speculations on literature.—It being rumoured that Mr. *Dennie* had been denominated, by the *British* Reviewers, the *American Addison,* the following ludicrous paragraph appeared in the *Aurora Gazette.*†

" Exult ye white hills of *New Hampshire,*
" redoubtable *Monadnock* and *Tuckaway!*

[* "The Lay Preacher of Dennie and his articles in the Portfolio seem to me feeble and affected, though occasionally marked by considerable excellence. For several years after the death of Brockden Brown, I believe he was the only man in the country who made literature a profession." Griswold, *Prose Writers of America,* p. 40. "Literature in America is an amusement only, not a profession." *Some Information respecting America, collected by Thomas Cooper, late of Manchester.* Dublin, 1794, p. 64.]

[† *The Aurora and General Advertiser,* of which Benjamin Franklin Bache was the editor. Those were political times. The *Portfolio* was Federalist and the *Aurora* was Democratic (Republican).]

" Laugh ye waters of the *Winiseopee* and
" *Umbagog Lakes!* Flow smooth in heroic
" verse ye streams of *Amorioosack* and *Andro-*
" *scoggin, Cockhoko* and *Coritocook!* And
" you *Merry Merrimack* be now more
" merry! "

Mr. *Dennie* passed his mornings in the shop of Mr. *Dickins,* which I found the rendezvous of the *Philadelphia* sons of literature. *Blair,* author of a poem called the *Powers of Genius; Ingersoll,* known by a tragedy, of which I forget the title; *Stock,* celebrated for his dramatic criticisms; together with several Reviewers, *chartam consumere nati,* assembled with punctuality in *North Second Street,* to the great annoyance of Mr. *Dickins,* who could scarcely find room to sell his wares. But I thought Mr. *Dickins* not inferior to any of the constellation; * he was remarkable for the gentleness of his manners, and displayed not less his good sense by his discourse, than his moderation by his silence.

I have seldom been at any city in the *United States,* without forming an acquaintance that has ripened into the intimacy of friendship. My love of the gallic idiom having led me to the shop of Mr. *Dufief,* a *French* bookseller,

[*Asbury Dickins, interested with Dennie in the *Portfolio.* It was John Blair Linn (1777-1804) who wrote the *Powers of Genius.* Charles J. Ingersoll, (1782-1862), member of Congress &c., and mover of one of the first railroad bills in this country, published in 1801 a tragedy, *Edwy and Elgiva.*]

in *North Fourth Street;* I found his conversation and manners so perfectly agreeable, that I hesitated not to accept an invitation to dine with him at his lodgings.

Though Mr. *Dufief* had emigrated from *France,* he was not inferior to any of the *Philadelphia* citizens in the pertinacity of his diligence. He had discovered that it was a position not only in *Europe,* but *America,* that the man who wanted money, was in want of everything; and directing his course toward the same goal for which so many millions were panting, he practised every art by which he could honestly put money in his purse. He opened a bookseller's shop, and placed an unsaleable bust of *Voltaire* over his door; he published a *French* grammar, on a plan entirely new; and taught *French* to those who would learn it. In a word, when I became acquainted with Mr. *Dufief,* he was about to open a lounging room for the *Muscadins* of *Philadelphia.*

Mr. *Dufief* did me the honour to shew me every place, in or near, *Philadelphia,* that it was fashionable to visit. The *Museum, Gray's Gardens,* the *Quaker's Meeting,* and

[* Cf. Wansey's *Journal,* pp. 134-136; p. 154,—"At Peale's Museum, I was entertained for two or three hours, in viewing his collection of artificial and natural curiosities. But what particularly struck me at this place, was portraits (kit-cat length) of all the leading men concerned in the late revolution, which after a century hence will be very valuable in the

State-House-Yard; together with the Water-works at *Schuylkill,* and Wax-work in *Shippen-street,* were familiar to the boundless curiosity of my attentive companion. Nor did he forget the ox, whose bulk was so unusual to animals of the same species on the *American* continent. Indeed it ought not to escape notice, that when an ox in the United States attains the ordinary growth of one in *England,* it becomes a source of riches to the proprietor, by a private exhibition.

The round of amusements at *Philadelphia,* did not make me neglect the *Wanderings of William.* But Mr. *Dickins* waved his claim to the copyright in favour of Mr. *Thompson,* who put it to the press before I left *Philadelphia.* Mr. *Thompson* had just printed a superb edition of the *Notes on Virginia;* and was exceeded by no man in the typographical elegance of the works that issued from his press.*

But the honours that awaited me at *Washington* employed principally my thoughts; I

eyes of posterity"—"On our return we stopped at Grey's Gardens, a place of entertainment, like Bagnigge Wells. It stands at the ferry of the Skuylkill, almost four miles from the city, and is much frequented by parties of pleasure from thence." Cf. also, William Priest, *Travels in the United States from 1793 to 1797.* London, 1802, p. 34.]

[* Sabin describes the edition of the *Notes on Virginia,* 'Philadelphia, 1801. For R. T. Rawle,' as perhaps the best edition before 1846. Cf. Brissot, *New Travels in the United States,* 1788, I. 97—'Isaiah Thomas (of Worcester, Massachusetts,) is the *Didot* of America.']

reproached myself in secret for not hastening my departure from *Philadelphia;* and, resolved not to be *dainty in taking leave* of my new friends; I left them to bewail my absence, and envy my exaltation!

I travelled in the coach, and was put down, with another passenger, to stop the night, at a tavern, built on a bank of the river *Susquehannah.* It was delightfully situated, commanding the prospect of *Chesapeak Bay,* and the little town of *Havre de Grace.* The accommodations at the tavern were elegant, and a Mulatto girl waited at supper, whose beauty entitled her to a better office than that of brushing away flies from the guests with a peacock's feather.

I repined at being waked before it was light by the horn of the driver; but I was repaid for the disturbance of my morning slumbers by the spectacle of the rising sun. His first rays gilded the herbage, yet humid with the dews of night; and the carol of the mockingbird, though faint, saluted the return of day.

We prosecuted our journey to *Baltimore,* in charming spirits, a happy constitution of temper made every place alike to my companion; and his advance in years seemed only to have brought with them a higher relish for life.

At *Baltimore* I separated from Mr. *Paine,* whose profession I had not discovered, but whom I suspect to have been what *Americans* call, *A speculator in lands*.

The next morning I resumed my journey for the city of *Washington*, passing in my way thither through no place of any note, unless it be a little town called *Bladensburgh*, built on the water of the *Eastern Branch* of the *Potomac*.

Washington, on my second journey to it, wore a very dreary aspect. The multitude had gone to their homes, and the inhabitants of the place were few. There were no objects to catch the eye, but a forlorn pilgrim forcing his way through the grass that overruns the streets; or a cow ruminating on a bank, from whose neck depended a bell, that the animal might be found the more readily in the woods.

I obtained accommodations at the *Washington* tavern, which stands opposite the Treasury. At this tavern I took my meals at the public table, where there was every day to be found a number of clerks, employed at the different offices under Government; together with about half a dozen *Virginians*, and a few *New England* men. There was a perpetual conflict of opinions between these southern and northern men; and one night, after supper, I was present at a vehement dispute, which terminated in the loss of a horse, a saddle, and a bridle.

The dispute was about Dr. *Franklin;* the

man from *New-England,* enthusiastic in what related to *Franklin,* asserted that, the Doctor being self-taught, was original in every thing that he had ever published.

"Sir," replied the *Virginian*, "the writings "of *Franklin,* so far from being original, "exhibit nothing but a transposition of the "thoughts of others. Nay, *Franklin* is a "downright plagiarist. Let him retain only "his own feathers; let those he has stolen be "restored to their lawful possessors, and, "*Franklin,* who now struts about expanding "the gayest plumage, will be without a single "feather to cover his rump." (A loud laugh from the whole party.)

New-England Man. If accusation without proof can condemn a man, who, Sir, shall be innocent? Sir, you are a *Virginian*. I intend no personal reflection, but it is notorious that the southern people do not hold the memory of *Franklin* in much estimation. But hear what a *Latin* writer says of him. *Eripuit cœlo* something—Gentlemen, I have forgot the most of my *Latin;* I cannot quote so correctly now as I did once; but this I can assure you, and you may rely on my word for it, that the compliment is a very fine one.

Virginian. I know the line you advert to; it was an eruption of mad enthusiasm from the disordered intellect of *Turgot.* But this is digressing from our subject; I maintain, and can prove, that *Franklin* is a plagiarist; a downright, bare-faced, shameless plagiarist.

New-England Man. *Franklin,* perhaps, Sir, had not that stoical calmness, which a great man in your State is remarkable for; he did not endeavour to catch applause by baiting his hook with affected diffidence. *Franklin* was above it. His penetration discovered, and his candour acknowledged, that sheer impudence was at any time less injurious than mock-modesty.

Virginian. Sir, an oracular darkness accompanies your discourse. But why retreat? Why not stand your ground? Why not evince yourself the champion of *Franklin?* Again I throw down the gauntlet! *Franklin,* I maintain was a shameless plagiarist.

New-England Man. Have you a horse here, my friend?

Virginian. Sir, I hope you do not suppose that I came hither on foot from *Virginia.* I have, Sir, in Mr. *White's* stable the prettiest *Chickasaw* that ever trod upon four pasterns. I *swopped* for her a roan horse; Mr. *Gibbs,* you remember my roan (turning to a man in company), I say, I swopped for her a roan with *Mad-Dog,* the *Chickasaw* Chief, who lives on the *Mississippi.*

New-England Man. And I have a bay mare here, that I bought of *Nezer Mattocks,* at *Salem.* I gave ninety dollars in hard cash for her. Now, I, my friend, will lay my bay mare against your *Chickasaw,* that Doctor *Franklin* is not a plagiarist.

Virginian. Done! Go it! Waiter! You waiter!

The waiter obeyed the summons, and making the *Virginian* a bow, replied, You call, Mossa *Ryland?*

Virginian. Yes, *Atticus.* Bring down my portmanteau out of my room. I never travel without books. And it critically happens, that in my portmanteau, I have both *Franklin's* Miscellanies, and *Taylor's* Discourses.

The trunk being opened, the *Virginian* put *Franklin's* Miscellanies into the hand of the disputant, and desired he would read the celebrated Parable against persecution.

New-England Man (reading). " And it
" came to pass, after these things, that *Abra-*
" *ham* sat in the door of his tent, about the
" going down of the sun. And behold a man,
" bent with age, coming from the way of the
" wilderness leaning on his staff! And *Abra-*
" *ham* arose and met him, and said unto him:
" Turn in, I pray thee, and wash thy feet, and
" tarry all night; and thou shalt arise early in
" the morning, and go on thy way, and the
" man said, Nay; for I will abide under this
" tree. But *Abraham* pressed him greatly;
" so he turned, and they went into the tent—

"and *Abraham* baked unleavened bread, and "they did eat. And when *Abraham* saw that "the man blessed not God, he said unto him, "wherefore dost thou not worship the Most "High God, Creator of heaven and earth? "And the man answered, and said, I do not "worship thy God, neither do I call upon "his name; for I have made to myself a god, "which abideth in my house, and provideth "me with all things. And *Abraham's* zeal "was kindled against the man; and he arose "and fell upon him, and drove him forth with "blows into the wilderness. And God called "unto *Abraham,* saying, *Abraham,* where is "the stranger? And *Abraham* answered and "said, Lord, he would not worship thee, "neither would he call upon thy name; therefore have I driven him out from before my "face into the wilderness. And God said, "Have I borne with him these hundred and "ninety and eight years, and nourished him, "and cloathed him, notwithstanding his rebellion against me; and couldest not thou, "who art thyself a sinner, bear with him one "night?"

The *New-England Man* having read the parable, he turned to the company, and with tumultuous rapture, exclaimed, "What a noble lesson is this to the intolerant! Can any thing speak more home? Why the writer appears inspired."

And inspired he was, cried the *Virginian*. There is nothing in that parable, Sir, natural; every word of it was revealed. It all came to *Franklin* from Bishop *Taylor*. There, Sir, read and be convinced. This book was printed more than a century ago; it is a volume of Polemical Discourses.

New-England Man (reading). "When " *Abraham* sat at his tent door, according to " his custom, waiting to entertain strangers, " he espied an old man stooping and leaning " on his staff, weary with age and travel, com- " ing towards him, who was an hundred years " of age. He received him kindly, washed " his feet, provided supper, and caused him " to sit down; but observing that the old man " ate and prayed not, nor begged for a blessing " on his meat, he asked him why he did not " worship the God of heaven? The old man " told him, that he worshipped the fire only, " and acknowledged no other god. At which " answer *Abraham* grew so zealously angry, " that he thrust the old man out of his tent, " and exposed him to all the evils of the night, " and an unguarded condition. When the old " man was gone, God called to *Abraham*, and " asked him where the stranger was? He re- " plied, I thrust him away, because he did not " worship thee. God answered him, I have " suffered him these hundred years, although " he dishonoured me; and couldest not thou

" endure him one night, and when he gave " thee no trouble?" *

The *New-England Man* having done reading, the Virginian leaped from his seat, and, calling the waiter, exclaimed, "*Atticus!* Tell " the ostler to put the bay mare in the next " stall to the *Chickasaw,* and, do you hear, " give her half a gallon of oats more upon " the strength of her having a new master."

Here followed a hearty laugh from the audience; but the *New-England Man* exhibited strong symptoms of chagrin. " Devil " take *Franklin*," said he. " An impostor! a " humbug." " If he ever obtains the wish he " expresses in his epitaph, of undergoing a " new edition in the next world, may his pla- " giarisms be omitted, that no more wagers " may be lost by them."

"*His* epitaph, did you say, Sir?" cried the *Virginian.* " I hardly think he came by that " honestly."

New-England Man. Sir, I will lay you my saddle of it; a bran new saddle. *Jonathan Gregory,* of *Boston,* imported it from *London.*

Virginian. My saddle, Sir, is imported too.—I *swopped* a double-barrelled gun for it with Mr. *Racer,* of *Fairfax* County. And I will not only lay my saddle against your's, Sir, that *Franklin* did not come honestly by

[* Dr. Franklin is specific. The story is doubtless a Talmudic legend.]

his epitaph; but I will lay my snaffle-bridle, and my curb, my plated stirrups and stirrup leathers—aye, and my martingale into the bargain.

New-England Man. Done! Go it! Now for your proof.

Virginian. Is there any gentleman in company *besides myself,* who understands *Latin.* If there is, let him have the goodness to speak.

New-England Man. This gentleman who came with me from *Salem,* is not only a *Latin,* but a *Greek* scholar. He was reared at *Cambridge.** He will talk *Latin* with Professor *Willard* an hour by the clock.

Virginian. Then, Sir, I believe, he will adjudge to me your imported saddle. Will you do me the favour to introduec me to your companion.

New-England Man. This, Sir, is Mr. *Meadows.* He is the author of an Ode on the Clam Feast.†

Virginian. Mr. *Meadows,* give me leave. Within the cover of this book you will find the epitaph which passes as *Franklin's.* I entreat you to read it aloud.

---

* An University near *Boston.*

† The first emigrants to *New England,* appeased their hunger, upon landing on the shore of *America,* with some shell-fish they found on the beach, known in popular language by the name of *Clams.* The anniversary of this day is every year celebrated on the spot, by their descendants, who feast upon Clams.

Mr. *Meadows* (reading).

"THE BODY

of

BENJAMIN FRANKLIN, Printer,

(Like the cover of an old book,
Its contents torn out,
And stript of its lettering and gilding)
Lies here, food for worms.
Yet the Work itself shall not be lost:
For it will (as he believ'd) appear once more
In a new
And more beautiful Edition,
Corrected and Amended
By
The Author."

New-England Man. Well, Sir! And what objection can you make to this? Does it not breathe humility? Is it not a lecture on mortality?

Virginian. Sir, it was not honestly come by. *Franklin* robbed a little boy of it. The very words, Sir, are taken from a *Latin* epitaph written on a bookseller, by an *Eton* scholar. Mr. Meadows, do, Sir, read the epitaph which I have pasted on the other cover.*

* If it should be objected that *Franklin* was ignorant of *Latin*, let it be told that, an *English* translation of this epitaph may be found in the Gentleman's Magazine, for *February*, 1736. The source, probably, from which *Franklin* got his thought.

Mr. *Meadows* (reads).

> "Vitæ *volumine* peracto,
> Hic finis JACOBI TONSON,
> Perpoliti Sosiorum principis:
> Qui, velut obstetrix musarum,
> In lucem edidit
> Felices ingenii partus.
> Lugete, scriptorum chorus,
> Et frangite calamos;
> Ille vester, *margine erasus, deletur!*
> Sed hæc postrema inscriptio
> Huic *primæ* mortis *paginæ*
> *Imprimatur,*
> Ne *prelo sepulchri* comissus,
> Ipse editor careat titulo:
> Hic jacet bibliopola,
> *Folio* vitæ delapso,
> Expectans *Novam Editionem*
> *Auctiorem* et *Emendatiorem.*"

Virginian. Well, Mr. *Meadows,* what say you? Is this accidental or studied similitude? What say you, Mr. *Meadows?*

Mr. *Meadows.* The saddle, Sir, is yours!

On hearing this laconic, but decisive sentence pronounced by his friend, the *New-England Man* grew outrageous—which served only to augment the triumph of the *Virginian.* Be pacified, cried he. I will give you another chance. I will lay you my boots against your's, that *Franklin's* pretended discovery of calming troubled waters by pouring upon them oil, may be found in the third book of *Bede's* History of the Church; or that his facetious essay on the air-bath, is poached word for word from *Aubrey's* Miscellanies. What say you?

Why I say, returned the *New-England Man,* that I should be sorry to go bootless home, and therefore, I will lay no more wagers about Doctor *Franklin's* originality.

At the *Washington* tavern I found seven *Cherokee* Chiefs, who had attended the President's levee on the 4th of *July,* they came to be instructed in the mode of *European* agriculture.

Of this circumstance Mr. *Jefferson* speaks in his Message to Congress: " I am happy
" to inform you, that the continued efforts to
" introduce among our *Indian* neighbours, the
" implements and practice of husbandry, and
" of the household arts, have not been without
" success: that they are become more and more
" sensible of the superiority of this dependance
" for clothing and subsistence, over the pre-
" carious resources of hunting and fishing: and
" already we are able to announce that, in-
" stead of that constant diminution of their
" numbers produced by their wars and their
" wants, some of them begin to experience an
" increase of population." *

If agriculture be deserving the attention of the *Indians,* it has also a powerful claim to that of the people of the United States; for it may be considered the firmest pillar of their national prosperity.

[* First Message, Dec. 8, 1801.]

It is, I think, to be wished that the principal citizens of the United States would enrol themselves into what might be termed a *Georgical Society,* which should be divided into four classes. The first should comprehend experiments made to ascertain the peculiar qualities, and comparative value of plants, together with the purposes to which they ought to be applied. The second should relate to the culture of plants, and the ascertaining the effects of different manures in facilitating their growth. The third should include experiments to determine the peculiar qualities of different soils. The fourth should be devoted to experiments for facilitating the operations of agriculture by improvements in machinery, and the distinguishing of what animals are the best adapted to labour, as it relates to climate.*

In such a Republic of Planters and Farmers, how would the knowledge of the most useful of all arts be promoted. Hints would be improved into experiments; the speculations of the theorist would be confirmed, or overthrown, by an appeal to practice; observations would be produced, that still tended to more useful inquiries; and even errors would lead

[* Cf. Washington's Speech to both Houses of Congress, Dec. 7, 1796, Sparks, XII, 70; Ford, XIII, 348. Experiment stations for North America are recommended *passim* in *American Husbandry.* London, 1775. 2 vols.]

to important truths, by stimulating the ardour of inquiry to refute them.

Without such a Society what agricultural improvements can be expected? Planters at present have no incitements to consult books, or alter their mode of husbandry. They are contented to tread tamely in the footsteps of their forefathers, and consider as mere visionaries the writers on agriculture.

I return from this digression to my business at *Washington,* which was to wait on the Secretary of the Treasury, by whom I expected to be invested without delay in some *diplomatic* department. Bear witness, ye powers, with what visions of greatness I feasted my imagination, as I walked from the tavern to the Treasury! The door-keeper desired to know my business. I wanted to see Mr. *Gallatin;* but Mr. *Gallatin* was engaged in an audience with the seven *Cherokee* Chiefs, who called every Monday morning at the Treasury for their weekly stipend from Government. I was somewhat chagrined that Mr. *Gallatin* should suffer *the savages of the wilderness* to take precedence of me, (I had sent up my name), but my chagrin soon gave place to an admiration of his policy; for I recollected these War Captains wore their tomahawks, and that they were men of an irascible temper.

In a few minutes, these warriors of scalping memory, descended the Treasury-stairs, which groaned under their giant-limbs; and I was ushered into the room where the Secretary in solemn greatness settled the expenditures of the nation.

Mr. *Gallatin* heard the object of my mission with patience; when he with the utmost composure observed that " the organization of the " offices in the Treasury, under the preceding " Administration, had been too complicated, " and that far from having any place to give " away, the employments of inferior diplo- " matic agency were yet to be diminished. Yet " he was sorry, very sorry, I should travel so " far to encounter disappointment. But the " Vice-President had certainly misunderstood " him. He had not the pleasure of knowing " me. It was another person of the same " name, whom he had spoken of to Mr. *Burr;* " but even for him there was now no office, " as all such offices were in future to be regu- " lated by legislative power, and legislature " thought the ramifications of office too mul- " tiplied. But he was sorry, very sorry, I had " travelled so far to no purpose."

During this speech my colour went and came.

Obstupui! steteruntque comæ et vox faucibus hæsit! *

But recovering from my stupor, I replied, that I had not travelled to no purpose, for

[* Aeneid, II, v. 774.]

I had not only seen the city of *Washington,* but also Mr. *Gallatin;* and making him a very low bow, I again walked down the Treasury-stairs!

My ambition was now blasted, and I learned how little dependance was to be placed in the magnificent promises of greatness. Yet I was determined my happiness should not be irrecoverably destroyed by a single blow, and instead of resigning my mind to gloom and despondency, I immediately built another castle in the air, not less desirable than the one I had missed on firm ground; for I had not yet lost the knack of comparing my possible with my actual condition.

Finding a schooner at *George-town,* ready to sail for *Alexandria,* I put my trunk on board of her, and left without regret the *Imperial City,* where I had encountered only disappointment.

The wind being contrary, we had to work down the *Potomac.*—The river here is very beautiful. *Mason's Island* forms one continued garden; but what particularly catches the eye is the Capitol, rising with sacred majesty above the woods.

Our boat turned well to windward, and in an hour we landed at the *Widow Bull's* house, which may be considered half way to *Alexandria.* Here having quaffed and smoked together under the shade of a spreading locust tree, we once more committed ourselves to the waters of the *Potomac*.

In approaching *Alexandria*, we passed an house on our right, in which the Paphian goddess had erected an altar. Some damsels were bathing before the door, who practised every allurement to make us land; but we treated their invitations with the insolence of contempt. Oh! Modesty! supreme voluptuousness of love! what charms does a woman lose when she renounces thee! What care, if she knew thy empire over the breast of man, would she take to preserve thee, if not from virtue, at least from coquetry.

It was easier landing at *Alexandria* in *America*, than *Alexandria* in *Egypt;* and I found elegant accomodations at *Gadesby's* hotel. It is observable that *Gadesby* keeps the best house of entertainment in the United States.

It was the middle of *July*, when I landed at *Alexandria*, and the heat was excessive. The acrimony of the bilious humours was consequently excited, and the diarrhœa and dysentery prevailed among the inhabitants; yet the taverns were frequented, for, *Americans* to preserve health, adopt the *Brunonian* system of keeping up the excitement.

The splendour of *Gadesby's* hotel not suiting my finances, I removed to a public-house kept by a *Dutchman*, whose *Frow* was a curious creature. I insert a specimen of her talk:

"This hot weather makes a body feel odd.
"How long would a body be going from
"*Washington* to *Baltimore?* How the mos-
"quitoes bite a body, &c." But I left the body
of my landlady to approach that of her daughter, whose body resembled one of those protuberant figures which *Rubens* loved to depict.

To what slight causes does a man owe some of the principal events of his life. I had been a fortnight at *Alexandria,* when, in consequence of a short advertisement I had put in the Gazette, a gentleman was deputed to wait on me from a Quaker, on the banks of the *Occoquan,* who wanted a Tutor for his children. Mr. *Ridgeway* was what is called a *supple Quaker*. With those of his own sect, none could be more formal; but among men of the world, he could practise all the arts of conciliation; and knew how to flatter a lady from the lustre of her eyes down to the taste of her shoe-string.

A Quaker accompanied him to the door, with whom he exchanged only the monosyllables, yea and nay; but no sooner had he turned his back, than Friend *Ridgeway* introduced himself to me with the bow of a dancing-master; expressed the earnest desire Mr. *Ellicott* had to engage me in his family, and lavished his eloquence on the romantic beauties of the river *Occoquan,* and the stupendous mountains that nodded over its banks.

The following evening, I left *Alexandria* on horseback, to visit the abode of Mr. *Ellicott*. But I had scarce ridden a couple of miles, when a violent storm of rain overtook me, and I sought shelter in a tailor's shop by the way-side. The tailor laid down his goose at my approach, and we soon entered into a political discussion, which ended with his lamentations over the miseries of the times, and a determination to support the Rights of Man.

It was six o'clock before the rain subsided, and I was in suspense whether to return to *Alexandria,* or prosecute my journey, when the tailor informed me, that only two miles further lived a very honest farmer, who accomodated Travellers with a bed. His name was *Violet.*

But why, said the tailor, not go on to *Mount Vernon?*

What, friend, should I do there?

Why, Sir, a gentleman is always well received.

I made the tailor an inclination of my head; but *Mount Vernon* was as remote from my thoughts as *Mount Vesuvius.*

I pursued my journey, but, after riding two miles, instead of reaching the farm of Mr. *Violet,* my horse stopped before the door of a log-house, built on the brow of a hill. The man of the house was sitting under an awning of dried boughs, smoking in silence his pipe;

and his wife occupied a chair by his side, warbling her lyrics over the circling wheel.

Will you alight, Sir, said the man, and rest yourself in the shade? Your horse looks well, Sir. He appears to be a mighty well-conditioned brute. What, if I may be so bold, Sir, did he cost you?

Why, Sir, the creature is worth a hundred and fifty dollars. The horse is young, quite young; he will be only five years old next Spring. Do put your hand into his mouth.

Excuse me, Sir. I never trust my hands in a horse's mouth: the brute may be vicious. But should you ever want any thing done to him, I shall be happy to serve you. My name is *Kaiting*. I have long been used to cutting and splaying all kinds of creatures.

Can you fox and nick a horse, Mr. *Kaiting?*

Aye, Sir, and cure all sorts of distempers; whether spavins, or ringbones, or cribs, or yellow-water, or blind-staggers, or weak eyes, or glanders.

Hum! What a catalogue of complaints is horse-flesh heir to. But can you inform me how far it is to the house of Farmer *Violet*.

I suspect it is a mile.

Come, none of your suspicions, but tell me candidly, my friend, do you think I can be accomodated there for the night.

Aye, as elegantly as you would be at *Gadesby's!*

And how shall I know the house?

It has a chimney at each end like my own.

The house, you say, is like your's.

Psha! It is better than mine; it is weather boarded. I pay no taxes for my house; the tax-gatherers value it below a hundred dollars.

I had not time to reply, before a goose waddled out of the house towards the place where Mr. *Kaiting* and his wife were sitting, followed by a tame frog that jumped in concert with his feathered companion. It was a singular spectacle, and would have afforded little pleasure to an unreflecting mind. But it was to me a most pleasing speculation, to behold this worthy couple extending their protection to a goose and a frog; it verified the remark of *Sterne,* that *the heart wants something to be kind to.*

Then, Sir, said I, you do not consider the frog a nuisance? You would not kill it?

Kill it! I should as soon think of putting an end to my own life. There was a gentleman from *Fredericksburg,* who stopped last week at my house to give his horse a bite of clover. He had hardly sat down under the awning, when the frog came out of the house, and hopped towards his chair. *That's a cursed impudent frog,* says he, and lifting up his arm, he made a blow at the animal with his whip. We were all in consternation. My wife screamed; I held out my leg to intercept the blow; and the goose, who seldom quits the frog, flew at the man with the strength and fury of an eagle. It was lucky his whip missed the frog, for had he killed him, there would not have been a dry eye in the house for a week.

I would willingly have protracted my conversation with so humane a person, had not the sky, which was overcast, indicated there was no time to be lost. I, therefore, put spurs to my nag, and departed at a gallop. It was not quite twilight, and my situation brought to my recollection a passage in the Poet of Nature.

> *The West yet glimmers with some streaks of day:*
> *Now spurs the lated Traveller apace,*
> *To gain the timely Inn.*

But I had scarce proceeded a mile when a storm of rain, lightning, and thunder, gave me some solicitude for my night's lodging; I could perceive no house; and the only alternative left was to scour along the road, while the tempest howled wildly from the woods on both sides.

At length, I descried a light, which, I flattered myself blazed from the window of Mr. *Violet's* house; but instead of dismounting at the portico of a mansion that vied in magnificence with *Gadesby's* hotel, I found myself before the door of a miserable log-house.

A mulatto woman, with a child at her breast, put her head out of the door as I alighted from my horse. We don't keep tavern here, said this olive beauty, in an accent not the most conciliating.

No! but you have a roof to your house, said I, dismounting, and that in a storm is a sufficient invitation.

The log-house was not empty. A mulatto-girl, of seventeen, was sitting in one corner in dalliance with a white youth of about thirty-five, who discovered no confusion at my unexpected entrance. But the olive Dulcinea was less confident in her aspect, and played the woman to perfection. One while she endeavoured to conceal her face from view, another she repulsed the caresses of her lover, and anon she clung to him as if seeking his protection.

Do you go to *Powheek* church, *Sylvia*, tomorrow? said the enamoured swain.

Who preaches there? If Parson *Wems* preaches, I won't go. He always preaches up matrimony.

You don't like matrimony, then, *Sylvia?*

Not I. There's time enough to be in trouble. I am, however, a friend to the Gospel. But, *Jemmy,* why don't you go to church? Ah! you need not smile! I know you are a *Deister!* People in your *spear* of life be all *Deisters*.

Here the girl looked round at me; but not being disposed for a theological controversy, I again mounted my horse, and no longer interrupted their innocent amour. The tempest was over; a beautiful night succeeded; and the moon with unusual lustre lighted me on my way. As I looked towards the silver orb, I exclaimed in the words of the most pathetic of writers,

> *For me! pale eye of evening! thy soft light*
> *Leads to no happy home!*

But I was waked from my musing by the barking of the dogs at *Colchester,* and having crossed the bridge, which is built over the *Occoquan,* I alighted at the door of Mr. *Gordon's* tavern.

Having ordered supper, I gazed with rapture on the *Occoquan* river, which ran close to the house, and, gradually enlarging, emptied itself into the capacious bosom of the *Potomac.* The fishermen on the shore were hawling their seine, and the sails of a little bark, stemming the waves, were distended by the breeze of night. The sea-boy was lolling over the bow and the helmsman was warbling a song to his absent fair.

The next day I proceeded to *Occoquan;* but so steep and craggy was the road, that I found it almost inaccessible. On descending the last hill, I was nearly stunned by the noise of two huge mills, whose roar, without any hyperbolical aggravation, is scarcely inferior to that of the great falls of the *Potomac,* or the cataract of *Niagara.* My horse would not advance; and I was myself lost in astonishment.

On crossing a little bridge, I came within view of the Settlement, which is romantic beyond conception. A beautiful river rolls its stream along mountains that rise abruptly from its bank, while on the opposite rocky shore, which appears to have been formed by a volcano, are seen two mills enveloped in foam and here and there a dwelling which has vast masses of stone for its foundation. The eye for some time is arrested by the uncommon scene; but it is soon relieved by a beautiful landscape that bounds the horizon. In a word, all the riches of nature are brought together in this spot, but without confusion.

Friend *Ellicott* and his wife received me with an unaffected simplicity of manners, whom I was happy to catch just as they were going to dinner. An exquisite *Virginia* ham smoked on the board, and two damsels supplied the guests with boiled *Indian* corn, which they had gathered with their own hands. Friend *Ellicott,* uncorrupted by the refinement of modern manners, had put his hat to its right use, for it covered his head. It was to no purpose that I bent my body, and made a hundred grimaces. *Mordecai* would not bow to *Haman,* nor would Friend *Ellicott* uncover his head to the Cham of *Tartary.*

Our agreement was soon made. Quakers are men of few words. Friend *Ellicott* engaged me to educate his children for a quarter of a year. He wanted them taught reading, writing, and arithmetic. Delightful task! As to *Latin,* or *French,* he considered the study of either language an abuse of time; and very calmly desired me not to say another word about it.

CHAP. VIII.

MEMOIR OF MY LIFE

ON THE BANKS OF THE OCCOQUAN.

Description of Occoquan Settlement.—Evening at Occoquan, an Ode.—Morning at Occoquan, an Ode.—A Party of Indians visit Occoquan.—Speech of a Warrior.—A War-Dance, and Scene of riotous Intoxication.—A Disquisition of the moral Character of the Indians.—Story of Captain Smith and Pocahontas—The Dispute between Buffon and Jefferson on the Subject of Beards satisfactorily decided.—The Midnight Orgies of the White-Man of America dramatized, &c.

> *Lo! the moon its lustre lends,*
> *Gilding every wood and lawn;*
> *And the Miller's heart distends*
> *On the banks of Occoquan!*

IN the *Bull-Run Mountains* rises a river, which retains the *Indian* name of *Occoquan*, and after a course of sixty miles falls into the *Potomac*, near the little town of *Colchester*. In *America* there are few or no rivers without falls; and at those of *Occoquan*, are erected a couple of mills, which by the easy and safe navigation of the *Potomac*, the richness of the adjacent country, and the healthfulness of the climate, induced the Proprietor to project the plan of a city, and invite strangers to build on it; but his visions were never realized, and *Occoquan* consists only of a house built on a rock, three others on the riverside, and half a dozen log-huts scattered at some distance.

Yet no place can be more romantic than the view of *Occoquan* to a stranger, after crossing the rustic bridge, which has been constructed by the inhabitants across the stream. He contemplates the river urging its course along mountains that lose themselves among the clouds; he beholds vessels taking on board flour under the foam of the mills, and others deeply laden expanding their sails to the breeze; while every face wears contentment, every gale wafts health, and echo from the rocks multiplies the voices of the waggoners calling to their teams.

It is pleasant, says *Juvenal,* to be master of a house, though it stand not on more ground than a lizard would occupy. The schoolhouse at *Occoquan* was entirely my own. It was a little brick structure, situated about three hundred yards from the house on the rock. The front casements looked upon the *Occoquan* river, and commanded the variegated prospect of hill and dale.

It is so seldom an author gets a house that it should excite no wonder if he loves to describe it. *Pliny* has described his house so minutely in one of his elaborate epistles, that he appears to be putting it up for sale; and *Pope* luxuriates in the strain that treats of his thickets being pierced, his grotto entered, his chariot stopped, and his barge boarded; that posterity may not be ignorant of the extent of his possessions.

I mingled seldom with the people of *Occoquan*, but, shut up in my profound habitation, sought an oblivion of care in writing, reading, and tobacco. Often when the moon-light slept upon the mountain near my dwelling, have I walked before my door, and gazed in silent rapture upon the orb of night, whose beams trembled on the stream that gave motion to the mill; while the tall bark was seen dancing on the waves at a distance, and the mocking-bird in a saddened strain was heard from the woods. It was during one of these nights, that recalling the images of the evening, I combined them in an Ode:

EVENING AT OCCOQUAN.

AN ODE.

SLOW the solemn sun descends,
Ev'ning's eye comes rolling on;
Glad the weary stranger bends
To the Banks of Occoquan!

Now the cricket on the hearth,
Chirping, tells his merry tale;
Now the owlet ventures forth
Moping to the silent gale.

Still the busy mill goes round,
While the miller plies his care;
And the rocks send back the sound,
Wafted by the midnight* air.

Lo! the moon with lustre bright,
In the stream beholds her face;
Shedding glory o'er the night,
As she runs her lofty race.

See! the bark along the shore,
Larger to the prospect grow;
While the sea-boy bending o'er
Chides the talking waves below.

Now the mocking-songster's strain
Fills the pauses of her brood;
And her plaints the ear detain,
Echoing from the distant wood.

Hanging o'er the mountain's brow,
Lo! the cattle herbage find;
While in slumber sweet below,
Peaceful rests the village hind.

Now the student seeks his cell,
Nor regrets the day is gone;
But with silence loves to dwell,
On the Banks of *Occoquon*.

I was never one of those *who sleep well at night*. All hours are of equal value, and the tranquillity of the night invites to study. Hence, I have been frequently compelled to change my lodgings where the good woman of

[* From the author's *Errata*: '*for midnight r. balmy.*']

the house was in fear that her curtains might catch fire, and set the dwelling in a blaze.

But the houses in *Virginia* are not very superb.* The people were never under any solicitude for the habitation I occupied; and had it been burnt to the ground, a few boards and a proportionate number of shingles would soon have constructed another. I never yet occupied a house that was not exempt from taxes; it was always valued by the tax-gatherers below a hundred dollars (about 20*l*. sterling), and, by an act of Assembly, for a house not worth a hundred dollars there is no tax to pay.

From the platform of my house at *Occoquan,* there was a subterraneous passage which led to a kind of kitchen. In this underground apartment dwelt Rachel, a negro-woman, who was left a widow with eleven children; but her numerous offspring were all provided for. Mr. *Carter,* to whom the whole family belonged, had taken upon him this benevolent office; for he had sold one to Mr. *A,* another to Mr. *B,* a third to Mr. *C,* a fourth

[* Cf. Isaac Weld, *Travels through the States of North America.* 3rd ed. London. 1800, Vol. I, p. 156—"Though many of the houses in the Northern Neck are built, as I have said, of brick and stone, in the style of the old English manor houses, yet the greater number there, and throughout Virginia, are of wood; amongst which are all those that have been built of late years. This is chiefly owing to the prevailing, though absurd opinion, that wooden houses are the healthiest."]

to Mr. *D,* and so on, nearly half round the alphabet.

The student who values his health will practise study and exercise alternately. After reading a scene in *Hamlet,* I took a few strides across the room, and amused myself by repeating a part of his soliloquies. Such, for example, as

> "How weary, flat, stale and unprofitable
> "Seem to me all the uses of this world!"

Rachel, who dwelt underneath, marvelled greatly at the noise. Her penetration made her immediately conclude that I was busied in praying; and in the morning my character was established for religion. "Ah!" said the old woman to her gaping auditors; "they may "talk about this parson, or that parson, or the "other parson, but our new coolmossa beats "them all by a heap. Why, 'tis as true as the "mill is now going round that he walks up and "down, and prays the whole night long!"

Rachel, without carrying about her the mockery of woe, mourned very sensibly her husband. Let my page record the words of her affliction.

"I was reared at *Port Tobacco.* A heap of "likely young fellows courted me, but I re- "fused them all for the head coachman of "Counsellor *Carter.* He was a good hus- "band; he made me the mother of eleven chil-

"dren. Woe to *Rachel* when he died. Oh!
"how I clap my hands and cry! but he's gone
"to the great *Jehovah.* I shall never forget
"it; 'twas at the pulling of corn-time. The
"poor creature was a little out of his head.
"He asked me if the corn was in tassel. In
"tassel, says I! God help you, you had some
"yesterday for dinner. But he changed the
"discourse, and he talked of the hymn-book,
"and Parson *Wems,* and *Poheek* church. It
"was as good as any sarment! Dear sweet
"honey! He was a friend to the gospel; he
"loved the Church of *England,* and nobody
"can say they ever saw him go to the Quaker-
"meeting. Alack! Alack! My poor husband
"died the next morning; I knew his time was
"come; the Whip-poor-will cried all night
"by the house, and I could not drive him
"away. God help us. *Die* come in every
"part of the world; *Virginia, Maryland:*
"black man! white man! all one day or an-
"other get their mouth full of yellow clay!"

Occoquan scarcely supplied more literature
than *Ovid's* place of banishment on the *Black
Sea.* But at *Clearmount,* near *Fauquier
Court-house,* lived a *French* gentleman of the
name of *Gerardine,** whose reputation for the

[* Cf. Isaac Weld, *Travels through the States of North
America* Vol. I. pp. 175-176.—" Among the inhabitants [of
Norfolk, Virginia,] are great numbers of Scotch and French.
The latter are almost entirely from the West Indies, and prin-

Belles Lettres, induced me to write to him from my solitude. I chose the *French* language for the vehicle of my thoughts, and enclosed in the letter the little book of poems I had published at *New-York.* The answer of Mr. *Gerardine* discovers an elegant mind.

" Monsieur,
" Dans cette Solitude ou les Muses se font
" si rarement entendre, vous conceverez aisé-
" ment que l'envoi de vos jolis Poemes a du
" exciter à la fois la surprize et le plaisir. Je
" compare votre present inattendu à un joli
" parterre dans un Desert inculte et sauvage,
" dont l'email se seroit offert continuellement
" à ma vue.
" Continuez, Monsieur, à caresser les Muses
" avec *Horace* and *Anacreon;* le tems repren-
" dra ses âiles, vos heures en couleront plus
" doucement, et vous ajouterez de nouvelles
" fleurs á la Guirlande Poetique dont vous
" etes deja couronneé. *Ovide* chantoit encore
" sur les bords lontaines où la tyrannie
" *d'Auguste* l'avoit enchainé, et vous avez
" celebré *Coosohatchie.*
" Je me suis fait un devoir de repondre à
" votre Lettre obligeante dans une langue que
"vous ecrivez si bien, et que sans l'envoi de ce

cipally from St. Domingo. Between two and three thousand were in Norfolk at one time; most of them, however, afterwards dispersed themselves throughout different parts of the country."]

" que vous appellez trop modestement vos
" Bagatelles, je vous eusse assurément pris
" pour un de mes Compatriotes.
  " J'ai l'honneur d'être, Monsieur,
    " Votre très obeissant, très humble
      " Serviteur,
            " C. GERARDINE."

It was now I felt the bliss of having an enlightened friend to whom I could pour out my soul on paper, and enjoy the intercourse of spirit without the mediation of an earthly frame. My friendship with Mr. *George* was still unimpaired, and I consider it no small felicity that I have been able to preserve so many of his letters amidst the casualties to which the life of a Wanderer is subject. The gloom of my solitude at *Occoquan,* was cheered by the sincerity of his friendship, and the sprightliness of his wit.

" An epistle from *Ovid* among the *Getæ* to
" his friend at *Rome,* could not have imparted
" half the delight that your letter from *Occo-*
" *quan* has given the companion of your ad-
" versity at *New-York.* I had long expected
" a missive from ' the City in the Woods,' *
" and could only ascribe your silence to the
" distraction of business in your new office of
" Secretary's Secretary; when suddenly is
" brought me a letter dated at a place, which,

* " Washington."

" however acute my researches into the Ge-
" ography of *America,* I never heard men-
" tioned before. I thank you for the ode you
" did me the favour to enclose, it is an happy
" imitation of *Cunningham's* manner; but the
" images are more pleasing from having the
" grace of novelty to recommend them. Nor
" should I neglect to observe, how much you
" have shewn your skill in making the word
" *Occoquan* the burden of your exordial and
" concluding stanzas; a practice never to be
" dispensed with in local poetry, as, without
" it, the poem would have no particular appli-
" cation, were the title to be lost.

" But it is useless to write anything for
" *Americans.* Taste has not so diffused its
" influence through this hemisphere as to
" cause the Poet to be cherished; and though
" an *Orpheus* might have power to charm the
" woods, yet the inhabitants would be insen-
" sible to the harmony of his lyre. In this
" region the minuteness of the politician takes
" place of the elevation of the poet.

" *Occoquan,* from your description of it,
" must be a delightful spot, and in prophetic
" language I would declare, that your abode
" on the banks of the river will make the
" stream classical in the annals of literary
" history.

" Let us continue, without failure, to write
" to each other. It will give life to our friend-

" ship, and soften the rigours of existence.
" Whatever we write must partake much of
" the spirit of the places in which we live; but
" sentiments may arise from solitary reflection,
" which the multitudinous (a word you taught
" me) uproar of a city would rather suppress
" than excite.

" Is it possible that you live in a family of
" Quakers, or that a Quaker should have
" selected you from the crowd to bring up his
" children in the way they should go? Alas!
" you will be writing wicked rhyme when you
" should be expounding to them scripture; and
" set before them the vanity of compliments
" when they should utter yea and nay!"

It was my custom every Saturday to ride to *Alexandria,* where I read the northern papers at the Coffee-room, and at *Thomas' "Book Store,"* regaled myself with the new publications imported from *Philadelphia.** But I sought in vain for the advertisement that was to announce the diffusion of the *Wanderings of William,* and looked forward with solicitude for the moment that was to reward my labour with emolument, and satisfy my vanity with praise. In this state of suspense I wrote my friend *Dufief* an elaborate epistle in

[* " The catalogue of books for sale in this city, [Philadelphia], contains upwards of 300 sets of Philadelphia editions, besides a greater variety of maps and charts than is to be found any where else in America."
Dr. Morse's *American Gazetteer,* 2nd Ed. 1804.]

French, execrating the honeyed-promises of the great men in power, who had doomed me to the obscurity of *Occoquan;* and earnestly demanding intelligence of *William,* who occupied my waking and sleeping thoughts. The lively answer of *Dufief* will amuse those who understand *French;* and they who are ignorant of the language can find some linguist among their friends to interpret it.

" Mon cher Favori d'Apollon, j'ai été plus
" faché que surpris d'apprende que vous
" aviez fait un demarche inutile. Je ne voyois
" rien de moins sur que ce dont vous vous étiez
" flatté; et c'étoit la parole du Colonel *Albert,**
" qu'il falloit avoir pour être sûr d'une Lieu-
"tenance dans son Regiment. .

" Je vous aurois engagé amicalement à at-
" tendre parmi nous une Lettre, mais étant
" près des Vacances, je n'ai vu dans votre
" Voyage qu' un moyen agréable de passer un
" tems de desœuvrement.

" J'ai pensé plus d'une fois à *William,* tant
" pour le lire moi-même, que pour vous en
" vendre, si je puis, beaucoup d'exemplaires.
" Chacun a ses tribulations dans ce monde.
" J'ai à present le chagrin de voir que mon
" Commerce ne va aucunement: pour y faire
" diversion je me suis jetté dans le profon-
" deur de la Metaphisique avec *Lock* et *Con-*
" *dillac..*

[* Secretary Gallatin.]

" Adieu: portez vous bien. Je vous Salue
" en *Pope* & en *Shakespear*.
"Votre affectioné,
" N. G. DUFIEF.
" Le 5, d'Août, 1801."

They who delight in walking, must, during the summer in *Virginia,* embrace the night to stimulate their muscular energies. The fierceness of the sun would suspend the steps of the hardiest Traveller; but amidst the freshness of the night, he breathes only odours in journeying through the woods.

No walk could be more delightful than that from *Occoquan* to *Colchester,* when the moon was above the mountains. You traverse the bank of a placid stream over which impend rocks, in some places bare, but more frequently covered with an odoriferous plant that regales the Traveller with its fragrance.

So serpentine is the course of the river that, the mountains, which rise from its bank, may be said to form an amphitheatre; and nature seems to have designed the spot for the haunt only of fairies; for here grow flowers of purple dye, and here the snake throws her enamelled skin. But into what regions, however apparently inaccessible, has not adventurous man penetrated? The awful repose of the night is disturbed by the clack of two huge mills, which drown the song and echoes of the mocking-bird, who nightly tells his sorrow to the listening moon.

Art is here pouring fast into the lap of nature the luxuries of exotic refinement. After clambering over mountains, almost inaccessible to human toil, you come to the junction of the *Occoquan* with the noble river of the *Potomac,* and behold a bridge whose semi-elliptical arches are scarcely inferior to those of princely *London.* And on the side of this bridge stands a tavern, where every luxury that money can purchase is to be obtained at a first summons; where the richest viands cover the table, and where ice cools the Madeira that has been thrice across the ocean.*

The *English* bewail the want of convenient taverns in the United States; but the complaint is I think groundless; for I have found taverns in the woods of *America,* not inferior to those of the common market towns in *England.* My description of the tavern at the mouth of the *Occoquan* partakes of no hyperbolical amplification; the apartments are numerous and at the same time spacious; carpets of delicate texture cover the floors; and

[* Cf. La Rochefoucauld, *Travels in North America.* London, 1799, Vol. II, p. 588,—" The war, in which all the commercial powers have been engaged for five years more or less, keeps their trade in a state of almost total stagnation. The United States are a kind of temporary *depot* of the produce of all countries. The commodities over and above the consumption of the United States are re-exported."]

glasses are suspended from the walls in which a *Goliah* might survey himself.

No man can be more complaisant than the landlord. Enter but his house with money in your pocket, and his features will soften into the blandishments of delight; call and your mandate is obeyed; extend your leg and the boot-jack is brought you.

Having slept one night at this tavern, I rose with the sun and journeyed leisurely to the mills, catching refreshment from a light air, that stirred the leaves of the trees. The morning was beautiful, and my walk produced a little Ode, which will serve as a counterpart to that I have already inserted.

MORNING AT OCCOQUAN

AN ODE

IN the barn the cock proclaims
That the East is streaked with gold;
Strutting round the feather'd dames,
Who the light with joy behold.

Sweet! oh! sweet the breath of morn!
Sweet the mocking-songster's strain;
Where the waving stalks of corn
Bend beneath the 'ripen'd grain.

Lo! the martins now forsake,
For a while their tender brood;
And the swallow skims the lake,
Each in search of winged food.

See the cottage chimneys smoke,
See the distant turrets gleam;
Lo! the farmer to the yoke,
Pairs his meek submissive team.

Here no negro tills the ground,
Trembling, weeping, woeful—wan;
Liberty is ever found,
On the banks of *Occoquan!*

But not the muses, nor walks, nor the melody of birds, could divert my mind from the publication of my Novel, which had been so long in the press at *Philadelphia,*

"Demanding life, impatient for the skies."

Suspense is ever an uncomfortable state of the mind; and I addressed *Dufief* in another letter, whose answer calmed my solicitude.

"*A Philadelphie,* ce 15, *de Septembre,*
"1801.
" Mon cher & ingénieux Romancier,
" Monsieur *Thompson* m'a remis douze Ex-
" emplaires du volage *William.* Si le Public
" goute l'ouvrage comme j'ai fait les premi-
" eres pages (car mes occupations multipliceś
" ne m'ont pas encore permis d'en lire davan-
" tage) vous pouvez être assuré d'un prompt
" débit.
" Je suis *entousiasmé* de votre francois.
" Vous feriez honte en verité à beaucoup de

" nos nationeux qui se piquent cependant de
" bien ecrire cette langue.*

" Faites-moi part de ce qui vous arrivera
" d'heureux dans un pays si peu fait pour vos
" talens.

" Adieu. Portez-vous bien, et acceptez les
" assurances de mon devouement.
       " N. G. DUFIEF."

My publisher soon after sent me a dozen copies of my novel, together with a number of the *Port Folio,* which contained some remarks on the volume. Mr. *Dennie,* my former panegyrist, now wielded his bull-rush against me; but I fear that, only glancing over the contents, like the student in *Gil Blas,* he did not dig deep enough to discover the soul of the Licentiate.—I insert his remarks.

" The author of Poems written chiefly in
" *South Carolina,* and the translator of *Buona-*
" *parte's* campaign in *Italy,* has just published
" a novel, entitled the *Wanderings of William,*
" or the *Inconstancy of Youth.*

" The author dedicates it to *Flavia* in a
" strain which seems to foretell the complex-
" ion of the work. His words are, " *Avail*

---

*This passage of Mr. *Dufief's* letter alludes to a *French* Essay, which I had enclosed for his inspection. I cannot resist the impulse of subjoining it. And I subjoin it without deprecating the strictures of criticism. The prayers of an author to his reader never yet averted his destiny; if his writ-

" *yourself of the moment that offers to indulge*
" *in the perusal of this book. Take it, read it,*
" *there is nothing to fear. Your Governess is*
" *gone out, and your Mamma is not yet risen.*
" *Do you hesitate? Werter has been under*

ings be bad, no supplications, however moving, will preserve them from contempt. I think it is *Despréaux*, who says,

> *Un auteur à genoux, dans une humble préface,*
> *Au lecteur qu'il ennuye a beau demander grace.*

I have never been in France. I therefore enjoy a particular advantage; for my style, formed only upon writers, can be infected with no colloquial barbarisms.

Séjour dans les Bois de la *Caroline* du Sud.

Sur la route de *Charleston* à *Savannah*, et presque à moitié chemin, se trouve un petit village qu'on appelle *Coosohatchie*. Ce fut à cinq milles de cet endroit que je passai l'hiver de 1798, et la plus grande partie du printemps de l'anné suivante.

Ma demeure étoit chez un *Planteur* qui m'avoit proposé l'education de ses enfans. Je m'accoutumai peu-à-peu a mon esclavage. Tout alloit à merveille. J'étudois l'esprit de mes éleves, et je réussissois auprès d'eux. J'en avois trois, dont deux étoient filles. La cadette, qui pouvoit bien avoir neuf ou dix ans, etoit d'une vivacité charmante. Son sourire exprimoit d'avance ce qu'elle alloit vous dire. Ses beaux yeux bleus peignoient toujours la situation de son cœur. C'étoit un charmant enfant, dont la beauté naissante promettoit d'egaler celle de sa mere. Sa soeur plus agée de cinq ans, quoique moins jolie, avoit ce qui peut faire valoir la beauté. Elle étoit douce, aimable, sans etourderie. A l'égard de Monsieur le frere, c'étoit un garcon tres-interessant; l'esprit ouvert, vif & joyeux. Je voulus m'attacher à ce petit bon-homme, le former, travailler à son education, mais sans me donner un air imposant, un œil severe, ou une voix rude & menacante pour me faire redouter.

Mon eleve aimoit la chasse en vrai *Americain*. Je me souviendrai des battemens de cœur qu'il éprouvoit au vol des premiers canards, & des transports de joie avec lesquels il tuoit un cerf dans les bois. Seul avec son chien, chargé de

"*your pillow, and the Monk* has lain on*
"*your toilet.*

" It was our design at first to have abridged
" the story of the Work; but the inutility of
" the task overcame our benevolence; for the

son fusil, de son fourniment, de sa petite proie, il revenoit le soir aussi heureux qu'il soit possible de l'être.

Pendant que mon éleve s'amusoit à la chasse, je me livrois aux objets purs & simples de la Nature. Avec quel transport je suis allé dans les bois d'alentour chercher la première violette, & épier le premier bourgeon. Que le chant de l'Oiseau Moqueur me faisoit tressaillir d'aise! Je prolongeois ainsi ma promenade, sans m'appercevoir que la nuit régnoit deja depuis long temps. Il est si doux de se trouver seul dans des lieux peu frequentés, & de s'abandonner à ses rêveries!

Voici un souvenir bien distinct qui me reste d'une de mes promenades solitaires. Après un doux sommeil je me levai avec l'étoile du matin, qui conduisit mes pas vers *Savannah*, Le chant du coq se faisoit entendre, & les travaux des negres recommencoient dans les plantations voisines. Le charmant plaisir que celui de respirer la frâiche haleine du matin! Avec quelle douce émotion je voyois les premiers rayons de l'aurore percer le crepuscule, tandis que mes pieds chassoient devant eux la rosée qui baignoit le gazon. Je marchois legerement dans ma route, animé par le spectacle enchanteur du lever du soleil, qui répandoit sur ma promenade un attrait délicieux. Je marchai dix milles pour le moins sans trouver d'autre batiment que les ruines d'une eglise, mais vers midi je m'arretai devant la porte d'une maison isolée, ou le joli son d'un violon m'enchanta les oreilles. Je fus recu á merveille du maitre du logis, qui me fit entrer dans une chambre ou il y avoit trois demoiselles, elégamment mises, dansant au son de l'instrument dont jouoît M. leur Maitre de danse. Ces jeunes personnes s'arreterent un moment pour me faire une reverence, and recommencerent encore leur danse avec une grace inexprimable. Elles étoient toutes trois pleines de charmes, mais la plus jeune étoit si jolie! elle mettoit tant de graces dans sa

---

[* Matthew Gregory Lewis's very successful novel *Ambrosio or the Monk.* 4th ed. London, 1798. 3 vols.]

" author sacrifices reflection to mirth; and his
" page, however it may be read with interest,
" will not be remembered with advantage."

On the north bank of the *Occoquan* is a pile of stones, which indicate that an *Indian* war-

danse & dans ses gestes, en tournoyant & en sautant legerement tantot sur un pied, & tantot sur l'autre! je fus stupefait d'admiration. Je la considerai dans un ravissement de cœur. De grands yeux noirs, un nez tant soit peu rétroussé, une bouche mignonne, des levres fraiches & vermeilles, une taille leste & svelte, une jambe faite au tour, le bras, la main, le pied moulés par les Graces, formoient l'assemblage le plus parfait qu'on puisse concevoir. *Constance* alloit compter quinze ans, & deja la nature lui avoit fait part de ces boutons charmans que l'hymen seul a le droit de cueillir. Son petit corset, qui les réceloit avec peine, garantissoit ce trésor naissant de toute profanation. L'ensemble de cette jeune fille me fit souvenir de quelques vers de *Boursaut*.

> *Elle a bien quatorze ou quinze ans,*
> *Fiere, mais sans être farouche.*
> *Les cheveux blonds, les yeux percans,*
> *Une gorge naissante, & surtout une bouche!*

J'appercus avec plaisir que mon hote étoit francois, & que ces jeunes personnes etoient ses trois filles. *Constance* ne parloit que francois; son accent seul eut suffit pour me tourner la tête. La danse se prolongea jusqu'á une heure, lorsque M. le maitre de danse prit congé de ses douces eleves avec un ah! ca, Mesdesmoiselles! au plaisir! monta à cheval, & partit au petit galop. Me voilá donc libre d'entretenir trois belles demoiselles en mauvais francois, & parlant á peu prés comme le beau Léandre. L'ainée de ces trois sœurs étoit une fille faite, dont l'embonpoint donnoit dans la vue, & dont les grands yeux noirs sembloient aller á la petite guerre. Sa figure réunissoit ce que les brunes ont de plus piquants, & les blondes de plus voluptueux. Le bon diner que je fis avec M. *Rencontre* et ses charmantes filles! Je m'assis entre *Constance* & la sœur dont je n'ai pas encore parlé. C'étoit une blonde aux yeux bleus, extrêmement timide, qui rougissoit aux moindres louanges qu'on lui donnoit. Mais ce qui m'in-

rior is interred underneath. The *Indians* from the back settlements, in travelling to the northward, never fail to leave the main road, and visit the grave of their departed hero. If a stone be thrown down, they religiously re-

teressa davantage fut qu'elle avoit une tournure tout-à-fait francoise.

Qu'on juge du regret avec lequel je quittai la famille de Monsieur *Rencontre*. Que nos adieux furent touchants! Les yeux de *Constance* rencontrerent les miens en partant avec une expression qui redoubla l'agitation de mon coeur.

She gas'd as I slowly withdrew,
My path I could scarcely discern;
So sweetly she bade me adieu,
I thought that she bade me return!

Qu'on nie l'existence de cette douce sympathie qui agit sur deux persones sensible, faits l'un pour l'autre, & qui se rencontrent pour la première fois. Ce n'est pas pour de tels lecteurs que je prends la plume.

Revenons à mes occupations. Depuis le jour ou j'arrivai chez M. *D.*— jusqu'au retour du printemmpts, je passai toujours la soirée & une partie de la matinée soit à lire ou à ecrire devant un bon feu dans ma chambre. Je commencois par quelque livre *Latin*, comme *Horace, Virgile, Ovide*; & finissois par les Confessions de l'éloquent Citoyen de *Geneve*. Un des plus grands ecrivains du dix-huitième siécle fut assurément M. *Rousseau*. Que ses recits sont touchants quand il parle de ses chères Charmettes, de ses bosquets, de ses ruisseaux. On est toujours présent à chaque scene dont il fait le tableau. Que le caractère de Maman est peint d'apres Nature. Il met tout ce qu'il raconte sous les yeux du lecteur. On ne croit plus lire, on croit voir. Le gout que je pris à la lecture des Confessions m'inspira le desir d'écrire en francois; dont les qualités distinctives sont la clarté & la precision. Je ne sai si j'y ai reussi.

Que ma vie eut éfé heureuse au sein de cette famille, si j'avois su en jouir. Mais il me restoit encore une humeur un peu volage, un desir de voyager & de parcourir le monde. Enfin degouté de ma vie, & plein des plus beaux projets

store it to the pile, and, sitting round the rude monument they meditate profoundly; catching, perhaps, a local emotion from the place.

A party of *Indians,* while I was at *Occoquan,* turned from the common road into the woods, to visit this grave on the bank of the river.

The party was composed of an elderly Chief, twelve young War Captains, and a couple of Squaws. Of the women, the youngest was an interesting girl of seventeen; remarkably well shaped, and possessed of a profusion of hair, which in colour was raven black. She appeared such another object as the mind images *Pocahontas* to have been. The people of *Occoquan,* with more curiosity than breeding, assembled round the party; but they appeared to be wholly indifferent to their gaze; the men amused themselves by chopping the ground with their tomahawks, and the women

pour l'avenir, je partis de la *Caroline* du Sud vivement emu des larmes de mes eleves que je quittois pour toujours.

Coosohatchie adieu! O demeure tranquille, chambre ou j'ai tant écrit, planchers que j'ai tant arrosés de mes pleurs, je vous salue! Je vous quitte, calme retraite, ou j'ai vecu loin du tumulte & du bruit. Restez toujours ouverte au voyageur egaré; recevez-le; qu'il trouve sous votre toit un abri contre la persecution, & que ce Monument que je vous ai erigé dans une langue etrangere, fasse connoitre à son coeur attendri que vous futes habitée par un infortuné.

[" Je laisse toutes ces choses de la jeunesse: on voudra bien les pardonner."—note of Chateubriand's in the second edition of his *Travels in America.* John Davis omitted his French essay from the later edition of his book.]

were busied in making a garment for the Chief.

Among the whites was a young man of gigantic stature; he was, perhaps, a head taller than any of the rest of the company. The old *Indian* could not but remark the lofty stature of the man; he seemed to eye him involuntarily; and, at length, rising from the ground, he went up to the giant stranger, and shook him by the hand. This raised a loud laugh from all the lookers-on; but the *Indians* still maintained an inflexible gravity.

When I saw the squaws a second time, they were just come from their toilet. Woman throughout the world delights ever in finery; the great art is to suit the colours to the complexion.

The youngest girl would have attracted notice in any circle of *Europe*. She had fastened to her long hair a profusion of ribbons, which the bounty of the people of *Occoquan* had heaped upon her; and, the tresses of this *Indian* beauty, which before had been confined round her head, now rioted luxuriantly down her shoulders and back. The adjustment of her dress one would have thought she had learned from some *English* female of fashion; for she had left it so open before, that the most inattentive eye could not but discover the rise and fall of a bosom just beginning to fill. The covering of this young woman's feet rivetted the eye of the stranger with its novelty and splendour. Nothing could be more delicate than her *mocasins*. They were each of them formed of a single piece of leather, having the seams ornamented with beads and porcupine quills; while a string of scarlet ribbon confined the *mocasin* round the instep, and made every other part of it sit close to the foot. The *mocassin* was of a bright yellow, and made from the skin of a deer, which had been killed by the arrow of one of the *Indian* youths. Let me be pardoned for having spoken of this lady's foot, with such minuteness of investigation. A naturalist will devote a whole chapter to the examination of a bird, count the feathers in its wings, and declaim with the highest rapture on its variegated plumage, and a Traveller may surely be forgiven a few remarks on the seducing foot of an *Indian* beauty. *Utrum horum mavis accipe!*

Of these *Indians,* the men had not been inattentive to their persons. The old Chief had clad himself in a robe of furs, and the young warriors had blackened their bodies with charcoal.

The *Indians* being assembled round the grave, the old Chief rose with a solemn mien, and knocking his war-club against the ground, pronounced an oration to the memory of the departed warrior.

"Here rests the body of a Chief of our

" nation, who, before his spirit took its flight
" to the country of souls, was the boldest in
" war, and the fleetest in the chace. The arm
" that is now mouldering beneath this pile,
" could once wield the tomahawk with vigour
" and often caused the foe to sink beneath its
" weight. (*A dreadful cry of Whoo! Whoo!
" Whoop! from the hearers.*) It has often
" grasped the head of the expiring enemy, and
" often with the knife divested it of the scalp
" (a yell of *whoo! whoo! whoop!*) It has
" often bound to the stake the prisoner of war,
" and piled the blazing faggots round the vic-
" tim, singing his last song of death. (A yell
" of *whoo! whoop!*) The foot that is now mo-
" tionless was once fleeter than the hart which
" grazes on the mountain; and in danger it
" was ever more ready to advance than retreat.
" (A cry of *whoo! whoo! whoop!*) But the
" hero is not gone unprovided to the country
" of spirits. His tomahawk was buried with
" him to repulse the enemy in the field; and
" his bow to pierce the deer that flies through
" the woods."

No orator of antiquity ever exceeded this savage chief in the force of his emphasis, and the propriety of his gesture. Indeed, the whole scene was highly dignified. The fierceness of his countenance, the flowing robe, elevated tone, naked arm, and erect stature, with a circle of auditors seated on the ground, and in the open air, could not but impress upon the mind a lively idea of the celebrated speakers of ancient *Greece* and *Rome*.*

Having ended his oration, the *Indian* struck his war-club with fury against the ground, and the whole party obeyed the signal by joining in a war-dance;—leaping and brandishing their knives at the throats of each other, and accompanying their menacing attitudes with a whoop and a yell, which echoed with ten-fold horror from the banks of the river.

The dance took place by moonlight, and it was scarcely finished when the Chief produced a keg of whiskey, and having taken a draught, passed it round among his brethren. The squaws now moved the *tomahawks* into the woods, and a scene of riot ensued. The keg was soon emptied. The effects of the liquor began to display itself in the looks and motions of the *Indians*. Some rolled their eyes with distraction; others could not keep on their legs. At length, succeeded the most dismal noises. Such hoops, such shouts, such roaring, such yells, all the devils of hell seemed collected together. Each strove to do an outrage on the other. This seized the other by the throat; that kicked with raging fury at his adversary. And to complete the scene, the old warrior was uttering the most

[* Cf. Jefferson's *Notes*. 3rd Am. ed. (1801), p. 94.]

mournful lamentations over the keg he had emptied; inhaling its flavour with his lips, holding it out with his hands in a supplicating attitude, and vociferating to the bye-standers *Scuttawawbah! Scuttawawbah!* More strong drink! More strong drink!

A disquisition of *Indian* manners cannot but be interesting to a speculative mind. The discovery of *America,* independent of every other circumstance, is of vast importance to mankind, from the light it has enabled us to throw upon man in his savage state;* and the opportunity it has afforded us to study him in his first degrees of civilization. It has even been advanced that before the discovery of the western continent, the natural history of the human species was very imperfect. The ancient philosophers had no other resources but to study the characters of the *Scythians* and *Germans;* but in the *Indians* of *America* a much wider field is opened to investigation. The moral character of the *Scythians* and *Germans* was

[* Cf. Philip Freneau, Introduction to the Abbé Robin's *New Travels through North America,* Philadelphia, 1783.—" Most of those accounts of North America, given to the public by British explorators and others, previous to the Revolution, are generally taken up with the recital of wonderful adventures, in the woods beyond the Lakes, or with the Histories and records of the wild Indian nations, so that by the time the reader gets through one of those performances he never fails to be better acquainted with the Ottagamies . . than with the most interesting particulars relative to the *inhabitants* of the *then* colonies."]

brutish insensibility; the moral character of the *American Indians* discovers little of that quality.

The *Indians* dwell in wigwams, which are formed of mats or bark, tied about poles, that are fastened in the earth; and a hole is made at the top to let out the smoke. Their principal diet is *Nokehick;* parched meal diluted with water; but, where the woods invite hunting, they kill, and devour the deer, the bear, the moose and racoon. Their meat and fish they do not preserve by salting but drying.

Every man is his own physician; but in dangerous cases the patient requires the co-operation of a priest. There is but one mode of cure for all disorders. The sick man descends into a heated cave, or sweating-room; from whence, after having evacuated much of the morbid matter through the pores, the patient is dragged to the river and plunged over head and ears. Should the case be desperate, a *Powaw* or Priest is summoned, who roars and howls till the patient either recovers, or his pulse ceases to beat.

They cross rivers in canoes, which are constructed sometimes of trees, which they burn and hew, till they have hollowed them: and sometimes of bark, which they can carry overland. It will be readily credited that their astonishment was very great on first beholding a ship. They were, says a pious colonist, *scared out of their wits, to see the monster come sailing into their harbour, and spitting fire with a mighty noise out of her floating sides.*

The men in domestic life are exceedingly slothful. The women perform all the household drudgery; they build the wigwams, and beat the corn. The active employment[s] of the men are war and hunting.

The division of their time is by sleeps, moons, and winters. Indeed, by lodging abroad, they have become familiar with the motions of the stars; and it is remarkable that they have called *Charles Wain, Paukunnawaw,* or the Bear; the name by which it is also known to the astronomers of *Europe*.

Of the first settlers in *Virginia*, the most distinguished character was Captain *Smith*, a man who seemed to inherit every quality of a hero; a man of such bravery and conduct, that his actions would confer dignity on the page of the historian. With the life of this gallant colonist, the reader is admitted to so much knowledge of *Indian* manners, that this appears a very proper place to take a view of his adventures. But I have yet a stronger motive. With the history of Captain *Smith* is interwoven the story of *Pocahontas,* whose soft simplicity and innocence cannot but hold captive every mind; and this part of my volume, many of my fair readers will, I am persuaded, hug with the tenderest emotion to their bosoms.

It was on the 26th of April, 1606,* that the ship in which Captain *Smith* had embarked, came within sight of the *American* coast; and it had by accident got into the mouth of that bay, which is now so well known by the name of *Chesapeak*.

This bay is the largest in the world. The distance between its Capes is about twelve miles, but it widens, when entered, till it becomes thirty miles in breadth; when it diminishes again to its head, and is generally from fifteen to five miles over. It is five miles broad at its extremity, where the *Elk* and *Susquehannah* fall into it; and here its length from the sea is three hundred miles, through the whole of which vast extent the tide ebbs and flows.

This mighty bay receives the streams of four large rivers from the west, all of which are navigable, and have their source in the same mountains.

Of these the southernmost is James river, called *Powhatan* by the natives; the next York river, named by the *Indians Pamunkey;* the third the *Rappahanock,* which preserves its aboriginal title; and the northernmost the

[* " The six and twentieth day of Aprill (1607), about foure a clocke in the morning, wee descried the Land of *Virginia*."]

Potomac which also flows under its first name through countries of vast extent.

The land which the colonists had come within sight of, was uncommonly low. It appeared at a distance like the tops of trees emerging above the water;* and as the ship approached the coast, there was not the smallest acclivity visible; the prospect never rising above the height of the pines that everlastingly covered the soil.

Of the promontories of the bay, they named the southernmost *Cape Henry,* and the northernmost *Cape Charles,* in compliment to the sons of their reigning Monarch; and, having got their ship into a harbour, they chose for the place of their settlement a peninsula on the north side of the river *Powhatan,* to which they very consistently gave the name of *Jamestown.*

It is only in active life that men can estimate their qualities, for it is impossible to answer for that courage which has never encountered danger, or that fortitude which has never had any evils to support. The situation of the Colonists was now the touchstone of their moral character, for they were encompassed on every side with imminent calamities. A scanty supply of provisions, and the uncertainty of recruiting them, in a country where every imagination was filled with

[* Cf. Smyth, *Tour in the United States of America,* p. 7.]

the barbarity of the natives, disquieted the breasts of those whose nerves were not firm.

In this situation of affairs, there was wanting a support for the infant colony, and Captain *Smith* was elected Ruler by unanimous consent. The conduct of *Smith* justified the wisdom of their choice. By his judgment, courage, and industry, he saved the new establishment; for by his judgment he discovered and defeated the schemes devised by the *Indians* for its destruction; by his courage he became their terror; and by descending to manual labour, his example produced a spirit of patient toil among his companions.

One of the tributary streams to the river *Powhatan,* is that of *Chickahominy,* which descended about four miles above the infant settlement. It was an object with the Colony to discover its source; but the dread of an ambush from the *Indians* deterred the majority from the undertaking. *Smith,* ever delighting in enterprise, gallantly undertook himself to discover the head of the river; having found six others who were willing to become the partners of his danger. Having with much labour cleared a passage for his barge, by felling the trees on the borders of the river, he reached a broad bay, the middle of which was beyond the reach of an arrow from either side. Here he moored the barge, and accompanied by two of his men, *Robin-*

son and *Emry,* proceeded up the river in a canoe; strictly enjoining the people left in the barge not to land on any condition. But no sooner had *Smith* departed, than the crew gratified the impulse they felt to land; and were received by a discharge of arrows from an ambush of *Indians* under the command of *Opechancanough,* a subtle and savage barbarian, who had vigilantly watched their motions. Each man now sought safety in flying to the water side, and swimming off to the boat; but one *George Cassen,* who could not swim, was overtaken by the *Indians,* who having extorted from him the way his Captain had gone, scalped him upon the spot, and then went in pursuit of *Smith.*

Captain *Smith* had gone about twenty miles up the river, and had discovered its source amongst swamps and marshes. Here he left the canoe to the care of *Robinson* and *Emry,* and penetrated the woods with his gun, in search of provisions. In the mean time *Opechancanough* was not backward in the pursuit. He traced the course which *Smith* had taken, and came upon the canoe, in which he found the two men, overcome with fatigue, fast asleep in the boat. These they dispatched with their war-clubs, and scalping them in haste, prosecuted their search after *Smith.* It was not long before the gallant adventurer found himself beset by these barbarians; but the imminent danger to which he was exposed, only animated him to more heroism, and he determined to die with a resistance worthy his former reputation for courage. So warmly did he receive the attack of his savage enemies with his musquet, that he laid six of them dead on the spot, and wounded several others. A panic seized the whole; none dared advance; and *Smith* keeping the *Indians* thus at bay, endeavoured to gain his canoe. But unacquainted with the nature of the soil, he, in his retreat, got into a morass, from which finding it was impossible to extricate himself, he threw away his arms, and made signs that he had surrendered.

When *Smith* was dragged from the morass, he asked for the Chief of the party, and being shewn *Opechancanough,* he presented him with a round ivory double compass dial, which our adventurer had taken with him to determine the course of the river. The savage was astonished at the playing of the fly and needle, which he could see so plainly, and yet not touch, because of the glass that covered them. But when *Smith* explained by it the roundness of the earth, the skies, the sphere of the sun, moon and stars, with other doctrines unknown to them, the whole party greatly marvelled.

For some time the compass excited the wonder of the *Indians,* but it subsided with its novelty; and there appeared to be a profound consultation among these barbarians respecting the manner in which they should dispose of their prisoner. After much vehement debate, they tied him up to a tree, and assembled in order to shoot him; but just as an archer was drawing his bow-string, *Opechancanough* held up the compass, and with the same smile of fondness that a child bestows on his rattle, suspended by his command the arm of the executioner.

Opechancanough was a person of distinction. He was brother to *Powhatan,* a powerful king of *Pamunkey,* whose will was a law among his numerous subjects. To *Powhatan* he had formed the resolution of delivering his prisoner, but first he wished to lead him in show and triumph about the country. For this purpose they bent their course again for *Orapakes,* lying on the upper part of *Chickahominy* swamp, from whence they had come. The *Indians,* in their march, drew themselves up in a file, and *Opechancanough* walked in the centre, having the *English* swords and muskets carried before him. *Smith* followed the Chief, led by a couple of *Indians,* holding him fast by each arm; and on either side went six in file, with their arrows cautiously notched.

When the *Indians* had arrived within hearing of the town, they set up different cries to give their countrymen notice of the event of their expedition. They uttered six dismal yells to announce that six of their party had been slain; and sent forth one war-hoop, to proclaim that they had brought home a prisoner.

The yell of these *Indians* resembled the sound of Whoo, whoo, whoop, which was continued in a long shrill tone till their breath was exhausted, when they suddenly paused with a horrid shout. The war-hoop was a cry yet louder, which they modulated into notes, by placing the hand before the mouth. They could be both very distinctly heard at a considerable distance.

It was evening when the *Indians* approached the town of *Orapakes* with their prisoner. The moon was walking in brightness, the firefly was on the wing, and the melancholy note of the *Muckawiss* * was heard from the woods.

The whole village came out to learn the particulars of what they had only heard in general terms; and now a widow was to be seen mourning her husband, a mistress bewailing her lover, and children crying for their fathers.

But unspeakable was the astonishment of the women and children on beholding the prisoner, who was so unlike any human being

* Whip-poor-will.

they had ever before seen. They gazed with speechless wonder at him; some clasping their hands in dumb admiration; some contrasting the redness of their own colour with the whiteness of his; and others unbuttoning his clothes and buttoning them again with a loud laugh.

The men, however, betrayed, or affected to betray, no emotions of surprise. The old people sat with stoical composure in separate circles on the ground, smoking their calumets by moonlight, and conversing with profound gravity; while the young fellows pursued the exercises that engaged them, shooting arrows at a mark, throwing the hatchet, wrestling, and running. All the domestic drudgery devolved on the women. Of these some were busied in splitting wood, some bearing logs from the forest, and some kindling fires.

When the wonder produced among the women by the novelty of *Smith's* appearance subsided, they all joined in a *yo-hah,* or huzza, which was not deficient in harmony. An elder then rose and harangued the female multitude. The object of his speech was to enjoin them to satiate their revenge on the back of the prisoner, who was sentenced to run the gauntlet, for the War Captains whom he had slain. The women then provided themselves with twigs, and having drawn themselves up in two lines, *Smith* was stripped, and compelled to run the gauntlet through the crowd.

Cruelty was succeeded by kindness. A repast of *Indian* corn was placed before him, on which having fed, half a dozen of the prettiest squaws in the village, who had washed and adorned themselves with much coquetry, were presented to the stranger, for him to select a mistress. But *Smith,* whose back still smarted under the lashes they had so prodigally bestowed upon him, felt very little disposed for dalliance; and he turned away unmoved by their seducing attitudes.

It is not to be supposed that the slumbers of *Smith* were very soft; but, however he might have been inclined to sleep, the horrid noises that prevailed through the night in the village would have rendered it impracticable; for the relations of those whom he had slain never remitted their yells; but when one was exhausted, another prolonged the clamour.

Smith passed the night in the wigwam of *Opechancanough,* and here he was witness to the mode of carrying on an *Indian* intrigue. When *Opechancanough* and his family were snoring on the ground, a young *Indian* stole softly through the door, walking on his hands and feet, somewhat after the manner of a bear. *Smith,* who was not ignorant of the implacable resentment of the *Indian* character, was led to suppose it was some assassin coming to revenge the death of a relation, and seizing a tomahawk which lay on the ground, he prepared to resist the murderer; but he soon discovered that a softer passion than revenge stimulated this nocturnal visitor. The *Indian* gently approached the embers of the fire which was not quite extinguished, and, lighting a splinter of wood, advanced with great caution towards a young *squaw,* who was reposing in the wigwam; he then uncovered her head, and jogged her till she waked, or pretended to wake. The nymph rising up, the lover held to her the light, which he had carefully concealed in the hollow of his hand; and which she immediately blew out. This act inflamed the respectful lover to boldness; for it discovered that the heart of his mistress was not cruel.

Smith passed the night in a conflict of hope and fear; but the next morning, while his mind was still filled with the horrors of an imaginary death, he was on the brink of experiencing a real one. An *Indian* Chief, whose son during the night had been seized with a delirious fever, hid himself behind a tree, and when *Smith* approached it, conversing with *Opechancanough,* threw a hatchet at his head, which underwent a rotary motion as it flew through the air, and had not *Smith* stooped providentially at the moment to gather a flower, his soul had certainly been dispatched to the region of ghosts. The superstition of the savage had ascribed his son's disorder to the sorcery of the prisoner; whom the *Indians* conducted to the raving man, imploring he would recover him. *Smith,* having examined the fellow, assumed a profound look, and informed the bystanders, that he had a water at *James-town,* which, in such a disorder, never failed to produce a cure; but *Opechancanough* had more cunning than to allow him to go and fetch it.

Smith found the *Indians* at *Orapakes* making the greatest preparations for an assault upon *James-town.* To facilitate their designs, they desired *Smith's* advice and assistance; holding out to him the alluring rewards of life, and liberty, and lands, and women. But he represented to them the danger of the attempt with such hyperbolical amplification; and described the springing of mines, great guns, and other warlike engines, with such an aggrandizement of horror, that the hearers were exceedingly terrified and amazed. And then he persuaded some of them to go to *James-town,* under the pretence of obtaining toys; and in the leaf of a table-book he apprized the Colonists of the warlike preparations of the beseigers, directing them to affright the messengers with the explosion of bombs, and not to fail sending the things that he wrote for. Within three days the messengers returned, greatly astonished themselves, and filling the hearers with astonishment, at the dreadful explosions they had witnessed; nor less wondering how the prisoner could divine, or make the paper speak; for all things were delivered to them as he had solemnly prophesied.

The meditated attack upon *James-town* being laid aside, *Opechancanough* led *Smith* in triumph through the country; exhibiting him with high exultation to the *Youghtanunds,* and *Mattaponies,* the *Piankatanks,* and *Nantaughtacunds.* They afterwards conducted him through the country of the *Nominies;* and when, for several weeks, he had raised the wonder of some, and provoked the laughter of others, they brought him to *Opechancanough's* chief settlement, on the river *Pamunkey.*

This place was much larger, and more populous than *Orapakes;* the wigwams were built with more care, and that appropriated to *Opechancanough* exhibited a rude magnificence. The curiosity of the women was here again excited; and the *Indians,* in conducting *Smith* through the crowd, performed with triumphant antics their military exercise; throwing themselves into a war-dance with every distortion of body; and yelling out the most diabolical screeches and notes.

Here *Smith* was confined three days in a separate wigwam; during which time the inhabitants came in crowds with frightful howlings, and hellish ceremonies, conjuring him to declare whether he intended them good or ill. After this they brought him a bag of gunpowder, and desired to know what kind of grain it was; for they judged it to be the produce of the earth, and carefully preserved it to plant the next spring.

At length, Captain *Smith,* was conducted to *Werowocomoco,* where *Powhatan,* the Emperor lived in savage state and magnificence. When *Smith* was brought into the presence of *Powhatan,* he was sitting upon a wooden throne resembling a bedstead, cloathed with a flowing robe of racoon skins, and wearing on his head a coronet of feathers. He was about sixty years of age, somewhat hoary, and of a mien that impressed every beholder with awe. On each side of him sat a young *squaw,* who practised every endearing softness of her sex, and contended for the caresses of her venerable Sovereign. It was ludicrous to behold the bald-headed letcher relax from his ferocity, and, waxing wanton, pinch the cheek of the damsel who most conciliated him.

When *Smith* entered the royal *Wigwam,* the whole Court gave a shout; and the Queen of *Appamattox* was appointed to carry him water to wash, while one of the concubines left the throne, and brought him a bunch of feathers instead of a towel to dry himself.

Hence *Smith* was received more like a guest than a prisoner; and, after an abundant supper, a skin was spread for him to sleep upon.

During the night a centinel was placed at each corner of the royal *Wigwam,* who every half hour was heard to shout; shaking his finger between his lips to give more horror to the sound. If there was any one found remiss in making this clamour, the Captain of the watch immediately took a cudgel and beat him over the head and shoulders till he roared with anguish.

The person of *Smith* was extremely prepossessing; to a figure comely from nature was superadded that external grace which he had acquired in the court and the camp of *Great Britain;* and several ladies of distinguished rank had heaped upon him unequivocal marks of their tenderness. The influence of the passions is uniform, and their effects nearly the same in every human breast; hence love operates in the same manner throughout the world, and discovers itself by the same symptoms in the breasts of beings separated by an immeasurable ocean. When *Smith* appeared before *Powhatan,* the first impression he made decided favourably for him on the minds of the women. This his knowledge of the sex soon discovered; but his attention was principally attracted by the charms of a young girl, whose looks emanated from a heart that was the seat of every tenderness, and who could not conceal those soft emotions of which the female bosom is so susceptible. It is in vain to attempt opposing the inroads of the blind god; the path of love is a path to which there is no end; in which there is no remedy for lovers but to give up their souls.

This young girl was the daughter of the Emperor *Powhatan*. She was called *Pocahontas;* and when *Smith* was engaged by the interrogations of the King, and she thought herself unobserved, never did the moon gaze more steadfastly on the water than she on the prisoner.

The next day a long and profound consultation was held by the King and his Privy Council, when a huge stone was brought before *Powhatan,* and several men assembled with clubs in their hands. The lamentations of the women admonished *Smith* of his destiny; who being brought blindfolded to the spot, his head was laid on the block, and the men prepared with their clubs to beat out his brains. The women now became more bitter in their lamentations over the victim; but the savage Monarch was inexorable, and the executioners were lifting their arms to perform the office of death, when *Pocahontas* ran with mournful distraction to the stone, and getting the victim's head into her arms, laid her own upon it to receive the blow. Fair spirit! thou ministering angel at the throne of grace! If souls disengaged from their earthly bondage can witness from the bosom of eternal light what is passing here below, accept, sweet Seraph, this tribute to thy humanity.

Powhatan was not wanting in paternal feeling; his soul was devoted to his daughter *Pocahontas;* and so much did his ferocity relent at this display of innocent softness in a girl of fourteen, that he pronounced the prisoner's pardon, and dismissed the executioners. Indeed, every heart melted into tenderness at the scene. The joy of the successful mediator expressed itself in silence; she hung wildly on the neck of the reprieved victim, weeping with a violence that choaked her utterance.

The breast of *Smith* did not yield to this act of female softness and humanity; it excited an emotion of gratitude, but it kindled no passion in his heart. Formed for action and enterprize, he considered love an imbecility unworthy of a great mind; and although his person could inspire tender sentiments, his mind was not ductile to them. His penetration, however, foresaw the uses to which the passion of *Pocahontas* for him might be converted; and his solicitude for the success of the Colony, which was much nearer his heart, made him feign a return of that fondness which every day augmented in the bosom of the Princess.

It was the custom of *Powhatan* when he was weary of his women, to bestow them among those of his courtiers who had ingratiated themselves into his favour; nor could his servants be more honoured than by this mark of his esteem.

Powhatan had conceived a very high predilection for Captain *Smith*. He caused his person to be adorned with a robe of racoon skins, similar to that which he wore himself; and when he was glutted with the possession of the two women, who sat at his throne, he signified it to be his royal pleasure to consign one of them to his guest.

No sooner did this intelligence reach the ears of the *squaws,* than a bitter controversy took place between them respecting which of the two was the more worthy of pre-eminence. Jealousy cannot like other passions be restrained by modesty or prudence; a vent it will have; and soon it burst forth from these women with the impetuosity of a torrent. They had neither nails, nor fingers enough to scratch with; nor a volubility of tongue sufficient to deliver the abuse that laboured with convulsive throes to come forth from their bosoms.

At length, *Powhatan* separated the combatants, and told *Smith* to make his choice.

But *Smith,* who was a man that never forgot the respect due to himself, declined with cold civility the honour his Majesty intended him; to the unspeakable joy of *Pocahontas,* who had awaited the event in solitude and tears.

Two days after *Powhatan* disguised himself in the most frightful manner his imagination could suggest. He then caused Captain *Smith* to be carried to a great wigwam in the woods, and there be left alone on a mat by the fire. Not long after, from behind a kind of arras that divided the apartment, was made the most doleful noise his ears had ever heard; and, presently *Powhatan,* with about two hundred more *Indians* in masquerade, came from behind the arras, and informed *Smith* they were now friends, and that he should immediately go to *James-town,* and send him one of those engines of war whose loud voice could mimic the thunder of the clouds; that he would give him the country of *Capahowsick* in exchange for it, and ever after esteem him next to his son *Nantaquas.* Captain *Smith* reposed but little confidence in his words; he expected every minute to be put to some savage death; but *Powhatan* sent him away immediately with twelve guides, and, having lodged that night in the woods, he arrived the next morning early at the fort.

And thus Captain *Smith,* after a seven weeks' captivity, returned to *James-town;*

improved in his knowledge of the country, and the language of the natives. He behaved to his guides with the most flattering attention, and, having shewn *Pawhunt,* the confidential servant of *Powhatan,* a brass nine-pounder, desired he would carry it with his compliments to the King. The weight of the cannon soon deterred him from the attempt; but when the *Indians* saw him discharge it, loaded with stone, among the bows of a large oak, they ran with wonder and dismay from the engine of terror.

Finding every effort ineffectual to transport the gun to *Powhatan,* their curiosity was turned to the toys Captain *Smith* exhibited before them. With these he loaded his guides, after selecting the most dazzling as presents for *Powhatan, Opitchapan* his brother, *Nantaquas* his son, and the tender *Pocahontas.*

When *Smith* returned to *James-town,* he found the colony in the utmost confusion. They considered their affairs desperate, and were fitting out a bark to return to *England.* Our adventurer exerted his abilities to frustrate the execution of this project. He lost no occasion to adorn with every embellishment of imagination, the beauty and fertility of the country he had travelled through; he dwelt with admiration on the grain reposited in the store-houses of the natives; and in fact, represented it to be a second *Canaan,* a land that flowed with milk and honey. His eloquence was not without the desired effect. He prevailed upon the bravest of his companions to alter their resolution, and by their assistance he overawed the extravagant projects of the rest.

The Colonists, therefore, thought once more of maintaining the fort; and in this resolution they were confirmed by the coming of *Pocahontas* with a numerous train of attendants, loaded with *Indian* corn and other grain of the country.

The Colonists flocked with eager curiosity to behold an *Indian* girl, who had saved by her interposition the life of their Chief; nor was their admiration less excited by the beauty of her person, than the humanity of her disposition.*

---

* *Pocahontas* was eminently interesting both in form and features. Her person was below the middle size, but admirably proportioned. Her waist resembled that of the *French* Monarch's mistress; it was *la taille à la main.* Her limbs were delicate; and her feet were distinguished by exquisite insteps, such as of those women whom *Homer* calls λισφυρους.

It has been remarked, says *Hawkesworth*, (this single sentence is of more value than the folios of *Lavater*), that the predominant passion may generally be discovered in the countenance, because the muscles by which it is expressed, being almost perpetually contracted, lose their tone, and never wholly relax; so that the expression remains when the passion is suspended.

Sensibility had left its signature upon the countenance of *Pocahontas.* It needed no Ghost, to inform him who delights

The acclamations of the crowd affected to tears the sensibility of *Pocahontas;* but her native modesty was abashed; and it was with delight that she obeyed the invitation of Captain *Smith* to wander with him, remote from vulgar curiosity, along the banks of the river. It was then she gave loose to all the tumultuous extasy of love; hanging on his arm, and weeping with an eloquence much more powerful than words.

The same year Captain *Newport* arrived from *England* with a reinforcement of men, and a supply of provisions. The ship also brought a quantity of such trinkets as the *Indians* are captivated with, and she was sent back loaded with cedar, skins, and furs.

It was the opinion of many chimerical heads in *England,* that the bay of *Chesapeak* had its source not far from the *South Sea. Smith,* however he discredited this idea, was ever ready to promote discoveries; and, in a boat adapted to the voyage, he traced the bay to its very head. He also sailed up the *Potomac* river to its falls; and having an eye for the

---

to read the *human face divine,* that the softer passions had produced a mechanical effect on the aspect of this *Indian* Maid. The characters were too plain not to be understood; they gave a turn and cast to her features that made a forcible impression on the mind of the beholder. Her beauty did not depend on mere features, but temper and sentiment. And we ought not to wonder that her looks afterwards captivated a man of elegant education.

wonders of nature, beheld with awful admiration the vast volume of water obstructed by irregular rocks, over which it broke with a roar that filled the country around.

In the absence of Captain *Smith, Powhatan* having taken offence at some act of the Colonists, sent them a hatchet, which was a token of defiance; and laid waste to the fields of corn, which he judged it might be difficult to protect. When *Smith* returned to the fort, he found his people reduced to a state bordering on famine; and that there was no alternative left but to invade a neighbouring town, and levy contributions on their grain. A detachment of the bravest men was selected from the Colonists, and an early hour of the morning was fixed for their departure; but the crafty *Powhatan* by the means of his spies anticipated their march; the oldest warriors were posted in ambush to wage among them unseen destruction; and the whole party would inevitably have been destroyed by the *Indians,* had not the kind, the faithful, the lovely *Pocahontas,* in a dismal night of thunder, lightning, and rain, stole through the woods, and apprized *Smith* of his danger.

Can the wild legends of rude ages, or the sentimental fictions of refinement, supply an heroine whose qualities would not be eclipsed by the *Indian Pocahontas?*

The return of Captain *Smith* restored to

the colony its former importance. His care, courage, and vigilance, not only defeated the projects of the neighboring *Indians,* but inspired even *Powhatan* with awe; and the Colonists no longer entertained any fear from the incursions of the natives.

But at this period an accident happened to Captain *Smith,* which deprived the colony of his services. From the sea to the falls of James river, the face of the country is uniformly level; but where the water becomes obstructed the land swells into the prospect of hills rising over hills.

Smith finding it necessary, from the great influx of emigrants to the colony, to establish a new Settlement, made choice of this spot; and assisted himself in throwing up a fortification. But while he was lying asleep one night in his boat, a spark from a fire which had been kindled by a boy, communicated to his powder-bag, which blew up, and tore the flesh from his thighs and part of his body, in a manner that endangered his life.

In this deplorable condition Captain *Smith* was carried to *James-town,* where, there being neither a Surgeon nor Surgeon's chest, he embarked in a ship that had brought over a supply of men, and was preparing to sail for *England.* It was on Michaelmas day, 1609, that Captain *Smith* bade farewell to that shore on which he had founded a Colony, that was decreed in the progress of time to become an independent empire, and confederating itself with other Colonies, to hold a distinguished rank among the nations of the earth.

Though the breast of *Pocahontas* cherished the deepest affection for Captain *Smith,* yet, such is the native modesty of the sex in all countries, that she could not collect resolution to tell him of her love; and the Captain, like a true soldier, unwilling *to put his unhoused free condition, into circumscription and confine,* though he ventured her endearments, never dropped the slightest hint about marriage. *Pocahontas* had, however, the discernment to perceive that among people of a civilized nation, no bonds but those of marriage could secure to a woman the object of her affections; and that little confidence was to be reposed in the fond assurances of a lover till he evinced their sincerity by becoming a husband. Averse to any solemn engagement with *Pocahontas,* yet, conscious of her own ardour for such an union, *Smith* devised an expedient that could not fail to cure her of her passion. He embarked privately for *England,* and enjoined the Colonists as they valued their own safety, to represent that he was dead; for *Smith* knew the mischief every woman feels an impulse to perpetrate whose passion has been scorned; but he also remembered the position, that where there was no hope there could be no longer love; and the breast, which, knowing him to be living, would glow with an impatience of revenge, would, on the belief of his death, be accessible only to the softness of sorrow. The project of our adventurer was founded on an acquaintance with the human heart; for when *Pocahontas* again, under pretence of carrying provisions to the fort, gratified her secret longing to meet her beloved *Englishman,* she yielded to every bitterness of anguish on hearing of his death. A Colonist of the name of *Wright,* undertook to practise the deceit.* He pretended to shew the afflicted girl the grave of Captain *Smith,* recounting the tender remembrance he expressed for her in his dying moments, and the hope he fondly indulged to meet her in the world of spirits. Love is ever credulous; but *Pocahontas* listened to this artful tale with catholic faith. She prostrated herself on the pretended grave, beat her bosom, and uttered the most piercing cries.

Mr. *John Rolfe,* one of the Colonists, was young, brave, generous, but of impetuous passions. His fine talents had been cultivated by a liberal education; but his feelings, ever tremblingly alive to external impressions,

[* "They did tell us alwaies you were dead, and I knew no other till I came to *Plimoth* . . Your Countriemen will lie much."]

made him resentful of even an involuntary design to offend; and an affair of honour with a superior officer had driven him to the shores of the new world.

Possessing a supreme contempt for the vulgar, there were few of the Colonists whose company he could endure. The only companion of his social hour for a long time had been *Smith;* but when that gallant soldier returned to *England, Rolfe* constructed for himself a log-house in the woods, and, when not upon duty at the fort, was to be found there solitary and sad.

Though the breast of *Rolfe* possessed not the ambition of *Smith,* it was infinitely more accessible to the softer emotions. He beheld with interest the tender sentiments which *Pocahontas* cherished for Captain *Smith,* and participating in her sorrow, his own heart became infected with a violent passion. He delighted in the secrecy of his solitude, where he could indulge undisturbed the emotions that *Pocahontas* had excited; he wandered dejected by moon-light along the banks of the river; and he who once was remarked for dressing himself with studied elegance, now walked about with his stockings ungartered.

Ominia vincit amor; et nos cedamus amori.
Virg.

Love, through all the world, maintains resistless sway,
Love conquers all, and Love we must obey.

The mind of *Rolfe* warmed with the ideal caresses of *Pocahontas,* produced often in his walks a poem to his *Indian* beauty. Of these effusions I have three in my possession; they rise, I think, above mediocrity; and as every thing that relates to the lover of *Pocahontas* will excite curiosity, I shall not withhold them from the public. They mark very strongly the climax of his passion.

TO POCAHONTAS.

WHY, sweet Nymph, that heart-fetch'd sigh,
Which thy heaving bosom rends?
Whence that pensive, down-cast eye,
Whose magic glance soft transport sends!

Sure thy roving thoughts recal,
A faithless Lover to thy mind;
Whose heart thy charms did once enthrall,
But now inconstant as the wind.

Ah! disclaim his fickle love,
Take some more deserving swain;
The tale he whisper'd in the grove,
Heed not when he tells again.

The second poem in my little collection bears a striking similitude to a *Latin* Quatrain of *Buchanan* * whose poems were extant in the reign of *James* I. But whether the resemblance be studied or casual, there is no external evidence to decide.

* *Rolfe* might have had recourse to the original Greek. [These verses doubtless are not Rolfe's.]

TO POCAHONTAS.

HE who thy lovely face beholds,
Where beauty every charm unfolds,
Is surely blest; but more so he,
Who hears thy voice of harmony!
But more than mortal is the bliss
Of him who ravishes a kiss,
In playful dalliance, from those lips,
Where glowing Love his empire keeps.
But quite a God is, sure the swain,
Who feels thee, blushing, kiss again;
And from that mouth the gift receives
Which all his soul of sense bereaves!

In the preceding little poem there will be found some lines unskilfully wrought; yet, so much more can we feel than imagine, and so much will truth predominate over fiction, that it will be, perhaps, recurred to without satiety, when the bundles of epic rhymes which now usurp the shelves of the bookseller, shall be transferred to their lawful claimants, the pastry-cook, and trunk-maker.

The third and last poem of Mr. *Rolfe,* was produced on the banks of the river *Powhatan.* In this his epigram and spriteliness have left him. He appears to be deeply wounded; not, indeed, by the arrow of an *Indian,* but the bow of a child. He seems to have received a death-wound; the very pin of his heart is cleft with the but-shaft of Cupid.

SONNET TO POCAHONTAS

WHERE from the shore, I oft have view'd the sail,
Mount on the flood, and darken in the gale,
Now wan with care, beneath the oak reclin'd,
Thy form, O! *Pocahontas,* fills my mind.
Here from my comrades, where the moon's soft beam,
Trembles in antic shadows on the stream;
Here the sad muse, in sympathy of woe,
Assists my grief in solitude to flow.
Here where the mocking-bird, the woods among,
Warbles with rolling note her plaintive song,
And the sad *Mucakawis'* ill-omen'd strain,
Rings from the woods, and echoes to the plain,
Here as I pensive wander through the glade,
I sigh and call upon my *Indian* Maid.*

It was during one of these nights, when Mr. *Rolfe* was sitting woe-begone under an oak, sighing and groaning, and coupling love with dove, that a foot wandering among the trees disturbed his profound thoughts. It was too light to belong to a man, and his prophetic soul told him it was the step of *Pocahontas.* He stole to the spot. It was SHE! It was *Pocahontas* strewing flowers over the imaginary grave of Captain *Smith.* Overcome with terror and surprize, to be thus discovered by a stranger, the powers of life were suspended, and she sunk into the arms of *Rolfe.* For what rapturous moments is a lover often in-

[* The author uses this sonnet again in his historical novel, *The First Settlers of Virginia,* p. 172. He does not there directly ascribe the lines to Rolfe.]

debted to accident! The impassioned youth clasped the *Indian* Maid to his beating heart, and drank from her lips the poison of delight. The breast of a woman is, perhaps, never more susceptible of a new passion than when it is agitated by the remains of a former one. When *Pocahontas* recovered from her confusion, a blush burnt on her cheek to find herself in the arms of a man; but when *Rolfe* threw himself before her on his knees, and clasping his hands to the moon, discovered the emotions that had so long filled his breast, the afflicted girl suffered him to wipe the tear from her eye that overflowed with sorrow, and no longer repulsed the ardour of his caresses. The day was now breaking on the summits of the mountains in the East; the song of the mocking-bird* was become faint,

* Of the feathered choir on the Western Continent, none is to be compared to the mocking-bird. When weary of mocking other birds, it luxuriates in an original strain; a strain characterised sometimes by merriment, and sometimes by tenderness. It delights, however, in cheerful tunes; and such is the sprightliness of the mocking-bird, that it will jump and dance to its own cadence.

No writer before me has ever introduced this songster warbling either by night or by day. *Brown* in his thousand and one novels, lays all the scenes in his native country, and yet, never once makes mention of this bird! Oh! what a sullenness against nature! And the Travellers from *England* seem more delighted with the bellowing of the bull-frog, on whose intonations they lavish all their eloquence.

In *Prince William County, Virginia*, I lucubrated late; and whenever the moon was visible, my feelings were always raised by the song of the mocking-bird. It generally perched

and the cry of the *Muckawiss* was heard only at long intervals. *Pocahontas* urged to go; but *Rolfe* still breathed in her ear the music of his vows, as he held her in his arms, or still rioted in the draught of intoxication from her lips. The sun had appeared above the mountains when *Pocahontas* returned through the woods.

In the early part of the year 1612, two more ships arrived from *England* with men and provisions. They found the colony much distressed for want of grain; they had no leader to stimulate them to industry by his example, and, relapsing into indolence, had neglected the cultivation of the earth. The provision brought them by the ships was not sufficient for them to subsist on long; and *Powhatan*, who was still at variance with the colony refused them a supply.*

within a hundred yards of my log-hut. Old Aunt *Patty*, the negro cook, was sitting on the threshhold of the next door, smoking the stump of an old pipe. "Please God Almighty," exclaimed the old woman, "how sweet that mocking-bird " sing! He never tire!"

* The distress of the Colonists appears ludicrous, when we search for the cause of the effect. It was a spirit of forming *Utopian* schemes of government, which heaped on them such calamities. It was agreed that no man should have any personal property in land or grain, but that every one should labour for, and be maintained by the public stock. The natural consequence was, that every man consumed as much of the public stock as he could come at, and contributed nothing to it by his labour but what he could not avoid. *Hinc illæ lachrymæ!*

In this critical situation of affairs, Captain *Argall,* who commanded one of the ships, devised an expedient to bring *Powhatan* to a compliance with their demands. His prolific brain was big with a stratagem, which, however unjustifiable, met with the concurrence of the Colonists. He knew the affection which *Powhatan* bore for his daughter *Pocahontas,* and was determined to seize her.

Argall, having unloaded his vessel at the fort, sailed up the *Potomac,* under pretence of trading with the *Indians* who inhabited its banks. But he had been informed that *Pocahontas* was on a visit to *Japazaws,* King of *Potomac,* and his real motive was to gain over the savage by presents, and make him the instrument of putting *Pocahontas* into his power.

Japazaws had his price. For the promised reward of a copper-kettle, of which this savage had become enamoured, he prevailed on *Pocahontas* to accompany him and his Queen in a visit on board the ship; when *Argall* detained the betrayed girl, and conveyed her, with some corn he had purchased, in triumph to the fort.

Rolfe was not sorry for the stratagem that brought *Pocahontas* to the fort. He had exposed himself to the most imminent danger by a mid-night expedition to the neighborhood of *Werowocomoco,* where his *Indian* beauty had promised to meet him in an unfrequented grove; and he would have been inevitably scalped by a party of the enemy, had not *Nantaquas,* whose friendship the lover had diligently cultivated, interposed his kind offices, and not only restrained the arms of his savage companions, but conducted him out of danger.

Pocahontas now put herself under the protection of *Rolfe,* who, by his tender, but respectful conduct, soothed her mind to tranquillity; while the Colonists, influenced by other passions, renewed their importunities upon *Powhatan,* demanding a supply of provisions in ransom for his child.

Powhatan, in solicitude for his daughter, and being informed that a formidable reinforcement of men and ammunition had arrived at the fort, not only complied with the terms of the ransom, but proposed to enter into an alliance with the Colonists.

It was *Nantaquas* who came to the fort with provisions to ransom his sister. *Rolfe* availed himself of the occasion to contrive a private interview with them, and propose himself in unequivocal terms as a husband to *Pocahontas.* The amiable girl was flattered by the preference of the young and accomplished *European. Nantaquas* urged the suit; and when *Rolfe* took the hand of *Pocahontas,* and with a look of inexpressible anxiety and tenderness repeated his proposal, the lovely *Indian* was melted to softness, and with blushing timidity consented to become his wife.

The ransom being paid, *Pocahontas* was now at liberty to return to *Werowocomoco*. But *Hymen* was not to be cheated of his prerogative; neither *Rolfe* nor *Pocahontas* were willing ever more to separate; and *Nantaquas* was dispatched to obtain the consent of *Powhatan*.

Powhatan did not withhold his consent; but adhering to the resolution he had made never to put himself into the power of the whites, he sent *Opitchapan,* the uncle of *Pocahontas,* with his son *Nantaquas,* to witness the marriage.

Rolfe was now happy in the arms of *Pocahontas;* nor did satiety necessarily follow from fruition. The *Indian* bride discovered in every question an eagerness of knowledge; and the elegant attainments of her husband, enabled him to cultivate the wild paradise of her mind. *Rolfe* found in *Pocahontas* that companion of his solitude for which he had so long sighed; and as she reclined her head on his shoulder before the door, and either made interrogation respecting *Europe,* or exchanged with him the glance of intelligence and affection, his eyes sparkled with fondness, and he caught her with transport to his breast.

Rolfe had brought with him into the woods

of *America,* a mind not inductile to wit and humour, but more often abstracted in the recollection of sentiment. When not employed at the fort, he indulged the impulse of his mind for composition, and wrote as the moment urged him, in prose or song. Of his poetical productions I shall submit one to my readers.

> Within *Powhatan's* calm retreat,
>   Repos'd beneath the woodland glade,
> I envy not the gaudy great,
>   Gay dance by night, or masquerade.
>
> For other thoughts my breast possess,
>   The joys that from reflection come;
> The bland discourse, the soft caress
>   Of her who makes this cot a dome.
>
> Then why exchange my sylvan seat,
> Impervious to unhallow'd feet,
> For crowds that ruder passions know,
> To me inelegant and low?

In the year 1616, several ships arrived at the Colony, from different parts of *England;* and *Rolfe,* being, by the death of his father, come to the inheritance of an estate in *Middlesex,* he embarked with his *Indian* bride in a vessel for *Plymouth.* *Pocahontas* had presented him with a son; and their infant offspring accompanied them across the *Atlantic.*

It was on the 12th of June, 1616, that Mr. *Rolfe* arrived at *Plymouth* with *Pocahontas.* He immediately proceeded with her to *London,* where she was introduced at Court to

James I. who, tenacious of his prerogative, was inflamed with indignation that one of his subjects should aspire to an alliance with royal blood. The haughty Monarch would not suffer *Rolfe* to be admitted to his presence; and when he received *Pocahontas,* his looks rebuked her for descending from the dignity of a King's daughter, to take up with a man of no title or family. The Ladies of the Court were, however, charmed with the unaffected sweetness of her manners; and spared no caresses nor presents to sooth her to complacency.

At length Captain *Smith* advanced to salute *Pocahontas;* at whose unexpected appearance, she expressed the utmost astonishment, which gave way to scorn.

Illa solo fixos oculos aversa tenebat.*

But in a private interview, the tender girl hung over *Smith* with tears, and reproached him in accents that breathed kindness, rather than resentment.

The smoke of *London* being offensive to *Pocahontas,* (and to what person is it not offensive who has been accustomed to the pure air of the woods,) *Rolfe* removed her to *Brentford,* where she breathed a less noxious atmosphere. Here she was often visited by ladies of distinguished rank, from the metropolis; and carriages, bearing coronets, were

[* Aeneid, VI, 469.]

often drawn up before her door. Good breeding is the offspring of good sense; it is a mode, not a substance; and *Pocahontas,* whose pentration was intuition, soon learned to receive her visitants with appropriate variations of deference.

But the hour was hasting when *Pocahontas* was to descend to that place *where the weary are at rest, and the wicked cease from troubling;* that bosom which had so often undergone perturbation for the sufferings of another, was soon to be stilled; that eye, which had so often overflowed with humanity, was soon to be closed; that hand which had been raised in supplication to avert the death of the prisoner, was soon to moulder in the grave.

Rolfe's right to his father's lands were disputed by another claimant, and not being of a temper to bear with the law's delay, he formed the resolution to embark again with *Pocahontas* for the shores of the new world. In *Virginia* he was entitled by the right of his bride, to lands of immeasurable extent;* and he was of opinion that, the return of *Pocahontas,* by rendering services to the Colonists, would give permanence to the Settlement, and increase the value of his possessions. The estates which had descended to *Poca-*

[* Cf. Phettiplace and Pots, Arber, p. cxvii,—" But her marriage could no way have entitled him (Smith) by any right to the Kingdome."]

hontas spread over a vast tract of country; they extended to the South nearly as high as the falls of the great rivers, over the *Potomac,* even to *Patuxent,* in *Maryland.*

But the inscrutable wisdom of Providence had decreed, that *Pocahontas* was never more to return to her native soil. *Rolfe* had gone with her to *Gravesend,* for the purpose of embarking in a convenient ship; but fate interposed between the design and execution, and at *Gravesend Pocahontas* died.

To express the grief which afflicted *Rolfe* at the death of his wife, who had now for three years been alike the sharer of his sorrow and his joy; who at the age of nineteen, when her mind was every day acquiring an accession of piety, and her person growing more lovely to the sight, was snatched from him prematurely, and borne to the grave; to express his grief were an hopeless attempt, and can be conceived only by him who has been both a husband and lover.*

* *Godwin* in his Memoirs of *Mary,* takes care to inform us, that during the whole illness of that *enlightened* woman, which brought her to dust, *not one word of a religious cast fell from her lips.* It was a female who shewed me the passage, and her comment on it was, " Perhaps *Mary* might have ap-"propriated to herself the exclamation of the King in "*Hamlet,*"
>Pray I cannot,
>Though inclination be as sharp as will;
>My stronger guilt defeats my strong intent.

As the biographer of *Pocahontas,* I could contrast her dying

Pocahontas left one son, from whom are descended, by the female line, two of the most respectable families now in *Virginia;* the *Randolphs* and *Bollings.*

Thus have I delivered to the world the story of *Pocahontas*; nor can I refrain from indulging the idea, that it was reserved for my pen, to tell with discriminating circumstances, the tale of this *Indian* girl. No Traveller before me has erected a monument to her memory, by the display of her virtues; for I would not dignify by that name the broken fragment which is to be found in the meagre page of *Chastellux.**

. In the progress of my story I have adhered inviolably to facts; rejecting every circumstance that had not evidence to support it. When I was in *Virginia,* I spared no pains to collect those materials, which I have now digested into a regular and connected series; and, not content with tradition, I obtained recourse to records and original papers. In this part of my volume, I doubt not of enchaining the attention of the reader; the dangers to which *Smith* is exposed awaken a lively curiosity; the humanity of *Pocahon-*

moments with those of *Mary.* This amiable *Indian* beheld her approaching dissolution with that peace of mind arising from a confidence in the mercy of God, through Him whom he sent to redeem the world; and the last words that faultered on her lips were praises of the Almighty.

[* *Travels in North America in 1780-1782.* Part II, Ch. 4.]

tas exacts emotions of tenderness; and the heart is interested in her history from the moment she suspends by her interposition the axe of the executioner, till she draws her last breath on the shore of a foreign country.*

In eloquence the *Indians* of *America* have eminently distinguished themselves. The speech of *Logan,* a *Mingo* Chief, exhibits the force and sententious brevity of a *Demosthenes.* I cannot repress the impulse I feel to insert this oration; but it will first be proper to state the incidents that produced it.

A white man having been murdered on the frontiers of *Virginia,* by two *Indians* of the *Shawanese* tribe, the Colonists undertook to avenge the outrage in a summary manner. A Colonel *Cresap* collected a party and proceeded down the *Ranhaway.* A canoe of women and children, with only one man, was perceived at a distance. *Cresap* concealed his boat in a recess of the river, and crept with his men along the trees that covered its banks. The unsuspecting *Indians* passed on, when *Cresap* and his people, singling out their victims, killed the whole party.

It was the family of *Logan,* who had long been a friend of the whites. Such unprovoked cruelty raised his vengeance; and, taking an active part in the war that followed,

[* The author has used Smith's *True Relation,* and *General History.*]

he slew many of the Colonists, and adorned his wigwam with their scalps.

At length a decisive battle was fought between the *Indians* and Colonists; the *Indians* were defeated and sued for peace. The pride of *Logan* would not suffer him to be seen among the suppliants; but lest the sincerity of a treaty should be distrusted from which so illustrious a Chief withheld himself, he sent by messenger a speech to be delivered to the white people.

" I appeal to any white man to say, if ever
" he entered *Logan's* cabin hungry, and he
" gave him not meat; if he ever came cold
" and naked, and he clothed him not? Dur-
" ing the last long and bloody war, *Logan*
" remained idle in his cabin, an advocate for
" peace. Such was my love for the whites,
" that my countrymen pointed as they passed,
" and said, *Logan* is the friend of the white
" men! I had even thought to have lived
" with you, but for the injuries of one man.
" Colonel *Cresap,* the last Spring, in cold
" blood, and unprovoked, murdered all the
" relations of *Logan,* not sparing even my
" women and children. There runs not a
" drop of my blood in the veins of any living
" creature. This called on me for revenge.
" I have sought it; I have killed many; I have
" fully glutted my vengeance. For my coun-
" try, I rejoice at the beams of peace. But

"do not harbour a thought that mine is the "joy of fear. *Logan* never felt fear! He "will not turn on his heel to save his life! "Who is there to mourn for *Logan?*—Not "one!"

The *Indians* of *America* want only an historian who would measure them by the standard of *Roman* ideas, to equal in bravery and magnanimity the proud masters of the world. The descendants of *Romulus* were ever engaged in a perpetual succession of barbarous wars. These wars, dignified by the historic page, are read with veneration by the multitude; but the philosopher contemplates them through the same medium that he would a bloody conflict between the *Chipeways* and *Mawdowessies,* on one of the *Ottowaw* lakes. I know not why a *Catawba,* or *Cherokee* Chief, should not be considered a rival in greatness with a *Roman,* or a *Latian* leader.

If I understand aright the *Roman* history, war seems to have been the trade of the ancient *Romans.* To war they owed their origin, and they pursued it as a system. Let us compare with these dignified butchers the depreciated *Indians* of *America;* and if a love of peace be the criterion of a great character, how will a *Roman* shrink at the side of an *Indian.* The *Romans* were ever found to sheath the sword with reluctance; the *Indians* have been always ready to lay down the hatchet.*

That in humanity and all the softer emotions the Indians of America will rival the most polished nations of the world let facts establish. When, after a sanguinary war between the whites and the *Indians,* a treaty of peace was concluded on, no scene could be more affecting than the sensibility with which the *Indians* restored their captives to the *British.* The *Indians* were of the tribes of *Muskingham,* and the event took place in the camp of General *Bouquet.*

It was with eyes full of tears that the *Indians* brought their captives into the camp of their countrymen. They visited them from day to day, bringing the horses, furs, and skins, which they had formerly bestowed on them, while they composed part of their families; accompanied with every act that could display sincerity of affection. Nay, some even followed their white inmates to *Fort Pitt,* hunting for them by the way, and delighting to supply their provisions.

But a young *Mingo* War Captain, evinced by his actions that the spirit of chivalry may be found in the forests of barbarous tribes. *Wampanoag* had formed a strong attachment for a female captive of the name of *Helen*

[* Cf. Jefferson's *Notes,* 3rd Am. ed., New York. 1801, pp. 94-96.]

Hopkins, and now at the risk of being killed by the surviving relations of the many unhappy victims whom he had scalped, he accompanied *Helen,* who rode his caparisoned horse to the very frontiers of his enemies; assisting her to ford the rivers, decorating her with the plumage of the birds he killed in the woods, and throwing into his looks all the tenderness of a lover. The girl from the prejudice of education, could not refuse to accompany the whites to *Fort Pitt;* but when the party were to separate at the *Ohio,* all the woman rushed to her bosom; she clung to *Wampanoag* with distraction, called him by the endearing name of husband, and with the most bitter lamentations was torn from his arms.

Of the captives that were restored, many had been taken when children by the *Indians.* These had been accustomed to consider the *Indians* as their only relations; they spoke no other language but that of the *Shawanese;* and beholding their new state in the light of captivity, they separated from their savage benefactors with mournful reluctance.

On the parting of the *Indians* from the *British,* a *Shawanese* Chief addressed the white men in a short but humane speech. " Fathers, said the *Indian* warrior, we have " brought your flesh and blood to you; they " are our children by adoption, but yours by

"natural right. Inmates with us from their
"tender years, they are wholly unacquainted
"with your customs and manners; and there-
"fore we beseech you to treat them with kind-
"ness, that at length, they may become recon-
"ciled to you." *

It was my design to have spoken only of the *Indian* in what bore a relation to his moral character, but as the world has been long agitated relative to a particular circumstance of his physical construction, I cannot neglect the opportunity to produce a testimony or two upon the subject.

"It has been said," observes Mr. *Jefferson* in his Notes, "that *Indians* have less hair than
"the whites, except on their heads. But this
"is a fact of which fair proof can scarcely
"be had. With them it is disgraceful to be
"hairy on the body. They say it likens them
"to hogs. They therefore, pluck the hair
"as fast as it appears. But the traders who
"marry their women, and prevail on them to
"discontinue this practice, say that nature is
"the same with them as the whites." †

He who can read the concluding part of this sentence, in which Mr. *Jefferson* still maintains that tone of philosophic gravity which breathes throughout his Work, without

[* Cf. *Historical Account of Bouquet's Expedition against the Ohio Indians*, Philadelphia 1766. Reprint: Cincinnati, 1868, p. 77; p. 90.]

[† *Notes on Virginia.* 3rd Am. ed., p. 93; and p. 301.]

a smile, must possess more stoical composure than I. The dispute which has been so long *sub judice,* was not respecting the physical woman, but the physical man of the new world. The question in point was about beards. It was contended for by the philosophers of *Europe,* that the *Aborigines* of *America* were without any hair to their chins, and that not all the warriors of the six nations could furnish one respectable beard. From this peculiarity in the *American Indian,* inferences were deduced by no means favourable to the other parts of his physical conformation; for when philosophers have once established a position they are seldom slow in building upon it.

But the dispute has at last been decided, and the red man of *America* is restored to his physical dignity; it has been discovered that nature has been not less liberal in her gifts to the *Indian* than the *European;* that the *Indians* would have beards but that they will not suffer them to grow.

On a subject of such magnitude; a subject that has called forth every acuteness of disquisition from a *Buffon* on one side of the *Atlantic,* and a *Jefferson* on the other; whatever positive evidence can be produced, is entitled to serious attention. It is, therefore, with satisfaction I lay before my readers three certificates of unquestionable authority.

COLONEL BUTLER'S TESTIMONY.

The *Indians* of the Six Nations have all beards naturally as have all other nations of *North America* which ever I saw. Several of the *Mohocks* shave with razors, as do likewise several of the *Panees,* who have had an intercourse with *Europeans.* But in general the *Indians* pluck out the beard by the roots from its earliest appearance; and as their faces are therefore smooth, it has been supposed they were without this characteristical mark of their sex. I am even of opinion that, if the *Indians* were to practise shaving from their youth, many of them would have as strong beards as *Europeans.* (Signed)

(True Copy)   JOHN BUTLER,
Agent of *Indian* Affairs.
Niagara, April 12, 1784.

CAPTAIN BRANT'S TESTIMONY.

The men of the Six Nations have all beards by nature; as have likewise all other *Indian* nations of *North America,* which I have seen. The generality pluck out the hairs of the beard by the roots as soon as they begin to appear, and hence they seem to have no beard, or at most only a few straggling hairs, which they have neglected to eradicate. I am, however, of opinion, that if the *Indians* were to shave, none of them would be without beards, and that some would have very thick ones.

(True Copy.)   (Signed),
JOSEPH BRANT.
Schenectady, April 19, 1793.

MAJOR WARD'S TESTIMONY.

I brought up in my family at *Flat-Bush,* a young *Indian* of the *Montauk* nation, who inhabit the East end of *Long Island,* and having read with interest both *Buffon's* and *Jefferson's* philosophic chapter on beards, I would not neglect the fair opportunity which offered to determine the dispute of these great men by an appeal to experience. Directly the chin of this *Montauk Indian* became razorable, I put a razor into his hand, and taught him to shave; inculcating with all my powers of rhetoric how much importance there was annexed by the world to a beard; that a beard had a kind of mechanical operation upon the mind; that in ages of antiquity no man could be a philosopher without one, and that (the fellow had received a pretty liberal education) it was the opinion of Doctor *Swift,* that the reason *Daphne* fled from *Apollo* was because he had no beard.

This mode of reasoning, together with my own example (I am obliged to shave every morning), induced my *Indian protegé* to encourage a beard; he at first shaved every other day, but in the lapse of a twelvemonth he was obliged to have diurnally recourse to his razor; he has now what may be termed a handsome beard; it is dark, bushy, and repulsive; and before he reaches the age of thirty (he is now only twenty-three) he may, I am of opinion, appear with dignity at the Court of the Grand Turk.

(True Copy.) (Signed) GUY WARD.*
Long Island, June 15, 1795.

Upon this subject there can now be no more controversy. Facts will ever supersede speculation; and, however the casuist may argue, truth vindicates itself. The page of *Buffon* that relates to the beards of the Six Nations, may eternally enforce homage by the dignified march of its periods; for the page of *Buffon*, whether his subject be the creation of the first man, the *Arab* wandering in the desert, or the

[* This important documentary evidence is not at once traceable. Its reappearance in 1801 was to be expected. Colonel John Butler was the famous New York Tory; Cf. Hough, *Proceedings, Commissioners of Indian Affairs (New York).* 1783-1790, p. 145.

"This renowned warrior (Captain Joseph Brant) is not of any royal or conspicuous progenitors, but by his ability in war, and political conduct in peace, has raised himself to the highest dignity of his nation, and his alliance and friendship is now courted by sovereign and foreign states."

Patrick Campbell: *Travels in North America in the Years 1791 and 1792.* Edinburgh 1793. p. 188. Campbell spent several days very agreeably at Brant's house—pp. 188-211.]

Mohock wanting a beard, is ever found to blaze with magnificence, and sparkle with illustration. But it can bring no conviction to him who submits his book to his reason, and not his reason to his book.

About eight miles from the *Occoquan* mills is a house of worship called *Powheek* Church; a name it derives from a Run * that flows near its walls. Hither I rode on Sundays and joined the congregation of Parson *Wems,* a Minister of the Episcopal persuasion, who was cheerful in his mien that he might win men to religion.†

A *Virginian* church-yard on a Sunday, resembles rather a race-ground than a sepulchral-ground;‡ the ladies come to it in carriages, and the men after dismounting from their horses make them fast to the trees. But the steeples to the *Virginian* churches were designed not for utility, but ornament; for the bell is always suspended to a tree a few

* A Run is the *American* for a Rivulet.

[† "Weems, the biographer of many heroes, in whose hands the trumpet of fame never sounded an uncertain blast"— Rector of Pohick Church, Fairfax County—best known as the author of *The Life of George Washington: with curious anecdotes, equally honorable to himself, and exemplary to his young countryman.* Duyckinck, Vol. I, p. 484.]

[‡ Cf. Bayard, *Voyage dans l'intérieur des États-Unis, à Bath, Winchester, dans la Valleé de Shenandoah etc., etc., pendant l'été de 1791.* 2º éd. Paris. 1798. p. 168,—" Le lendemain, j'allai au temple avec tous les voyageurs: c'était un édifice en bois, autour duquel on voyait rangés des chevaux de prix, enharnachés avec luxe. Les galeries étaient pleines de

yards from the church. It is also observable, that the gate to the church-yard is ever carefully locked by the sexton, who retires last; so that had *Hervey* and *Gray* been born in *America,* the Preacher of Peace could not have indulged in his Meditations among the Tombs; nor the Poet produced the Elegy that has secured him immortality.

Wonder and ignorance are ever reciprocal. I was confounded on first entering the church-yard at *Powheek* to hear

Steed threaten steed with high and boastful neigh.

Nor was I less stunned with the rattling of carriage-wheels, the cracking of whips, and the vociferations of the gentlemen to the negroes who accompanied them. But the discourse of Parson *Wems* calmed every perturbation; for he preached the great doctrines of salvation, as one who had experienced their power. It was easy to discover that he felt what he said; and indeed so uniform was his piety, that he might have applied to himself the words of the prophet: " My mouth shall

négresses et de noirs endimanchés. Dans le bas, se trouvaient leurs mâitres et mâitresses, dont l'extérieur annonçait que tous étaient pénétrés de la sainteté du lieu, et de la solennité de la cérémonie. En revenant du temple, j'observai que les portes des maisons étaient fermées : elles le furent pendant tout le jour. M^de B— et ses filles se retirèrent après le diner, pour lire quelques chapitres de l'ancien et du nouveau testament : c'est ainsi que dans toutes les villes des États-Unis on célèbre le jour du dimanche."]

" be telling of the righteousness and salvation
" of Christ all the day long; for I know no end
" thereof."

In his youth, Mr. *Wems* accompanied some young *Americans* to *London,* where he prepared himself by diligent study for the profession of the church.* After being some months in the metropolis, it was remarked by his companions, that he absented himself from their society towards the close of the day; and conjecturing that the motive of his disappearing arose either from the heat of lust, or a proneness to liquor, they determined to watch his conduct. His footsteps were traced, and they found him descending into a wretched cellar that augured no good. But their suspicions were soon changed on following him into his subterranean apartment. They found him exhorting to repentance a poor wretch, who was once the gayest of the gay, and flatered by the multitude, but now languishing on a death bed, and deserted by the world. He was reproving him tenderly, privately, and with all due humility; but holding out to him the consolation of the sacred text, that his sins, red as scarlet, would become by contrition white as snow, and that there was more joy in the angels of heaven over one sinner that

[* The Bishop of London was the Diocesan of Virginia before the Revolution. Parson Weems was in London for his studies after 1781.]

repented, than over ninety-nine persons whose conduct had been unerring.

Of the congregation of *Powheek* Church, about one half was composed of white people, and the other of negroes. Among many of the negroes were to be discovered the most satisfying evidences of sincere piety; an artless simplicity, passionate aspiration after Christ; and an earnest endeavour to know and do the will of God.*

After church I made my salutations to Parson *Wems,* and having turned the discourse to divine worship, I asked him his opinion of the piety of the blacks. "Sir," said he, " no people in this country prize the Sabbath " more seriously than the trampled-upon " negroes. They are swift to hear; they seem " to hear as for their lives. They are wakeful, " serious, reverent, and attentive in God's " house; and gladly embrace opportunities of " hearing his word. Oh! it is sweet preaching, " when people are desirous of hearing! " Sweet feeding the flock of Christ, when they " have so good an appetite!"

How, Sir, did you like my preaching? Sir, cried I, it was a sermon to pull down the

[* Cf. Dr. Coke's *Journals* &c. London. 1793, p. 18,—" I sometimes give notice immediately after preaching, that in a little time *Harry* will preach to the blacks; but the whites always stay to hear him. Sometimes I publish him to preach at candle-light, as the Negroes can better attend at that time. I really believe he is one of the best preachers in the world."]

proud, and humble the haughty. I have reason to believe that many of your congregation were under spiritual and scriptural conviction of their sins. Sir, you spoke home to sinners. You knocked at the door of their hearts.

I grant that, said Parson *Wems*. But I doubt (shaking his head) whether the hearts of many were not barred and bolted against me.

I had been three months at *Occoquan,* when I so often caught myself stretching, yawning, and exhibiting other symptoms of *Ennui,* in my chair, that I began to be of opinion it was time to change my residence. My condition was growing irksome. There was no light, airy vision of a female disciple, with expressive dark eyes, to consider my instructions oracular; but I was surrounded by a throng of oafs, who read their lessons with the same tone that Punch makes when he squeaks through a comb.

I, therefore, resigned my place to an old drunken *Irishman* of the name of *Burbridge,* who was travelling the country on foot in search of an *Academy;* and whom Friend *Ellicott* made no scruple to engage, though, when the fellow addressed him, he was so drunk that he could with difficulty stand on his legs.

I remonstrated with Friend *Ellicott* on the

impropriety of employing a sot to educate his children. "Friend," said he "of all the "schoolmasters I ever employed, none taught "my children to write so good a hand, as a "man who was constantly in a state that bor-"dered on intoxication. They learned more of "him in one month, than of any other in a "quarter. I will make trial of *Burbridge.*" *

CHAP. IX.

Return from Occoquan to New-York.—Visit to Mr. George on Long Island.—Meditations among the Tombs.—I go to Baltimore.—Mammoth Cheese.—An Exchange of Letters with the Vice-President.—A Walk to Washington.—Congress assembled.—Debates.—Politeness of the Vice-President.—A Journey on Foot into Virginia by the Great Falls of the Potomac.—Get benighted.—A Hospitable Reception at a Log-house in the Woods.—A cast-away Sailor restored to the bosom of his Family.—The Story of Jack Strangeways.

IT was not without emotion that I quitted the Banks of the *Occoquan;* those Banks on which I had passed so many tranquil hours in study and meditation. I was about to ex-

[* Cf. Goldsmith,
"Logicians have but ill defined
As rational the human mind; . .
Homo est ratione preditum
But for my soul I cannot credit 'em."]

change the quiet of solitude for the tumult of the world; and was posting I knew not whither, without any object to my journeying.

I pass over the common occurences of the road to *Washington;* the contributions levied on my purse by the landlords of *Alexandria,* and those of the imperial city; but at *Baltimore* an accident happened, which I have still, under every combination of circumstance, in my memory's eye.

I had left *Peck's* tavern in the stage-coach at a very early hour of the morning, when, before we had proceeded half way down Market-street, one of the fore-wheels came off. The driver, on whose presence of mind the safety of the passengers depended, deserted his post in the moment of danger, and leaped from his seat. The horses being without any check, accelerated their pace, and I can only compare their speed to the rapidity of lightning. This was an awful moment. I expected every moment to be dashed in pieces; and determined to make one effort for my life, I leaped from the carriage into the street; an example that was soon followed by two other passengers. In my eagerness to clear the wheels, I leaped further than was necessary, and received a bruise in my forehead: but one of the other passengers was mangled by the flints in the road.

On looking up I could perceive nothing but

a flame before me, produced by the horses whose shoes struck fire as they flew; I followed the carriage with the third passenger, who had escaped unhurt, solicitous to know the fate of a sailor and a boy whom we had left in the coach. We overtook it at *Chinquopin-hill,* where the horses in their ascent had slackened their pace; and found the sailor and the boy holding the panting cattle by the reins. I congratulated them on their escape, but when I asked the sailor, Why he had not jumped from the carriage? " Avast there," said the tar, " more people are lost by taking to the " boat, than sticking by the wreck; I always " stick to the wreck!"

A fresh coach and horses conveyed us to *Chester,* where I supped with Monsieur *Pichon,* Embassador from *France* to *America;* and the next morning arrived at *Philadelphia* to breakfast.

I sojourned a week at *Philadelphia,* collecting what money was due to me for the sale of my Novel, and enjoying the converse of that *Mammoth* of literature, *Joseph Dennie,* whom I found seated in all the splendour of absolute dominion among his literary vassals.

I called on *Dufief:* but I found him so occupied in teaching *French,* and selling books, that he had neither leisure nor disposition for

[* The Baron Louis André Pichon, Consul-General, 1800-1805.]

the offices of friendship. *Dufief* informed me, that Doctor *Priestly* had called at his shop, and exchanged with him half a dozen copies of *Godwin's Political Justice,* for the sermons of *Massillon,* and some other religious works. " This," said the lively *Frenchman,* " was poor " barter, and I resembled the hero in the *Iliad,* " who exchanged a shield of silver for another " of brass."

From *Philadelphia* I travelled to *New-York,* partly by water, and partly by land. In the passage-boat to *Burlington* was a sweet girl of seventeen, whose voice was music; and who observed that the *Pennsylvania* shore of the *Delaware,* was much more pleasant than the *Jersey* side.

We got to *Burlington* a little before the going down of the sun. It is built on the *Delaware,* and at a place so near *Philadelphia,* I did not expect to be put in the same bed with another passenger. This passenger was going to *Canada,* and was accompanied on the road with two wagons loaded with bale goods.

The next day we passed through *Hiat's-town,* which is composed of a meeting-house, a public-house, and a blacksmith's shop. The next place of any distinction was *Cat's Tail,* from which to *Allen-town* is a rugged and almost insurmountable road, called *Feather-bed-lane!* Strange names these for a Christian country.

From *Amboy,* which terminated our land-travelling, we embarked for *New-York,** where I found a kind reception at the house of Major *Howe.* The next day I hastened on the wings of friendship to Mr. *George,* who was still employed on *Long Island* in his sublime academy.

I found his bardship walking and meditating near the *Dutch* church. He received me with transports. We repaired to his house, where I recounted to him my adventures; but he was impatient of my recital, and eagerly changed the subject to *Homer,* whose *Iliad* he made his manual. Nor did he forget to inquire if I had multiplied my wealth by school-keeping at *Occoquan;* rightly reflecting, that *et genus et virtus nisi cum Re vilior alga est* †
or in plain *English,* the man who wants money wants everything.

I expostulated with my friend. I represented to him that a base metal dug out of the earth was unworthy the care of a philosopher, who ought to contemn every pursuit that was not intellectual; and that the accumulation of

[* "There is not a little town on all this coast, but what has this kind of packets going to New York: such as New Haven, New London, &c. They have all the same neatness, the same embellishments, the same convenience for travellers. You may be assured there is nothing like it on the old continent." J. P. Brissot de Warville, *New Travels in the United States of America performed in 1788.* London, 1794 (translation). Vol. I, §§ *Newport to New York.*]

[† Hor. *Sat.* II, 5, 8.]

riches tended neither to enlarge the comprehension, nor elevate the fancy. No, Sir, said I, let not an avarice of money make inroads on your heart; the wants of a philosopher are few, for there is more tranquillity in an unenvied condition, than the opulence of large possessions.

My friend did not hear a word that I uttered. He sat studious and abstracted. You have approved, said he, my Elegy over the grave of a stranger in the woods of *Owendaw*. I have made an Epitaph on a similar subject.

> Like a tree in a valley unknown,
> In a region of strangers I fell;
> No bosom my fate to bemoan,
> No friend my sad story to tell.

Come! the weather invites us abroad. Let us walk into the church-yard; I will put *Hamlet* in my pocket; a single reflection of *Hamlet* is of more value than all the meditations of *Hervey*.

Death, said *George,* has mowed down many a lusty fellow in your absence. In that grave reposes a countryman of mine, who died of the yellow fever; an *Hibernian,* who unfortunately brought with him to this climate his habit of hard-drinking. Often has the alehouse here rung with plaudits at his wit; and often has the landlord's daughter sighed on contemplating the vigour of his herculean form. A brave fellow! he would have taken the Grand *Turk* by the beard; at the broadsword and cudgels he was the first in the village annals; but Death——

Cudgelled, said I, his brains out at last!

Who sleeps there?

A *New-York* merchant: only last week he was sitting in his counting-house, feasting his imagination with visions of bags of dollars. His clerks bowed to him with submission, and his servants watched every motion of his hand. But Death is not practised in the arts of ceremony, and he refused his mournful supplications of—A little longer! Oh! let me live a little longer! The writings of the eloquent *Burke* will supply his grave with an epitaph.

What is that?

Why,—His God was his gold; his country his invoice; his desk his altar; his ledger his bible; his church his exchange; and he had no faith but in his banker!

Who lies in that grave? No flower grows near it.

A *New-York* Reviewer. He spared writers of no sex or condition; nor has Death spared him. He is gone himself to be reviewed by the Great Reviewer of Reviewers.

From whose awful tribunal, said I, there is no appeal.

Who reposes there?

A poor negro! He was slave to Parson

Vandyke, and now sleeps in as good a bed as his master one day will. Fate had imposed hard burdens on him; but Death has taken them from his shoulders.

Who lies prostrate there?

The head-board tells you. *Drinkwater* the *Newtown* school-master, of unclassical memory. Where be his frowns now? Obliterated! Where be the terror his looks inspired? Alas! remembered only to be mocked at. The very school-boy that once trembled at his nod, spurns him with his foot as he gambols round his grave.

Who reclines there?

The toast of the village, the fairest of the maidens. She never left the village but the enamoured swains watched her footsteps till she had gone down the hill, passed through the valley, and could be seen no more. Oh! she was beautiful to look upon!

And has now worms for her chamber-maids!

Alas! nothing now of her remains but what the tomb has concealed. She was cropped like a flower in its bloom by the scythe of the mower. Her lover wastes the day in tears, frantic in grief: but alas! what part of his happiness will grief restore?

To whom does this grave belong?

A soldier in that grave has taken up his quarters, whose ears will never be disturbed by the sound of another trumpet, but the trumpet at the day of resurrection. This man, Sir, guarded the baggage-waggons, in the rear of the *American* army, at the battle of *Brandywine,* and from the big looks he assumed, and the egregious lies he told, in reciting the story, you would be disposed to imagine he had, at least, been the second in command. I knew him at *Albany,* where he kept a boarding-house. He could tell you who stood their ground, who ran away, and relate how seven stout soldiers were blown up by the bursting of a cohorn.*

Were these all his battles? He was modest compared to other men of war.

No, Sir. He thrice very narrowly escaped being scalped; for in his youth he had fought against the *Ohios,* the *Shawanoes,* the *Hurons,* the *Utewas,* the *Nadouessians,* and the *Messegagues.*

O! brave! And he lies here at last?

Yes, not redoubtable even to a worm: which, I presume, will be the case of *Suwarrow,* and *Arch-Duke Charles,* who now spread terror through the world.

Who lies silent, there?

A man who, when living, delighted to be heard. He belonged to a club of Jolly Dogs, where it was his constant practice to sit from seven till eleven every night, with a pipe in his

[* ' Small mortar for throwing grenades.']

left hand, and the handle of a porter-tankard in the other. Thus would he sit smoking and drinking, and bawling out, To order! with the lungs of a jack-ass. But his smoking and drinking incur no reprehension, for it benefited rather than injured society, by hastening his death. The calamity was that he threw that money to a bloated landlady which should have purchased food and raiment for an amiable wife, and four small children. His end may be conjectured. His very coffin was seized by his creditors, and his family went on the parish.

A jolly dog! truly! And here at last he lies?

Yes! never more to fill the tap-room with smoke and noise, never more to knock his tankard on the table, and cry landlady! Replenish! Never more to fill a chair with his corpulence, and be dubbed President by the porter-washed wits of the club. Never more to carol a bawdy song, and be joined in chorus of the whole room. Where be your songs now, my jolly dog? Your long-winded tales, which you dealt out over your cups? Your egregious lies, which by so often repeating, you believed at last yourself? Where be your horse-laugh now, that would have out-done the ha! ha! of *Job's* steed of thunder? Now get you to the club, my friend, and tell each jolly dog though he drains his draught of porter down, to this state must he come; make them laugh loud at that!

Who reposes in that grave?

The fat-landlady, who kept the porter-house in *Pearl-street,** and dealt out her draughts of malt to the Club of Jolly Dogs. A dropsy had distended her to the size of one of her porter-buts.

And into this underground cellar she is thrust at last?

Yes! after a life passed in administering her porter to drunkards, and scoring down each tankard with a piece of chalk over the chimney. Disgrace to the memory of that man who ran in debt with her landladyship, and discharged not the reckoning. It was then she would unpack her heart with words. "A " pretty Captain! Yes! A pretty Captain! " truly! He almost drank my cellar dry, and " I never saw the stamp or colour of his coin. " He was a *Villian,* he must have been a *Vil-* " *lian* or he would never impose upon a de- " fenseless widow-woman. But I never had " the courage to ax him for the money. He " swore so, that I shook like a leaf; I trembled " like a rush. And he talked so much about " his ship, and how he took in his small kites " to engage a privateer, that I never doubted " of his honesty. He has paid me indeed.

* Pearl-street is the longest street in *New-York.* It has the irregularity of the Strand without its animation.

" Yes, he has paid me with his fore-topsail,
" and a fair wind—the wind a little upon the
" quarter. But I may catch him yet; and,
" when I do catch him, there's no snakes in
" *Virginia,* if I don't bring his nose to the
" gridiron."

I did not fail to visit my old friends on *Long Island.* Parson *Vandyke* was afflicted with jaundice, but his wife was still as notable and narrative as ever. Farmer *Titus* had lost none of his accustomed hospitality; nor was Farmer *Moore* less kind to the stranger within his gates. Mr. *Remsen* continued to regale his guests with Madeira, and his sons were increasing their ideas under the tuition of my literary friend. Nor were the daughters of these worthy people less lovely, or less amiable. Joy be to *Newtown;* Joy to its rosy damsels; and may Heaven preserve their charms from decay!

I remained a week on *Long Island,* enjoying a renovation of intellectual felicity with Mr. *George,* when impatient of being without any determined pursuit, I again departed for the southward. It was *September,* 21, 1801; a day I shall ever remember in the annals of my life, as it was a day of separation from a more than fraternal friend, whom I have never since seen.

I embarked in the passage-boat for *Amboy,* from whence I travelled in the stage-coach to

Burlington, with a sea faring man, and an Indian *trader.* I had never met with such blasphemous wretches. Indeed, something might be advanced in extenuation of the sailor, whose mode of life was not favourable to external decorum; but the *Indian* trader was a man of at least three score years, who had mingled with reputable society.

Five miles from *Burlington* we crossed Ancocus Creek, and at a public-house on its border stopped to refresh our cattle. The old reprobate as usual staggered to the bar, and as usual vociferated for a glass of *clear brandy*. The sailor proposed drinking with him, and an interchange of oaths followed between them to the manifest discomfiture of a family of wayfaring Quakers, who were sitting before the fire, and who began to groan in concert. But the old sinner had no regard for the feelings of the devout; he heaped his imprecations on the whole house, because his mandate for a glass of brandy had been neglected by the landlord. Such characters are injurious to society from the contagion of example. I observed a boy in the house who laughed with gust at the oaths uttered from the old man's lungs, which were ulcerated with blasphemy.

Resuming our journey, a few miles brought us to *Penhausen-creek,* remarkable for its circular form, and transparent stream; and a little beyond it we stopped at a public-house, where a very pretty lively young woman was rocking her babe to sleep.

Our journey was now soon terminated, for in another hour we reached the *Jersey* bank of the *Delaware,* and were conducted in a large boat across the river to *Philadelphia,* where I separated without regret from my ruffian companions.

The sun was going down, and I sought for lodgings without delay. I proposed myself a boarder to a Quaker woman, whom I saw standing at her door. The good matron told me she was cautious how she took strangers, and inquired my connexions. What, pray, said I, do you charge a week for boarding in your house? She replied, four dollars. I put the money into her hands, and she was no longer importunate on the subject of my connexions.

I did not continue long in my lodgings. The manners of the family petrified me. The melancholy ejaculations of the old woman, who was striving to work out her salvation by groaning, together with the woe-gone countenance of her husband, whose head would have furnished the model of a bust for one of the Sages of *Greece,* conspired to drive me in search of another lodging, and I was received into the house of Madame *de Florian*, in whose company I wanted no domestic entertainment.

The name of Madame *de Florian* announces her to be a *French* woman. She lived in North third-street, with her two daughters, of whom one was between seventeen and eighteen, the other three years younger, and a son of five. My introduction to this family was curious.

At *Fouquet's* gardens,* rambling one afternoon in the shade, puffing vulcanoes of smoke from my segar, and indulging the most splendid reveries; I suddenly came upon Madame *de Florian* and her two daughters, who were drinking peaceably their coffee in one of the alcoves, while the little boy was fondling a lap-dog on the grass.

The spectacle of this interesting groupe suspended my steps, which being observed by the child, the little rogue danced towards me, and insisted upon having my segar.

The mother and sisters rebuked the child, but I instantly delivered my cigar to him and bowing, was about to pursue my ramble round the gardens, when Madame *de Florian,* with that grace of manner so peculiar to a *French* woman, accosted me with *Peut etre, Monsieur nous fera l'honeur de prendre une tasse de caffe?*

I bowed my acquiescence, and seated my-

[*"Between 10th and 11th, and Arch and Race Streets, where mead and ice-cream were sold"—1800-1818. Watson's *Annals* (Hazard), III, 400.]

self next the eldest daughter, who welcomed my approach with a smile of enchantment. And now all that I had read of a *Mahometan* Paradise rushed into my mind. The garden of Monsieur *Fouquet* was the blissful region and Mademoiselle *de Florian* the houri.

It is to Mademoiselle *de Florian* and a few other of her countrywomen, that the young ladies of *Philadelphia* owe their present graceful mien. The revolution in *France* produced a revolution in the walk of the *Philadelphia* damsels. Formerly the *American* ladies did not sacrifice to elegance in their walk; or, more properly speaking, they were without a model to form themselves upon. But when the revolution drove so many of the *Gallic* damsels to the banks of the *Delaware,* the *American* girls blushed at their own awkwardness; and each strove to copy that swimming air, that *nonchalance,* that ease and apparent unconsciousness of being observed, which characterized the *French* young ladies as they passed through the streets.* Men and

[* Dr. Schoepf observes, Vol. I, 129-130, "Die Musik war vor diesem lezten Kriege noch ganz in ihrer Kindheit. . . . Während des Kriegs und nach demselben aber, hat, durch die von den verschiedenen Truppen zurückgebliebenen Musikkundigen, sich der Geschmack weiter verbreitet, und man hat nunmehro in den grössten Städten Concerte und mit volistängiger Musik besezte Bälle. Für Tanzmeister hat Frankreich gesorgt." Cf. Robin, *New Travels*, &c.,—"Our military music, of which they are extravagantly fond, is then played for their diversion. At such times, officers, soldiers, Americans, of both sexes, all intermingle and dance together."]

women ran to their windows, and involuntarily exclaimed, Oh! heaven! look at that girl! how beautifully she walks!

A spirit of imitation was now kindled, and as both men and women never appear more ridiculous than when they affect qualties to which they have no pretensions, many a *Philadelphia* lady provoked the malice of laughter, when she strained every nerve to command the homage of admiration. Some sprawled, some kicked, some frisked, and it is recorded that one girl in despair threw herself into the *Schuylkill*. But, then, on the other hand, many polished their natural ease into elegance.

An *American* girl commonly throws me into a fit of profound thought, and to think in the presence of a woman is an insult to her sex. The vision of a *French* girl on the contrary, banishes all abstraction from my thoughts; and the natural tendency of my *English* mind to dulness is improved into vivacity.

I accompanied Madame *de Florian* and her family home; nor did I discover without secret rapture that this lady took boarders. She confined her number to two; there was nobody now in the house but one old gentleman, for a young officer who had lately occupied *une chambre garnie,* was gone to *Saint Domingo*. There was consequently space left for another, but how to get possession of this enviable spot without an introduction was the rub. At length, the present lodger made his appearance in the shape of Monsieur *Lartigue,* —whom I had accompanied once from *Philadelphia* to *Charleston* in the packet. Not more astonished stood *Hamlet,* at seeing his royal father, than I on beholding Monsieur *Lartigue;* but our mutual astonishment was soon converted into joy, and the old man fell on my neck weeping like a school-boy. What coxcomb was it observed the *French* had no feeling?

The scene was affecting; and I could perceive the eye of my Houri brimful of tears.

I desired Mr. *Lartigue* to introduce me to Madame *de Florian* and her daughters; their countenances brightened; my proposal of becoming a lodger was accepted with, *You do us honour!* and when the porter brought my trunks, I heard *Adelaide* direct him what room to carry them into, with a kind of *Saint-Preuxish* emotion.

Month of happiness that I passed under the same roof with *Adelaide de Florian!* Happiness never to return beneath the cloudy sky that now frowns on me as I look towards it.

At the *Indian* Queen, in fifth-street, (every sign in the United States, is either an *Indian* Queen, or a Spread Eagle) I sometimes lounged away an hour with some young men from *Charleston.* " Where do you board," they all asked me,—" With a *French* lady."

"Some *Creole,* I suppose.—Why not take "your quarters up here? I hate *French* cus- "toms. They never drink tea unless they are "sick."

And what were the customs of these young gentlemen who plumed themselves on their knowledge of mankind, and their travelled air? When not engaged with eating, they were sitting in the street before the door of the *Indian* Queen, drinking punch cooled with ice, and obscured in volumes of tobacco smoke. It is true, their discourse did not turn on bullocks. But they were either laughing over their nocturnal adventures in *Mulatto Alley,* at *Charleston;* or recommending each other to different brothels at *Philadelphia.* Nor was the stream of their conversation ever diverted, unless some young lady (who, finding the pavement blockaded by their chairs, was compelled to walk in the carriage-road,) called forth the exclamation of "That's a fine "girl! So is that coming up the street now. "There are no snakes if *Philadelphia* does not "beat *Charleston* hollow! See there again, at "the tailor's window. Harry! I'll go over and get measured for a coat to-morrow." *

At this juncture (it was a beautiful moonlight night) an *American* girl from an opposite window sung, with uplifted sashes, a song to a circle of ladies and gentlemen in the room. This custom is very prevalent at *Philadelphia*

[* Cf. Philip Vickers Fithian, *Journal* &c. 1767-1774. p. 260.]

and *New-York;* and it evinces there is still left in those towns some simplicity of manners.

The voice was melodious; the shake * excellent. And when the song was concluded, the lads from *Charleston* gave it their applause. Some were in high raptures. Encore! Encora! Bravo! Bravissimo! followed close upon the warbling.

In some countries this insolence would have been resented. The gentlemen would have rushed down stairs, and exchanged a pass or two with the street critics. Here it was widely different. The ladies continued to warble in succession; the *Carolinians* grew tired of applauding; and at length, each crossed his arms and contented himself with puffing smoke from his segar.

Not being able to obtain any employment at *Philadelphia,* I thought it best to embark for *Baltimore,* and I took my passage in the *Newcastle* packet. The wind was fair, the sky serene, the water smooth, and we passed *Chester* and *Wilmington* with great rapidity.

A good dinner on board the Packet, and the conversation of a motley groupe, enlivened my spirits; and I provoked the laughter of the master of a ship lying at *Newcastle,* whose fore-top-sail was loose, and whose destination was *London.* How my heart danced at the sound of that name! How my fancy conjured

[* 'In music—a melodic embellishment; a trill.']

up the *Thames,* and the spires of the city to my view! How delectably did I behold myself seated in the bosom of my friends, and how appalled was I when these illusions vanished, and I perceived before me the shores of *Pennsylvania* and *New-Jersey!* Oh! if these are prejudices, let me hug them to my breast, and far away be the philosophy that would deprive me of my feelings.

We landed at *Newcastle,* and were bounded in two coaches to *French-town,* which is a journey of sixteen miles. We stopped to bait our cattle at *Glasgow,* and at *French-town* found a surly landlord, and sorry accommodations. Our number was sixteen; and for sixteen passengers there were only six beds; hence the large beds lodged three, and the small beds two passengers. For my part there being a good fire, I proposed to sit up all night and make an *Indian* file with our feet to the fender; but sleep overcame me, and I retired to bed, undisturbed by the nasal trump of my bed-fellow who snorted like a horse. It is not unworthy of remark, that the landlord would not suffer cards to be played in his house; and that the negro-girl, who waited at supper, wearing a man's hat; a Quaker in company aspired to be witty by calling her *Cæsar.*

The following morning we all embarked again for *Baltimore;* * and on the passage a

[* The Chesapeake and Delaware Canal was begun in 1804,

Yankee diverted the company by producing a favourite cat that he had stolen from the landlord, (who had refused him a pack of cards) and making the poor animal eat a yard or more of tobacco. His method was ingenious. He placed the cat over a chair, and confining forcibly her feet, untwisted a roll of tobacco; the cat in the agony of pain snapped at any thing that was offered her, and the Mountebank Traveller ministered his tobacco.

We dined again on the water. Among the passengers was a pretty, modest, blushing maiden of fifteen, whose manners were not inelegant; but it is somewhat curious that whenever she wanted the salt, or mustard, she begged some one to shove it to her.

Pool's Island is half way to *Baltimore,* which we passed about noon: but in the evening we got round *Fell's Point,* and at eight secured our vessel at *Bowly's* Wharf; having *Federal-Hill* on our opposite side.

It was the opinion of the ancient philosophers that nature endowed man with language to express his wants; but this notion has been exploded by the more enlightened moderns; for it is an observation founded on every day's experience, that no man is so likely to get his wants redressed as he who keeps them secret;

but the work was not completed until 1829. Cf. Scharf, *Hist. of Maryland,* Vol. II, p. 524.]

the disclosure of poverty exciting only the insolence of contempt.

The true use of speech, therefore, is not to express our wants but to conceal them; and in conformity with this maxim, I kept it a profound secret, on my landing at *Baltimore,* that I had very little money left in my pocket. I accompanied with affected gaiety a young fellow to the city of *Strasburgh,*[*] who told me he always lodged there, and extolled the house for its convenience of accomodation, and the landlord for the suavity of his manners.

Mr. *Wyant* received us with a smile of welcome, and supper being ready, ushered us into a room, where twenty guests were sitting at table, who appeared to be mutes; for no man uttered a syllable, but each seemed by his looks to have just come out from the cave of *Trophonius.*

During my sojournment at *Baltimore,* a cheese of no ordinary dimensions was landed from a vessel to be transported to Washington. It was a present from the farmers' wives and daughters of *Cheshire,* in *Massachusetts,* to the President of the United States; and was entrusted to the pious care of one Mr. *Leland,* a Baptist Minister, who is said to have smoked

---

[* The tavern seems to have been called 'City of Strasburgh.']

his pipe in solemn silence the whole of his travels both by land and by water.*

I know not the weight of the "greatest "cheese in the world," but it was I believe equal in circumference to the hind-most wheel of a waggon. Its extraordinary dimensions induced some wicked wag of a federalist to call it the *Mammoth Cheese;* and by this name it is known throughout the States of the Union.

The curiosity of the inhabitants of *Baltimore* was universally excited; men, women, and children flocked to see the Mammoth Cheese. The taverns were deserted; the gravy soup cooled on the table, and the cats unrebuked revelled on the custards and cream. Even grey-bearded shop-keepers neglected their counters, and participated in the Mammoth infatuation.

The cheese was drawn in a waggon to the city of *Washington* by four horses richly caparisoned, which were furnished the pious Mr. *Leland,* by the Republicans of *Baltimore;* and the President of the United States received the present with every polite acknowledgment, and invited the Republican Members of the Senate and House of Representatives *to tender it the homage of their respects, and the respects of their homage.*

[* John Leland, 1754-1841, who lived in Virginia from 1776 to 1790, and is said to have baptized 700 people there. The cheese weighed 1,450 pounds.]

I had advertised in the *Baltimore* Paper for the place of domestic Tutor, and one morning, while I was standing before the door of the city of *Strasburgh,* the bar-keeper brought me a note very carefully sealed. I eagerly took it from his hand, impressed with an idea that it was sent me by some opulent merchant who wanted an instructor for his children; and already was I delighting my fancy with the rewards of knowledge, when on opening the note it produced what *Rabelais* calls the most gloomy of all moments, the payment of a landlord's reckoning.

" SIR,
" According to the custom of the house, Mr.
" *Wyant* has requested me to send in your bill.
" To eight days board, at 9*s,* 4*d.*——£3 14*s.* 8*d.*
" I am, for Mr. *Wyant,*   John *Kellen.*"

I called Mr. *Wyant* into a private room. He obeyed the summons with a true *German* smile. Wait, Sir, said I, a few days. He started back, rolling wildly his eyes. " Mine Got! " cried he, " if I wait a few days, how " can I go to market? " I will give you, said I, my note of hand. Note of hand! cried he. Mine Got! I have a drawer full of notes of hand. Well, said I, pray leave your damnable face and I will pay you the cash tomorrow.

I had been informed that Mr. *Burr* was at

the Federal City; and the Federal City, as one of our Travellers in *America* solemnly remarks, is only forty-three miles from *Baltimore*. I was determined, therefore, to give him a missive by the post; and my missive was *a la Quin*.

Sir, I am at *Baltimore*.

The next mail brought me a letter from Mr. *Burr,* which dissipated the clouds that obscured the horizon of my life. He did not make answer, like *Quin's* correspondent, Stay there, and be d—d; but in a letter breathing kindness, and protestations of friendship, desired me to send him the estimate of the expences of my late travels, which he proposed immediately to reimburse.

I retired to my room, and computed, with *diplomatic accuracy,* my unavoidable expences on the road, from the day I crossed the *Hudson* till I descended the *Treasury*-stairs at the Imperial City. The answer of the Vice-President will evince that he did not think himself overcharged.

DEAR SIR,

You Men of Letters are the worst calculators in the world. I am persuaded I only discharge a just debt, when I enclose double your amount.

Accept the assurances of my regard,

AARON BURR.

At this letter my pride took alarm. It produced from me an answer, and a restitution of half the bills.

> SIR,
> As I cannot possibly descend from the respectability of a Creditor to the degradation, if I may be allowed the expression, of an Eleemosynarist; I decline receiving more than half of what you remitted me.
> I am,
> With profound respect, &c.

Being proffered a situation in a part of *Virginia* I had not visited, and having it in my power to journey at my leisure by the friendship of the Vice-President, I departed without regret from *Baltimore,* on foot and alone.

It was the latter part of *March* when I left the *once-flourishing town of Baltimore,*[*] and again directed my steps towards the imperial city. But my mind was somewhat altered. Experience had cured me of my illusions. I was no longer elated with the hope of being lifted above the crowd; but my ambition was contented with the harmless drudgery of teaching children their rudiments.

After walking a few miles, I turned into a wood to call at the house of a brother-peda-

[* Trade fell off after the establishment of peace in Europe. Course of Maryland exports: 1799, $16,299,609; 1801, $12,767,530; 1802, $7.914,225. Scharf, Vol. II, p. 604.]

gogue, who had invited me the preceding evening at a public-house, to visit him in his literary retirement. Boys and girls rent the air with their acclamations as I approached the dwelling; but the School-master's daughter, a lusty lass of nineteen, escaped into the woods, and I could only catch a glimpse of her flying across the green. I was not *Apollo* or I should have followed this *Daphne.*

The board placed above Mr. *Macdonald's* sylvan Academy diverted me not a little. " *Anthony Macdonald* teaches boys and girls " their grammar tongue; also Geography "terrestial and celestial.——Old hats made as " good as new."

But Mr. *Macdonald* was not at home; his daughter had fled and I trod back the path to the main-road, where I sought an asylum under the roof of the Widow *Smith,* who regales the woe-begone Traveller with whiskey; and

"Where the gaunt mastiff growling at the gate,
"Assaults the stranger whom he longs to eat."

Old age is garrulous, and the Widow did not want for talk. She *admired* that Miss *Macdonald* instead of staying in the house to receive a stranger, should run into the woods. For her part she was never *scared* at folks, however well-dressed; and yet all her life she had lived in the country.

Pursuing my journey, I arrived at *Elk-*

Ridge Landing, where I supped at a genteel tavern with the hostess and her sister, who are remarkable for the elegance of their conversation, and the amenity of their manners. I found the old Manor-house of *Charlotte Smith* lying on the table, of which the concluding part seemed to have been moistened with tears of sensibility.

The next day I resumed my walk; refreshing myself at *Spurrier's,* carousing at *Dent's,* and sleeping at *Drummond's;* three public-houses on the road, which the Traveller passes in succession. The weather was somewhat warm in the middle of the day; but this only made the springs more grateful, at whose waters I stopped to allay the thirst produced by walking.

Rousseau in enumerating the pleasures of pedestrian traveling, makes no mention of the joy with which the solitary walker beholds a spring on the road; from which omission I am inclined to believe that the foot-travels of the eloquent *Swiss* were performed round his chamber.

The next morning proceeding forward, I reached *Bladensburgh* before the going down of the sun; and at night-fall to my great satisfaction I entered the imperial city. The moon was rising from the woods, and I surveyed the Capitol by its light, meditating on the future state of the Western Empire; the clash of interests, the commotions of Demagogues, and the disunion of the States! But dumb be the Oracle of Prediction!

Congress was assembled at *Washington,* and I was constant in my attendance on the Senate and the House of Representatives. The Senate Chamber is by far the most superb room in the Capitol, but the House of Representatives is a detached and temporary building. Yet, I loved best to visit the House of Representatives; there seemed to be so much energy and freedom of debate. It is unknown I presume to few of my readers that the Vice-President of the United States is President of the Senate. Mr. *Burr* was presiding in the Chair, and no man knew better the routine of the House, or how to acquit himself with more dignity than he.

I watched an opportunity to make the Vice-President my salutations as he came out of the Capitol. I remembered the advice which old *Polonius* gave his son when he was about to travel and I was then travelling myself.

"The friends thou hast, and their adoption try'd,
"Grapple them to thy soul with hooks of steel."

The Vice-President demonstrated no little pleasure to see me, and his chariot being at the steps of the Capitol, he took me home with him to dine. I forget how many Members of Congress were present at the dinner; but, though Republicans, I did not think they had all an equal voice, for some spoke much louder than others.

A reduction had already taken place of the judiciary system of the United States; that is, the superfluous Judges were dismissed, who under the preceding Administration had unnecessarily augmented the expences of civil Government; and the object of the Republican party in the House of Representatives was to obtain a repeal of the Internal Taxes; comprehending excises, stamps, auctions, licenses, carriages and refined sugars.

The most eloquent in debate was Mr. *Randolph*. He was *Demosthenes,* but *Demosthenes* who had sacrificed to the Graces. He spoke full an hour for the repeal of the tax on domestic distilled liquors; that is, whiskey, and peach,* and apple brandy. At the conclusion of the debate the Speaker very solemnly exclaimed, " Those who are for the repeal are to say aye! and they who are against it are to say no." The affirmative monosyllable immediately resounded from every quarter of the building. Aye! Aye! Aye! followed

[* Cf. Castiglioni, *Viaggio negli Stati Uniti.* Milan. 1790, I, 217,—" Dove si fa molto uso dell' acquavite di pesco, e della birra di *Persimon*. I Peschi sono tanto abbondanti nella *Virginia,* che spesse volte tagliando un bosco di Pini, questi alberi fruttiferi, che prima non potevano moltiplicare per l'ombra, vi crescono ben tosto in tanta quantità, che in breve tempo coprono tutto il terreno."]

in rapid succession; upon which the Speaker with much gravity proclaimed, "The ayes "have it! The Bill has passed."

I took great interest in this debate, for I consider whiskey very cheering; but I thought it curious that a Member from *Virginia* should stand up for the repeal of the tax upon that liquor, which now it is become cheaper, will throw many of his countrymen off their feet!

Having amused myself a few days at the imperial city, I rose with the sun, and pursued my journey along the banks of the *Potomac*. About nine in the morning I reached the bridge at the *Little Falls;* a bridge that raises the admiration of an *American,* but provokes only the contempt of an *European.** In fact art in *America* would not detain an intelligent Traveller one hour; but nature would perhaps enchain his attention for years.

Near the bridge at the *Little Falls* my journey was suspended by the rain, and I found a reception in the tavern of Mr. *Slimner, a German,* who at the age of threescore was smitten by a young *English* woman, whom he

[* "Of the same kind as the bridge of Merrymack, near Newbury-port, in Massachusetts: the same architect was employed in both; . . . an immense quantity of timber and iron wasted on it." La Rochefoucauld, Vol. II, p. 334. "Mein Rath also ist die Gelehrten und Künstler bleiben zu Hause." *Der Freistaat von Nordamerika in seinem neuesten Zustand.* Dietrich von Bülow. Berlin. 1797. II, 107.]

had taken for his wife, and who had brought him a child; a child the darling of his dotage, which he ludicrously termed " his little young woman cut shorter."

The rain not remitting its violence, I was obliged to pass the night under the roof of this fond couple, whom, I, however, left at an early hour the next morning to prosecute my journey; purposing to take the more circuitous road of the *Great Falls* of the *Potomac*.

I pass over in silence the common occurrences of the road; the waggoners who returned no answer to my interrogations, and the plantation-curs that disturbed my reveries with their barking. About noon I reached the cross roads, and taking to the right, I could every minute hear more distinctly the roar of the *Great Falls*. At length I came to a spacious stream called " Difficult Run "; an appellation derived from the difficulty in crossing it. But no place could be more romantic. On one bank towered a majestic mountain, from the side of which rocks hanging in fragments menaced the Traveller with destruction; while others that had tumbled into the stream interrupted its course, producing a tumultuous roar that absorbed the cry of the water fowl hovering over the waves.

I was in suspense whether to ford this Run, or wait for a guide on its bank, when I descried two boys on the opposite shore who obeyed my call with alacrity; leaping from rock to rock till they reached the spot where I stood. With the assistance of a pole they conducted me to the opposite bank, where I learned that one of my young guides was called *Basil Hurdle,* and the other *Jack Miller.*

I now ascended a hill that led to the *Great Falls,* and on a sudden my steps were suspended by the conflict of elements, the strife of nature. I beheld the course of a large river abruptly obstructed by rocks, over which it was breaking with a tremendous roar; while the foam of the water seemed ascending to the clouds, and the shores that confined it to tremble at the convolution. I gazed for some time in silent awe at this war of elements, when having recovered from my admiration, I could not help exclaiming to the Great Maker of Heaven and Earth, " Lord! What is man " that thou art mindful of him; or the son " of man, that thou regardest him! "

For several hours I continued gazing at these Falls, lost in musing over the grandest object the Universe can supply; and when I beheld the wilderness around me, I could not but be impressed with the idea that nature delighted to perform her wonders in the secrecy of solitude.

The obstruction of these Falls to boats conveying the produce of the interior country to

Alexandria and the city of *Washington,* has been obviated with unremitted labour by the construction of locks; and large boats ascend and descend without much difficulty.) Of these locks it may be expected that I should give some account; but after the noble spectacle of the Falls, I had no disposition to examine an Aqueduct devised probably by the incitement of avarice or luxury. When I journeyed fifteen miles out of the beaten road, it was not art but nature that called me.

A little below the Falls, on the bank of the *Potomac,* stand a few scattered buildings, which form a kind of hamlet called *Charlotteville.* The first settler in this savage wilderness was the Lady of General *Lee,* from whose christian name the place takes its appellation.*

At a house of entertainment kept by Widow *Myers,* I was accommodated with a supper and a bed. This buxom Widow was by persuasion a Methodist, and possessed of considerable property.

Into what part of the world has not Love found his way? The goat herd in *Virgil,* discovered him to be an inhabitant of caverns; and the Widow *Myers* acknowledged his power in the Wilderness of the *Potomac Falls.* The muscular form of a young *Scotchman* enchained the glances of the pious Widow; whose eyes seemed to say to the brawny

[* This seems not to be fact.]

Caledonian, " Stay me with flaggons, comfort
" me with apples; for I am sick of love!"

On leaving the *Great Falls* of the *Potomac* I was followed by a dog, whose attendance I rather encouraged than repulsed. I was tired of travelling alone, and I wanted a companion.

An *European* who has confined his travels to his own country, can have but a very imperfect idea of the forest scenery of *America.* His imagination familiar only with open and clear grounds, will scarce form an adequate conception of the endless and almost impenetrable woods in the Western Continent: It was through such woods that I now journeyed with an accession of cheerfulness from the company of my dog; and smoking tobacco in my march, with which I never went unprovided.

I never remember to have felt a more perfect exemption from care than in my journey from the *Potomac Falls.* I rioted in health and I. walked forward *oblitus meorum et obliviscendus ab illis.* I embraced the Universe as my country, and it was wholly indifferent to me where I terminated my pilgrimage; for whether I ended my days in the wilds of the *Potomac,* or the close of *Salisbury, the earth and its bands would have been about me for ever.*

I eat my dinner in a log-house on the road. It was kept by a small planter of the name of

Homer. Such a tavern would have raised the thunder and lightning of anger in the page of my brother travellers in *America.* But the lamented scarcity of *American* inns is easily accounted for. In a country where every private house is a temple dedicated to hospitality, and open alike to Travellers of every description, ought it to excite surprize that so few good taverns are to be found? When, therefore, the Travellers through the United States, curse in their pages of calamity the musquitoes, and fleas, and bugs, and ticks that interrupt their slumbers, they make the eulogium of *American* hospitality.*

The inhabitants of these woods are remarkably prolific; they obey at least one of the divine injunctions,—they increase and multiply their species. Mr. *Homer* was out felling the lofty trees of the forest, but Mrs. *Homer* was sitting by the fire, surrounded by half a dozen girls and boys and giving a bosom of maternal exuberance to a child she held in her arms. A curly-pated boy and girl were eating their dinner on the hearth; it seemed to be short commons; for after thrust-

[* Cf. Wansey's *Journal,* p. 111,—"We entered the city [Philadelphia] by Front Street, and arrived at the city Tavern in South-second-street, about noon. I slept at this house two nights and met with my old tormentors, the bugs."—The author has reference particularly to Isaac Weld, who left the United States 'without the slightest wish to revisit the American continent.']

ing their fingers into the platter, they licked them with great gusto. Come, you eat the sop, cried the boy, the egg belongs to me. No it don't, said the girl, for mammy's hen laid it.

Leaving the hut of Mr. *Homer,* I walked vigorously forward, indulging the hope I should get to *Frying-Pan* before night. But before dusk I found myself bewildered in the woods, whose solitude was rendered more melancholy from the cry of the owl. I had given myself up for lost, and was taking the flint from my pocket to kindle a fire, and pass the night under a tree, when the sound of the axe chopping wood rejoiced my hearing. Not more delightful was sleep ever to the weary, or water to the thirsty, than the sound to my ear.

Guided by the noise of the axe, I got to a tobacco plantation; but I had scarce leaped the fence when a couple of huge dogs assailed me, barking, advancing and retreating, all in a breath. Now, thought I, if these curs were to devour me, what an ignominious death would terminate my pilgrimage on earth. Fear is not only an ignoble, but dangerous passion; and, had I turned and endeavoured to escape from these blood-hounds, it is a hundred to one but I had been seized in that part where honour is said to be lodged.

I, therefore, stood my ground, and called

lustily to the house. My cry was not unheard; the door was opened, and a lad advanced with a light, which he had fixed in a calabash.

The way, my friend, if you please, to *Frying-Pan*.

"*Frying-Pan!* 'Tis a right difficult road
" to find in the dark. You must keep along
" the worm-fence — *Jowler!* begone — hush
" your mouth, there, you *Rover!*—begone, I
" say, you bloody.—You must keep *strait*
" along the worm (i. e. *crooked*) fence, till
" you come to a barn—but I would advise
" you to avoid the brush-wood about the barn,
" because of a nest of rattlesnakes—and the
" old one is mighty savage.—Well—when you
" have left the barn on your right, take the
" path that leads into the woods, and keep the
" main road the whole way, without turning
" either to the right or left, till you come to
" the track of the wheel—then cross right over
" into the next wood, and that will bring you
" to *Frying-Pan* Run—and, then, you could
" not go wrong if you was to try at it." *

My friend, will you favour me with a draught of water?

Yes, sure. Come walk with me into the

[* Thomas Anburey, Letter 63, Feb. 12, 1779 (Vol. II, p. 338-39) gives at length similar directions furnished him, and remarks, "It requires the most retentive memory to be able to proceed at all, if unaccustomed to the roads." The Bœotian sometimes knows no better, and again he twits the foreigner of condescension.]

house. You *Rover,* hush your noise, you *negur.*—*Jowler!* if you don't hush, I'll make you rally for something.

On entering the log-house, I found a man sitting with his wife and five children, before a blazing fire of wood. My reader, do you not envy me the sensations with which the strings of my heart vibrated on beholding this domestic groupe? The weary Traveller, after losing his way in the awful woods of *America,* stoops to enter at the door of a little log-house, and happy to be once more in the society of his fellow-creatures, finds the roof under which he has got shelter large enough for his heart's desire.

Hospitality is the prominent feature in the character of a *Virginian:* and I had a presentiment that I was housed for the night. When I had drunk my water, which tasted the more delicious, from being administered to me by a fine girl of seventeen, (she had two pitch-balls stuck in her head for eyes,) I rose to depart; but the man of the house accosted me, saying, " Be content, I pray you, and tarry " here all night; the day is grown to an end: " to-morrow I will send my son to put you in " the way."

The children now considered me as one of the family, and moving their chairs, made room for me to come within their circle.

My dogs, said the man, gave you a rally.

But I reckon it was the little dog you brought with you, that made them so savage.

Oh! my! what a pretty little lap Foist, cried the eldest girl. Indeed, indeed, he's right beautiful.

Mary, said a boy about nine years old, he's for all the world like the little dog that *Jack Hatchet* bought of 'Squire *Carter's* driver. He's spotted just like him. I'll lay you he came out of the same bitch.

Do hush, *Bill,* said *Mary.* The gentleman brought the dog with him from *England.*

An *Englishman* once, said the eldest son, borrowed a dog of me, and he was ashamed to return him. He carried him to *England.* If I was ever to go there, I would make a point to find the dog out. How big, Sir, is *England?*

Nearly, Sir, as big as the State of *Virginia.*

(Oh! *Mary,* said the next sister, what a great big place!)

Then, said the young man, I should give it up for a bad job. I did not reckon that *England* had been bigger than *Prince William County.*

Supper (that is tea) was now got ready; nor was it without a grateful emotion that I beheld the mother of this worthy family unlock her Sunday cupboard, and hand her eldest daughter part of a loaf of sugar for the repast.

Wilmot, the eldest son, now departed. I

discovered afterwards that he was courting the daughter of Mr. *Strangeways'* neighbour, whom he never failed to visit after the labour of the day. It was plain he was a lover by the care he took in adorning his person; changing his *leggings* * for a pair of *Philadelphia*-made boots, and his frock for a fashionable *coatee*.† The first character of love is a diffidence of pleasing.

After supper we again drew round the fire. —I had for some time perceived an unusual blaze in the chimney; but supposing it to come from an oven, I said not a word.

At length the good woman exclaimed, The plague! there's our chimney on fire again. We must pull down the rubbish, or we shall get no peace.

Mr. *Strangeways* now rose with great composure, and seizing a large staff, went out to the back of the chimney, where he raked away the rubbish; while *Mary,* catching up a gourd, filled it thrice with water, and helped to extinguish the conflagration.

As the night advanced, I could not but meditate upon the place my worthy host designed for my repose.

I formed a hundred conjectures. He surely would not cherish me in the bosom of his numerous family? And yet I could perceive only one room in the house.

* *Indian* stockings.
† *Coatee* is the *American* for a short coat.

There were three beds in the room. Of these I discovered that the back one belonged to the two eldest girls; for while Mr. *Strangeways,* his wife, and I were yawning in concert over the fire, I perceived *Mary,* from the corner of my eye, steal softly to her nest, and slip in under the clothes; an example that was quickly followed by *Eliza,* who, with equal archness, crept in by her side.

Pure and simple innocence! To dread no eye, and to suspect no tongue, is the prerogative of the family to whom these manners belong.

At length Mr. *Strangeways* asked me if I was willing to go to bed, and upon my replying in the affirmative, he fetched a ladder from an out-house into the room, and having placed it against the wall, he ascended a few steps, and opened a trap-door in the rafters, which I had not perceived led to a cock-loft.

Did you ever mount a ship's ladder, said Mr. *Strangeways?*

I replied, that I had a thousand.

Then, said he, be kind enough to follow me.

I followed, without betraying the least emotion of surprise; none but a rustic would have uttered an exclamation at the novelty of the staircase. I found a decent bed in the room appropriated to my reception; and, when Mr. *Strangeways* had opened and closed the shutter of the window in a manner which, after travelling so long in *America,* I could not but understand; the worthy man bade me a good night, and left me to my repose. I soon fell asleep; nor were my slumbers disturbed by the vision of an exorbitant landlord, appearing, to levy contributions on my purse, with a long bill in his hand.

I rose the next morning with the sun, and descended my ladder. The family were all stirring. The father and sons were at the plough, the mother was getting ready breakfast, and the two girls were at their spinning-wheels. The sound of these instruments was not quite so harmonious as that of a piano; but I know not whether a woodland nymph giving rapid motion to her spinning-wheel, be not a more captivating object than a haughty town-dame running her fingers disdainfully over the keys of a harpsichord.

Mary's breast knew not the restraint imposed by the depravity of the world.

When I came down, she replied to my salutations of the morning, by saying, (her spinning-wheel still in rapid motion) Oh! Sir! I am so sorry! indeed! indeed! indeed!—upon my word and honour—your little dog is gone back home!

My dog, cried I, gone back home! I fear, Miss, you advised him to go.

No, Sir, returned the girl, indeed! indeed!

a double indeed! a hundred indeeds! I asked him to stay.

Do, *Mary,* said the mother, hush your nonsense. Could your asking make the dog stay?

Why, mother, said the girl, I reckoned by his going to lie down at the door, that he wanted to go back; so I talked to him, and told him if he knew when he was well off he would stop and be my dog.

Your dog, cried the mother. How comes that about?

Why, mother, replied the girl, did I not make the gentleman promise me last night, that he would leave the dog under my care till he travelled this road again. Pish! said the mother, you cannot child take care of yourself.

The brother entered just as the last sentence escaped the lips of the girl. What! *Mary,* said he. So you made the gentleman promise he would travel this road again!

Do, *Wilmot,* said the girl, hush. Don't take me up before I am down.

Fags! *Mary,* said *Wilmot,* I believe you will be both up and down often enough yet before you die. We have all our ups and downs in the world.

Do, mother, cried the girl, tell *Wilmot* to hush. I know what! I wont mend his coat that's out of elbows—I wont for spite—and then he can't go to the dance at *Newgate.*

Yes, said *Wilmot,* I can go to the dance at *Newgate.*

Yes, said *Mary,* but will *Rose* dance with you?

No matter, rejoined *Wilmot,* I will get *Eliza* to patch the elbows. You'll do it for me *Eliza*—I know now for a flying squirrel's nest—and I'll save the prettiest one for *Eliza.*

I'll patch your elbows for you, brother, said the other girl. Is the squirrel's nest on the plantation.

And when the stranger's dog, said *Mary* comes back, I shall be better off than *Eliza.*

And when the stranger comes back, said *Wilmot,* What then?

What then? Mr. Inquisitive, said *Mary,* why I reckon father will not shut his door against him.

Not I, said the father, putting on his coat as he entered the room. We are all fellow-travellers in this vale of tears; and it becomes us in our pilgrimage to behave with loving kindness to each other. The stranger shall always find a home under this roof.

Sir, said I, I acknowledge your hospitality. But no man ought to account himself at home till he enters into the house of his heavenly father.

Right, Sir, said the man. We are only sojourners here below. Our race is soon run. Our duty is to tarry here patiently till we are received into the house of our common father; and heaven will be doubly sweet to him who has borne afflictions without repining.

The family now sat down to breakfast, and the stranger within their gates. But where, said the father, is *Bill?*

Why I reckon, said *Wilmot, Bill* is gone to look for the gentleman's dog. I heard him halloo in the woods.

In a few minutes *Bill* returned, skipping like a young hart upon the mountains.

Well, *Bill,* said *Wilmot,* what is become of the dog. Why I reckon, cried *Bill,* he is gone back to the *Great Falls.* If I had know'd he intended to go, I would have tied him up in the stable. He was a right pretty dog. He was just such another as *Jack Hatchet* bought of 'Squire *Carter's* driver.

The morning was ushered in with rain, which continued throughout the day. It was the wet season in *April,* a time very favourable to the planting of tobacco.

I, therefore, continued housed. I had got into pleasant quarters; and I opposed but feebly Mr. *Strangeways,* who insisted with much hospitality that I should *tarry* another night under his roof.

I passed the day in talking with *Mary,* and gazing on her dark eyes. She had dressed herself with no little coquetry; and I could perceive when she contemplated her white frock and blue sash, that she thought herself a finer lady to-day than she was yesterday. Enviable Maid! with her, dress and happiness were synonimous terms.

We had breakfast next morning, and the old man was gone to cultivate his tobacco, when a pedlar came to the door. The appearance of *Sam Lace* lighted up joy in the eyes of *Mary* and *Eliza*.

The pedlar first exhibited his ballads. " Here," said he, " is the whole trial, examina-
" tion, and condemnation of *Jason Fairbanks*,
" who was executed at *Philadelphia* for cut-
" ting off *Peggy Placket's* head under a hedge
" on the road to *Frankfort*."

Lord! said *Eliza,* what a wicked fellow. I would not live in one of those great big towns for all the world! But I wonder whether it is true?

True! replied *Mary,* certainly it is. Don't you see it is in print.

" And here," cried the pedlar, " is the ac-
" count of a whale that was left ashore by the
" tide in the bay of *Chesapeak,* with a ship
" of five thousand tons in his belly, called
" the Merry Dane of *Dover.* She was the
" largest ship ever known."

And is that true, too,? said *Eliza*.

True! cried *Mary*. How can you ask such a question? Do you think they would put it in print if it was not true?

Come pedlar, said I, let us examine the contents of your box. Have you any ear-rings?

At this interrogation I could perceive the bosom of *Mary* rise to her chin.

Yes Sir, said the fellow, I have ear-rings that would be an ornament to the ears of the President's lady. I have them at all prices—from five dollars down to one and a half. My five dollar pairs are fit for the first tip top, quality breeding.

Let me see some, said I, that are fit for the first tip top, quality breeding.

There, said he, is a pair—and there is another, that a duchess need not be ashamed of. I sold the fellow pair last week to 'Squire *Cartwright's* lady in *Gloucester County*.

I thought the heart of *Mary* would have burst from its bondage. It made her little bosom heave up and down like a bird that was dying.

Mary, said I, do me the favour to accept that pair of ear-rings; and *Eliza,* I beg you will take the other.

Eliza had put on her little straw bonnet to visit Miss ——, at the shrine of whose beauty *Wilmot* was offering his incense; and she now danced off with an accession of happiness from the present I had made her. The pedlar strung his box over his shoulders, and seizing his staff, pursued his journey through the woods.

And now it was necessary to separate from the family of the log-house in the woods. Yet, I could not leave *Mary* without emotion. Oh! my reader, if you are a lover of a happy face, it would have done your heart good to have beheld the countenance of this *Virginian* damsel, when her mother had hung the earrings to her ears. The spinning-wheel no more revolved with the magic of her hand. *Mary* was sitting crosslegged (I hope I need not gut this naughty word of its vowels) in her chair; and had placed on her lap a little looking-glass, in which she was beholding herself. She uttered not a word. Real happiness is not loquacious; the mind under its influence is content with its own sensations.

I now rose to go. The mother and *Mary* were the only tenants of the log-house. I bade the Dame good bye.

I wish, said the worthy woman, that *Wilmot* was here. The gentleman will never find his way out of the woods. My daughter, do put on your bonnet, and shew the gentleman in the way to the main-road.

Mary rose with alacrity; she slipped on her bonnet: and having taken a parting look at the glass, conducted me through the plantation.

I gave the little wood-nymph my arm, and

we walked forward together. The mockingbird was singing; his song never appeared to me so sweet before.

At length, after walking half a mile, we emerged from the wood, and reached the track of the wheel.

And now, *Mary,* said I, once more farewell. Her cheek was crimsoned, and the redness of her lips heightened, from the exercise of walking. I would fain have tasted them; coral was not to be compared to their hue; and the nether one, a little more prominent than the other, looked as if some bee had newly stung it.

We both stood some minutes in silence. If peradventure, now, thought I, I should give a pressure to that lip, what effects might ensue. There may be a subtile poison lurking in its moisture. It might doom me to pass the remainder of my days in a house roofed with shingles.

Mary, said I, farewell. And let my advice go with you. Confide not for ornament in the rings that hang in thy ears, but in the virtue that dwells in thy bosom. For when thou art deceived though thou clothest thyself with crimson, though thou deckest thee with the ornaments of gold, though thou rentest thy face with painting, in vain shalt thou be fair.

After walking a mile and a half, I met a boy sauntering along, and whistling, probably, for want of thought. How far, my boy, said I, is it to *Frying-Pan?* You be in the pan now, replied the oaf. I be, be I, said I. Very well.

Frying-Pan is composed of four log-huts and a Meeting house. It took its name from a curious circumstance. Some *Indians* having encamped on the Run, missed their frying-pan in the morning, and hence the name was conferred on the place.

I did not deign to stop at *Frying-Pan,* but prosecuted my walk to *Newgate;* where in the piazza of Mr. *Thornton's* tavern I found a party of gentlemen from the neighbouring plantations carousing over a bowl of toddy, and smoking segars. No people could exceed these men in politeness. On my ascending the steps to the piazza every countenance seemed to say, This man has a double claim to our attention; for he is a stranger in the place. In a moment there was room made for me to sit down; a new bowl was called for, and every one who addressed me did it with a smile of conciliation. But no man asked me where I had come from, or whither I was going. A gentleman is in every country the same; and if good-breeding consists in sentiment, it was to be found in the circle I had got into.

The higher *Virginians* seem *to venerate themselves as men;* and I am persuaded there was not one in company who would have felt embarrassed at being admitted to the presence and conversation of the greatest Monarch on earth. There is a compound of virtue and vice in every human character; no man was ever yet faultless; but whatever may be advanced against *Virginians,* their good qualities will ever outweigh their defects; and when the effervescence of youth has abated, when reason asserts her empire, there is no man on earth who discovers more exalted sentiments, more contempt for baseness, more love of justice, more sensibility of feeling, than a *VIRGINIAN.*

At *Newgate* my pilgrimage was nearly at an end; for Mr. *Ball's* plantation was only distant eight miles,—and it was he whom I was going to visit. But it was now necessary to bestride a horse; for in *Virginia* no man is respected who travels on foot; and as a man of sense will conform with the customs of every country, (and at *Rome,* as my Lord Chesterfield elegantly observes, kiss either the *Pope's* great toe or his b—k—e,), I put myself to the expence of a horse, and with the argument of a stick I prevailed on him to advance.

CHAP. X.

MEMOIR OF MY LIFE

IN THE WOODS OF VIRGINIA

There be some sports are painful; but their labour
Delight in them sets off; some kinds of baseness
Are nobly undergone; and most poor matters
Point to rich ends. This my mean task
Would be as heavy to me, as odious; but
The mistress, which I serve, quickens what's dead,
And makes my labours pleasure.—Hear my soul speak!
I am in my condition, a Prince, *Miranda;*
I do think a King; and but for thee,
I would no more endure this wooden slavery,
Than I would suffer the flesh-fly blow my mouth.
The very instant that I saw you, did
My heart fly to your service; there resides,
To make me slave to it; and, for your sake,
Am I this patient log-man.
SHAKESPEAR.

Reception at Pohoke.—An Old Field-School.—A fair Disciple.—Evening Scene on a Plantation. Story of Dick the Negro, &c. &c. &c.

THE rugged and dreary road from *Newgate* to *New-Market,* in *Prince William County,* is bordered by gloomy woods, where the natives of the State, and emigrants from *New Jersey,* cultivate on their plantations *Indian* corn, wheat, tobacco, and rye. After passing *Bull Run,* a stream that takes its appellation from the mountains of the same name, the Traveller comes to the intersection of two roads, and is in suspense which to take. If he travels the left it will bring him to the unaccommodating town of *New-Market,* where publicans * and sinners waste the day in drinking and riot; but the right will conduct him to the hospitable plantation of Mr. *Ball,* who never yet shut his door against the houseless stranger.

Having come to *Bull Run,* I stopped at a kind of waggoner's tavern on its border, to inquire the way to the plantation. Old *Flowers* the landlord, reeled out of his log-hut towards my horse, but was too much intoxicated to make a coherent reply; so giving my steed his head, I was all passive to his motions, till overtaking an old negro man, I demanded the road to Mr. *Ball's.* The old negro was clad in rags, if rags can be called cloathing; he was a squalid figure of sixty, and halted as he walked; he was grunting somewhat in the manner of an old hog at an approaching shower of rain; and he carried a hickory stick in his right hand, with which he was driving the cattle home from pasture.

Is this the way, old man, to Mr. *Ball's?* Aye, Master, I'm going there myself; and should have got to the plantation a couple of hours before sun-down, but the red bull was

* Tax Gatherers.

strayed after old mother *Dye's* heifers, and it cost me a plaguy search to find him in the woods.

Good company on the road, says *Goldsmith,* is the shortest cut, and I entered into conversation with the negro.

Then you live with Mr. *Ball?*

Aye, Master, I live with the 'Squire, and do a hundred odd jobs for him. You're going to see him, I reckon; some friend it's like enough. The 'Squire is a worthy gentleman, and I don't tell a word of a lie when I say he would not part with me for the best young negro that was ever knocked down at vendue.* There was 'Squire *Williams* of *Northumberland* wanted to tempt him, by offering for me a young woman that was a house-servant, a *seamster*, and could work at the hoe. But old birds is not to be catched with chaff. No! No! says Master, I shant easily meet with the fellow of *Dick* again; he is a gardener, a flax-beater, and a good judge of horse-flesh. No! No! if I part with *Dick,* I part with my right-hand man.

Has your Master a large family?

Aye, a house full of children. Four and three makes seven. There's seven young ones altogether; four girls and three boys. Master *Waring* is a sharp one; he found a nest of bees in the woods, which I reckoned nobody

* Auction.

know'd anything about but myself; and will make nothing of climbing a hickory after an owl's nest, and pulling out young and old by the neck. Concern it, an owl always scares me. He'll turn his eyes round and round, and look all manner of ways at once!

Have you good hunting in the woods?

Aye, rat it, Sir, I reckoned you was coming to hunt with Master. But, God help us, hunting is all over; the *New Jersey* men have cleared the woods. When I was a lad, I used to track the wolves on the snow, and never tracked one that I did not catch.* Master, I don't tell you a word of a lie, if you'll believe me, when I say that in one winter I got fifteen dollars reward from the Justice at *New-Market,* for the heads of wolves. And then there was such mighty herds of deer; the woods was *fested* with them. We would not take the trouble to hunt them: all we had to do, was to tie a bell to the neck of a tame doe, and turn her into the woods. A little after sun-down, we got ready our guns, and stood behind the out-house. Presently we could see the doe trot towards home, followed by half a dozen bucks prancing after her. Then we

[* Cf. Dr. Coke's *Journals*, p. 42,—" So romantic a scene, I think I never beheld. The Wolves, I find, frequently come to our friend's fences at night, howling in an awful manner; and sometimes they seize upon a straying sheep. At a distance was the *Blue-Ridge,* an amazing chain of mountains."]

crack away at them all together, and hie! they come tumbling down by *hundreds!*

The conversation of the negro held me engaged till we got to the plantation; I then gave him my horse, and walked through the garden to the house.

In my way through the garden I passed two young ladies gathering roses, who, however immured in the woods, were clad with not less elegance than the most fashionable females of *Europe*. They were beautiful in face and form; I asked them with a bowing mien, whether Mr. *Ball* was at home. They replied, that their papa was in the parlour, and with much sweetness of manner directed me by the shortest path to the house.

Mr. *Ball* received me with undissembled accents of joy; he said he had long expected my coming and was gratified at last. A nod to a mulatto boy placed refreshments on the side-board, and in a few minutes the family assembled to take a peep at the Schoolmaster.*

The first impression made by Mr. *Ball* decided that he was a Gentleman; and I was not a little delighted with the suavity of his manners, and the elegance of his conversation.

[* The author seems to have had no trouble in finding employment. The matter of education was at this time still a difficult one. Cf. Richard Parkinson, *A Tour in America in 1798, 1799, and 1800*. London, 1805, Vol. II, p. 474,—"I one day called on a gentleman of the name of Benj. Delany, Esq., at Shooter's-Hill, near Alexandria; and when I was introduced

When the children withdrew, I entered on the terms of my proposed engagement, and presented to him a letter which I had been honoured with from Mr. *Jefferson*. I knew my host to be a *Virginian* who favoured the Administration, and thought a letter from the President would operate on him like witchcraft. But I was unacquainted with my man. Mr. *Ball* was not to be biassed by the whistling of a name; he read my letter more from complaisance than any motive of curiosity; observed, that a man's conduct could alone decide his character; congratulated himself upon the acquisition of a man of letters in his family; and offered to engage me for a twelvemonth, at a salary of a hundred guineas. I acknowledged the honour he did me, and engaged with him for a quarter of a year.

The following day every farmer came from the neighbourhood to the house, who had any children to send to my Academy, for such they did me the honour to term the log-hut in which I was to teach. Each man brought his son, or his daughter, and rejoiced that the day

to him, it was in a place at a distance from the house, in the garden, which he called his office. He was instructing his children. He told me he had been so troubled to get his children educated, that at last he had found more satisfaction in doing it himself than pursuing any other method. He told me his eldest son was at Annapolis College; and when he came home in the holidays, his manners were such, that he was disagreeable to him; and as for the boys he had at home, he had an intention of sending them to England."]

was arrived when their little ones could light their tapers at the torch of knowledge! I was confounded at the encomiums they heaped upon a man whom they had never seen before, and was at a loss what construction to put upon their speech. No price was too great for the services I was to render their children; and they all expressed an eagerness to exchange perishable coin for lasting knowledge. If I would continue with them seven years! only seven years! they would erect for me a brick seminary on a hill not far off; but for the present I was to occupy a log-house, which, however homely, would soon vie with the sublime College of *William and Mary,* and consign to oblivion the renowned Academy in the vicinity of *Fauquier Court-House.* I thought *Englishmen* sanguine; but these *Virginians* were infatuated.

I now opened what some called an *Academy,** and others an Old Field School; and, however it may be thought that content was never felt within the walls of a seminary, I, for my part, experienced an exemption from

* It is worth while to describe the *Academy* I occupied on Mr. *Ball's* plantation. It had one room and a half. It stood on blocks about two feet and a half above the ground, where there was free access to the hogs, the dogs, and the poultry. It had no ceiling, nor was the roof lathed or plastered; but covered with shingles. Hence, when it rained, like the nephew of old *Elwes,* I moved my bed (for I slept in my Academy) to the most comfortable corner. It had one window, but no glass, nor shutter. In the night to remedy this,

care, and was not such a fool as to measure the happiness of my condition by what others thought of it.

It was pleasureable to behold my pupils enter the school over which I presided; for they were not composed only of truant boys, but some of the fairest damsels in the country. Two sisters generally rode on one horse to the school-door, and I was not so great a pedagogue as to refuse them my assistance to dismount from their steeds. A running footman of the negro tribe, who followed with their food in a basket, took care of the beast; and after being saluted by the young ladies with the curtesies of the morning, I proceeded to instruct them, with gentle exhortations to diligence of study.

Common books were only designed for common minds. The unconnected lessons of *Scot*, the tasteless Selections of *Bingham*, the florid Harangues of *Noah Webster*, and the somniferous Compilation of *Alexander*,* were

---

the mulatto wench who waited on me, contrived very ingeniously to place a square board against the window with one hand, and fix the rail of a broken down fence against it with the other. In the morning when I returned from breakfasting in the " great big-house," (my scholars being collected,) I gave the rail a forcible kick with my foot, and down tumbled the board with an awful roar. "Is not my window," said I to *Virginia*, " of a very curious construction?" " Indeed, indeed, "Sir," replied my fair disciple, "I think it is a mighty "noisy one."

[* Caleb Alexander's *Young Ladies' and Gentleman's In-*

either thrown aside, or suffered to gather dust on the shelf; while the charming Essays of *Goldsmith,* and his not less delectable Novel, together with the impressive work of *De Foe,* and the mild productions of *Addison,* conspired to enchant the fancy, and kindle a love of reading. The thoughts of these writers became engrafted on the minds, and the combinations of their diction, on the language of the pupils.

Of the boys I cannot speak in very encomiastic terms; but they were perhaps like all other school boys, that is, more disposed to play truant than enlighten their minds. The most important knowledge to an *American,* after that of himself, is the Geography of his country. I, therefore, put into the hands of my boys a proper book, and initiated them by an attentive reading of the Discoveries of the *Genoese;* I was even so minute as to impress on their minds the man who first descried land on board the ship of *Columbus.* That man was *Roderic Triana,* and on my exercising the memory of a boy by asking him the name, he very gravely made answer *Roderic Random.*

Among my male students was a *New Jersey*

structor; William Scott's *Lessons in Elocution* and *English Grammar* was widely used at that time, both in this country and in England; Caleb Bingham's *American Preceptor* went through 64 editions, 640,000 copies.]

gentleman of thirty, whose object was to be initiated in the language of *Cicero* and *Virgil*. He had before studied the *Latin* grammar at an *Academy School* (I use his own words) in his native State, but the *Academy School* being burnt down, his grammar, alas! was lost in the conflagration, and he had neglected the pursuit of literature since the destruction of his book. When I asked him if he did not think it was some Goth who had set fire to his *Academy School,* he made answer, " So, " it is like enough."

Mr. *Dye* did not study *Latin* to refine his taste, direct his judgment, or enlarge his imagination: but merely that he might be enabled to teach it when he opened school, which was his serious design. He had been bred a carpenter, but he panted for the honours of literature.

Optat ephippia bos; piger optat arare caballus.
Hor.*

Such was the affectation or simplicity of this man, that he expressed his fears the *English* students would interrupt the acquirement of *Latin*. Not knowing whether to storm or laugh, I advised him to retire with his books into *Maddison's Cave.*

The *Blue Ridge Mountains* were in sight

[* Epist., I, 14, 43,—
 Optat ephippia bos piger, optat arare caballus.]

from the plantation of Mr. *Ball,* and the rays of the descending sun gilded their summits. But no situation could be more dreary. It had neither the wildness of nature, nor the uniformity of art; and in any month of the year would inspire an *Englishman* with thoughts of suicide.

I never saw slavery wear so contented an aspect as on *Pohoke* plantation. The work of the slaves was light, and punishment never inflicted. A negro, who had run away, being brought back by a person who recognized him, he was asked by Mr. *Ball* the reason of his elopement. Because, said the fellow, I was born to travel. This man I presume was a predestinarian.

On the Sabbath the negroes were at liberty to visit their neighbours. Woman, of whatever colour, delights in finery; and the girls never failed to put on their garments of gladness, their bracelets, and chains, rings and earrings, and deck themselves bravely to allure the eyes of the white men. Nor are they often unsuccessful; for as the arrow of a strong archer cannot be turned aside, so the glance of a lively negro girl cannot be resisted.

The verse of *Virgil* will apply to the people of Virginia:

Alba ligustra cadunt, vaccinia nigra caduntur.*

[* *Ecloga* II, v. 18. Cf. La Rochefoucauld, *Travels* &c. II, 42, 82.]

Several families from *New Jersey* were settled in the neighbourhood. The characters of men are best illustrated by comparison, and it may not be useless to compare the *Jersey* man with the native *Virginian*.

The *New Jersey Man* puts his hand to the plough; the *Virginian* only inspects the work of his farm. The *New Jersey Man* lives with the strictest economy, and very seldom visits or receives visits. The *Virginian* exceeds his income, loves to go abroad, and welcomes his guest with the smiles of hospitality. The *New Jersey Man* turns every horse out to labour, and walks whither he has to go on business; the *Virginian* thinking it degrading to be seen on foot, has always his riding nag saddled and fastened to the fence. The *New Jersey Man* is distinguished by his provincial dialect, and seldom enlarges his mind, or transfers his attention to others; the *Virginian* is remarkable for his colloquial happiness, loses no opportunity of knowledge, and delights to shew his wit at the expence of his neighbour. Neither a dancing-master, a pedlar, or a maker of air balloons, was ever encouraged by a *New Jersey Man;* but on a *Virginian* they never fail to levy contributions. The treasury of the pedlar is in vain laid open to the eyes of the *New Jersey Man:* neither the brilliant water of the diamond, the crimson flame of the ruby, nor the lustre of the topaz has charms to allure him; but the *Virginian* enamoured of ornament cannot gaze on them with impunity; he empties his coffers of every dollar to adorn the apparel of his wife and daughters.

Of my female students there was none equal in capacity to *Virginia*. The mind of this fair creature was susceptible of every culture; but it had been neglected, and I opened to her worlds of sentiment and knowledge.

Geography was one of our favourite studies. The greatest trifler can scarce inspect a map without learning something; but my lovely pupil always rose from it with a considerable accession of knowledge. Imparting such new ideas was no undelightful employment, and I often addressed my rose of May in an appropriate Ode.

ODE

TO VIRGINIA, LOOKING OVER A MAP

POWERFUL as the magic wand,
Displaying far each distant land,
Is that angel hand to me,
When it points each realm and sea.

Plac'd in geographic mood,
Smiling, shew the pictur'd flood,
Where along the *Red Sea* coast,[*]
Waves o'erwhelm'd the *Egyptian* host.

[* "Sea-coast" in text.]

Again the imag'd scene survey,
The rolling *Hellespontic* sea;
Whence the *Persian* from the shore,
Proudly pass'd his millions o'er.

See! that little Isle afar
Of *Salamis* renown'd in war;
Swelling high the trump of fame
With glory and eternal shame.

And behold to nearer view,
Here thy own lov'd country too;
Virginia! which produc'd to me,
A pupil fair and bright like thee!

It was my desire to open to my pupil the Treasures of *Shakespeare;* of that poet whose works will be studied with increasing rapture on the banks of the *Mississippi,* the *Ohio* and *Potomac,* when the language in which *Voltaire* reviled him shall have perished with the wreck of nations. But the Library of the plantation did not supply the poet of nature; and I was almost in despair, when on a shelf in a miserable log-house I found the first volume of *Theobald's* edition. The book I obtained for a trifle, and I removed it to my school.

I shall not easily forget the feeling with which my pupil read aloud that beautiful and natural scene in the Tempest, where *Miranda* sympathizes with *Ferdinand,* who is bearing logs to *Prospero's* cell. No scene can be more exquisitely tender, and no lips could give juster utterance to the speeches of its characters than those of my fair disciple. Her voice possessed more magic than *Prospero's* wand. I was transported into fairy land. I was rapt in a delicious dream from which it was misery to be waked. All around was enchantment. And what *Ferdinand* had before exclaimed on hearing the music of *Ariel*, I applied in secret to the voice of *Virginia*—

> *This is no mortal business, nor no sound*
> *That the earth owns!*

The female mind seems peculiarly adapted to relish tender poetry; and in the Elegy of *Gray* and the Ballad of *Goldsmith*, I spread before my pupil a rich banquet to exercise reflection. Such poets are ever read with advantage for they embellish nature and virtue with an elevated but chaste imagination.

My pupil was perhaps not a regular beauty; but her form was exquisitely delicate; and there were a spirit and expression in her countenance that charmed more than mere regular features. Her hair was rather light for eyes perfectly black.

> *Viola mon Eleve: il faut encore y joindre*
> *Un petit nez, mais un nez fait au tour,*
> *Nez retroussé comme le veut l'Amour.*

As the studies of my pupil never tired, so the relation of them will never fatigue me.

She learnt *French* with avidity, and it was no unpleasant task to hear her give utterance to the musical language of a *Sevigné*. The Epic Narrative of *Fenelon*, and the pathetic Tale of *Saint Pierre*, were the *French* books that most delighted her. But she thought the translation of *Paul* and *Virginia* from the pen of Miss *Helen Maria Williams*, more beautiful in her attire than that of the author. "The Sonnets," exclaimed *Virginia*, "are so "pretty. Indeed! Indeed! Sir, they are."

The Rose, the queen of flowers, and theme of the *Persian* poets, grew abundantly in the garden; and my girls never came to school without having gathered clusters of them to decorate their dress. Hence I breathed only fragrance in a circle of loveliness.

How unspeakably delightful was the employment of cultivating the taste of *Virginia!* By the magic of the Belles Lettres I was opening the avenues of her innocent heart to friendship and to pity; I was exciting its natural susceptibility for every mild and tender passion that can soften humanity.

Let the gloomy and austere moralist condemn woman to vegetate on the earth. Let him shut from her those sources of pure and exalted pleasure, arising from the contemplation of the sublime and the beautiful. Such inhibitions become the cynic in his cell; but let a man of the world and of elegant education ask his heart what conveyed to it such transports in the company of a particular female. Was it the lustre of the eye? the redness of the lip? or the peculiar conformation of the features? No. The beauty of countenance which captivates a soul exalted by education, depends not upon any known rule of proportion, but is connected with sentiment; it is the emanation of intellectual excellence, the beaming forth of that moral sense which imparts a magic to every look, and constitutes expression. Women, like men, without education, are not of a social but gregarious nature. They herd together, but they exchange no ideas. And there is certainly the same difference between an educated and unducated woman, as between one living and one dead.

Succession is only perceived by variation, and in the delightful employment of *teaching my lovely pupil all I knew,* the hours of the morning were contracted to a moment by the earnest application of my mind to its object; time took a new pair of wings, and the schooldoor, which faced the south, had the sun staring full upon it, before I recollected that my attention ought to be divided, and not consecrated to one scholar.

Hence I frequently protracted the studies of the children till one, or half past one o'clock; a practice that did not fail to call forth the exclamations both of the white and the black people. Upon my word, Mr. *Ball* would say, this gentleman is diligent; and Aunt *Patty* the negro cook would remark, "*He good cool-mossa that; he not like old "Hodgkinson and old Harris, who let the "boys out before twelve. He deserve good "wages!*"

Having sent the young ladies to the family mansion, I told the boys to break up; and in a few minutes they who had even breathed with circumspection, now gave loose to the most riotous merriment, and betook themselves to the woods, followed by all the dogs on the plantation.

Let the reader throw aside my volume, whose mind feels disgust from the images afforded by a school in the woods of *America*. I deprecate not his severity; I write not for such feelings. But, reader, if thou art a father, or if thy mind uncorrupted by the business and vanities of life, can delight in the images of domestic privacy, thou wilt derive more real satisfaction from the picture of a groupe of school-boys at play, than from the conflict of the *Austrians* with the *French* on the plains of *Maringo*.

There was a carpenter on the plantation, whom Mr. *Ball* had hired by the year. He had tools of all kinds, and the recreation of Mr. *Dye,* after the labour of study, was to get under the shade of an oak, and make tables, or benches, or stools for the Academy. So true is the assertion of *Horace*, that the cask will always retain the flavour of the liquor with which it is first impregnated.

Well, Mr. *Dye,* what are you doing?"

I am making a table for the *Academy-School*.

What wood is that?

It is white oak, Sir.

What, then you are skilled in trees, you can tell oak from hickory, and ash from fir?

Like enough, Sir. (A broad grin) I ought to know those things; I served my time to it.

Carpenter.—I find, Sir, Mr. *Dye* has done with his old trade; he is above employing his hands; he wants work for the brain. Well! larning is a fine thing; there's nothing like larning. I have a son only five years old, that, with proper larning, I should not despair of seeing a Member of Congress. He is a boy of *genus;* he could play on the Jew's-harp from only seeing *Sambo* tune it once.

Mr. *Dye.*—I guess that's *Billy;* he is a right clever child.

Carpenter.—How long, Sir, will it take you to learn Mr. *Dye* Latin?

Schoolmaster.—How long, Sir, would it take me to ride from Mr. *Ball's* plantation to the plantation of Mr. *Wormley Carter?*

Carpenter.—Why that, Sir, I suppose, would depend upon your horse.

Schoolmaster.—Well, then, Sir, you solve your own interrogation.—But here comes *Dick*. What has he got in his hand?

Mr. Dye.—A mole like enough. Who are you bringing that to *Dick?*

Dick.—Not to you.—You never gave me the taste of a dram since I first know'd you. Worse luck to me; you *New Jersey Men* are close shavers; I believe you would skin a louse. This is a mole. I have brought it for the gentleman who came from beyond sea. He never refuses *Dick* a dram; I would walk through the wilderness of *Kentucky* to serve him. Lord! how quiet he keeps his school. It is not now as it was; the boys don't go clack, clack, clack, like 'Squire *Pendleton's* mill upon *Catharpin Run!*

Schoolmaster.—You have brought that mole, *Dick,* for me?

Dick.—Yes, Master, but first let me tell you the history of it. This mole was once a man; See, Master, (exhibits the mole,) it has got hands and feet just like you and me. It was once a man, but so proud, so lofty, so puffed-up, that God, to punish his insolence, condemned him to crawl under the earth.

Schoolmaster.—A good fable, and not unhappily moralized. Did you ever hear or read of this before, Mr. *Dye?*

Mr. *Dye.*—Nay (a broad grin), I am right certain it does not belong to *Æsop*. I am certain sure *Dick* did not find it there.

Dick.—Find it where? I would not wrong a man of the value of a grain of corn. I came across the mole as I was hoeing the potato-patch. Master, shall I take it to the school-house?—If you are fond of birds, I know now for a mocking-bird's nest; I am only afeard those young rogues, the school-boys, will find out the tree. They play the mischief with every thing, they be full of *devilment*. I saw *Jack Lockhart* throw a stone at the old bird, as she was returning to feed her young; and if I had not coaxed him away to look at my young puppies, he would have found out the nest.

In conversation of this nature I sometimes employed an hour or two not unprofitably; for it brought me acquainted with characters which could, perhaps, be only found in the woods of *America*. Indeed human nature, when considered separately from contingent circumstances, is, I believe everywhere the same; but modified by custom and climate, its external qualities are varied.

On Saturday I was at leisure to ride or walk. On that day the bow was unbent, that it might become stronger in its future tension.

Yet, I confess, it was a day I rather dreaded than wished; for, without the company of *Virginia*, I gave myself up to despondency.

> Urit me Glyceræ nitor
> Splendentis Pario marmore purius:
> Urit grata protervitas,
> Et vultus nimium lubricus aspici.*)

Had I lived near the *Alps* I should certainly have adopted the plan of *Saint Preux*, and striven to dissipate my melancholy by climbing to their summit. The *Blue Ridge Mountains* were in sight, and why did I not ascend them? Alas! the manners of the *Blue Ridgers* possess none of that simplicity which characterizes the inhabitants of the mountains of *Switzerland*.

Finding the hours hang heavy, I bethought myself of some invitation that had been given me to a neighbouring plantation, and one visit leading to another, in my round of calling on one or another, I came to the house whither *Virginia* had gone before me. *Virginians* are ever hospitable; ever open-hearted to the stranger who enters their doors. The house of a *Virginian* is not less sacred to hospitality than the tent of an *Arab*. I was received always with transport. " Here, *Will,* take this " gentleman's horse. *Edward,* run up stairs,

[* Horace, *Odes*, I, 19, 5-9.]

" my dear, and tell your mother and the girls
" to come down."

(My recreation after school in the evening was to sit and meditate before my door, in the open air, while the vapours of a friendly pipe administered to my philosophy. In silent gravity I listened to the negro calling to his steers returning from labour, or contemplated the family groupe on the grass-plat before the dwelling-house, of whom the father was tuning his violin, the mother and daughters at their needles, and the boys running and tumbling in harmless mirth upon the green. Before me was an immense forest of stately trees; the cat was sitting on the barn door; the firefly was on the wing, and the whip-poor-will in lengthened cries was hailing the return of night.)

I was now, perhaps, called to supper, and enjoyed the society of Mr. *Ball* and his family till the hour of their repose, when I returned to my log-hut, and resumed my pipe before the door. The moon in solemn majesty was rising from the woods; the plantation-dog was barking at the voices of the negroes pursuing their nightly revels on the road; while the mocking songster mimicked the note of every bird that had sung during the day.

A skilful chymist will endeavour to extract good from every substance, and I declined not the conversation of a man because his face differed in colour from my own. Old *Dick,* the negro whom I had met on the road, never failed to visit my cell in the evening, and the purpose of his visit was to obtain a dram of whiskey. *Dick* said that *it comforted him,* and I never withheld my comfort from him.

As I considered old *Dick* a much greater philosopher than many of his white brethren who have written volumes on resignation under misfortunes, but could never bear the tooth-ache patiently; I always put him upon talking about himself, and one evening when he came to see me, I desired he would relate to me the story of his life.

STORY OF DICK THE NEGRO

" I was born at a plantation on the *Rappa-*
" *hannoc* River. It was the pulling of corn
" time, when 'Squire *Musgrove* was Governor
" of *Virginia.* I have no mixed blood in my
" veins; I am no half and half breed; no chest-
" nut-sorrel of a mulatto; but my father and
" mother both came over from *Guinea.*

" When I was old enough to work, I was
" put to look after the horses, and, when a boy,
" I would not have turned my back against the
" best negur at catching or backing the most
" vicious beast that ever grazed in a pasture.

" 'Squire *Sutherland* had a son who rode
" every fall to look at a plantation on *James*
" *River,* which was under the care of an over-

"seer. Young master could not go without
"somebody on another horse to carry his sad-
"dle-bags, and I was made his groom.

"This young chap, Sir, (here *Dick* winked
"his left eye,) was a trimmer. The first thing
"he did on getting out of bed was to call for
"a *Julep;** and I honestly date my own love of
"whiskey, from mixing and tasting my young
"master's juleps. But this was not all. He
"was always upon the scent after game, and
"mighty ficious when he got among the negur
"wenches. He used to say that a likely negur
"wench was fit to be a Queen; and I forget
"how many Queens he had among the girls on
"the plantations.

"My young master was a mighty one for
"music, and he made me learn to play the
"Banger.† I could soon tune it sweetly, and
"of a moonlight night he would set me to
"play, and the wenches to dance. My young
"master himself could shake a desperate foot
"at the fiddle; there was nobody that could
"face him at a *Congo Minuet;* but *Pat Hick-
"ory* could tire him at a *Virginia Jig*.

"The young 'Squire did not live long. He
"was for a short life and a merry one. He
"was killed by a drunken negur man, who
"found him over-ficious with his wife. The

---

* A dram of spirituous liquor that has mint in it, taken by *Virginians* of a morning.

† A kind of rude Guitar.

"negur man was hanged alive upon a gibbet.
"It was the middle of summer; the sun was
"full upon him; the negur lolled out his
"tongue, his eyes seemed starting from their
"sockets, and for three long days his only cry
"was Water! Water! Water!

"The old gentleman took on to grieve
"mightily at the death of his son; he wished
"that he had sent him to *Britain* for his educa-
"tion; but after-wit is of no use; and he fol-
"lowed his son to that place where master and
"man, planter and slave must all at last lie
"down together.

"The plantation and negurs now fell to the
"lot of a second son, who had gone to *Edin-
"burgh* to learn the trade of a Doctor. He
"was not like 'Squire *Tommy;* he seemed to
"be carved out of different wood. The first
"thing he did on his return from *Britain,* was
"to free all the old negur people on the plan-
"tation, and settle each on a patch of land.
"He tended the sick himself, gave them medi-
"cine, healed their wounds, and encouraged
"every man, woman and child to go to a Meet-
"ing-house, that every Sunday was opened be-
"tween our plantation and *Fredericksburgh.*
"Every thing took a change. The young
"wenches, who, in Master *Tommy's* time,
"used to put on their drops, and their brace-
"lets, and ogle their eyes, now looked down
"like modest young women, and carried their

"gewgaws in their pockets till they got clear
"of the woods. He encouraged matrimony
"on the plantation by settling each couple in a
"log-house, on a wholesome patch of land;
"hired a schoolmaster to teach the children,
"and to every one that could say his letters
"gave a Testament with cuts. This made me
"bold to marry, and I looked out sharp for a
"wife. I had before quenched my thirst at
"any dirty puddle; but a stream that I was
"to drink at constant, I thought should be
"pure,—and I made my court to a wholesome
"girl, who had never bored her ears, and went
"constantly to Meeting.

"She was daughter to old *Solomon* the
"Carter, and by moon-light I used to play
"my *banger* under her window, and sing a
"*Guinea* Love-song that my mother had
"taught me. But I found there was another
"besides myself whose mouth watered after
"the fruit. *Cuffey,* one of the Crop Hands,
"came one night upon the same errand. I am
"but a little man, and *Cuffey* was above my
"pitch; for he was six foot two inches high,
"with a chew of tobacco clapped above that.
"But I was not to be scared because he was a
"big man, and I was a little one; I carried a
"good heart, and a good heart is everything
"in love.

"*Cuffey,* says I, what part of the play is
"you acting? Does you come after *Sall?*

"May be, says he, I does. Then, says I, here's
" have at you boy; and I reckoned to fix him
" by getting the finger of one hand into his ear,
" and the knuckles of the other into his eye.*
" But the whore-son was too strong for me,
" and after knocking me down upon the grass,
" he began to *stomp* upon me, and ax me if
" I had yet got enough. But *Dick* was not
" to be scared; and getting his great toe into
" my mouth, I bit it off and swallowed it.
" *Cuffey* now let go his hold, and it was my
" turn to ax *Cuffey* if he had got enough. *Cuf-*
" *fey* told me he had, and I walked away to
" the Quarter.†

" My master the next day heard of my battle
" with *Cuffey*. He said that I ought to live
" among *painters* and wolves, and sold me to
" a *Georgia* man for two hundred dollars.
" My new master was the devil. He made me
" travel with him handcuffed to *Savannah;*
" where he disposed of me to a tavern-keeper
" for three hundred dollars.

" I was the only man-servant in the tavern,
" and I did the work of half a dozen. I went
" to bed at midnight, and was up an hour be-
" for sun. I looked after the horses, waited at
" the table, and worked like a new negur. But
" I got a plenty of spirits, and that I believe
" helped me.

* This is what is called Gouging.
† The place of abode for the negroes.

"The war now broke out, and in one single
" year I changed masters a dozen times. But
" I knowed I had to work, and one master to
" me was as good as another. When the war
" ended, I was slave to 'Squire *Fielding,*
" at *Annapolis,* in *Maryland.* I was grown
" quite steady, and I married a house-servant
" who brought me a child every year. I have
" altogether had three wives, and am the father
" of twelve children; begot in lawful wed-
" lock: but this you shall hear.

" My wife dying of a flux, I was left to the
" management of my children; but my master
" soon saved me the trouble, for directly they
" were strong enough to handle a hoe, he sold
" the boys to Mr. *Randolph* of *Fairfax,* and
" the girls to 'Squire *Barclay* of *Port Tobacco.*
" It was a hard trial to part with my little ones,
" for I loved them like a father; but there was
" no help for it, and it was the case of thou-
" sands besides myself.

" When a man has been used to a wife, he
" finds it mighty lonesome to be without one;
" so I married a young girl who lived house-
" servant to a tavern-keeper at *Elk Ridge*
" Landing. It is a good twenty-five miles
" from *Annapolis* to the Landing-place; but
" a negur never tire when he go to see his
" sweetheart, and after work on Saturday
" night I would start for *Elk Ridge,* and get to
" my wife before the supper was put away.

"*Dinah* was a dead hand at making of mush;*
"but she could not love it better than I.
"*Dinah,* says I, to her one night, if you was
"a Queen what would you have for supper?
"Why milk and mush, *Dick,* says she. Con-
"cern it, *Dinah,* says I, why if you was to
"eat all the good things what would there be
"left for me?

"I was not perfectly satisfied with my new
"wife; I had some suspicion that she gave
"her company, when I was away, to a young
"mulatto fellow; but as her children were
"right black, I was not much troubled. I
"never could bear the sight of a mulatto; they
"are made up of craft. They are full of im-
"pudence, and will tell a black man that the
"Devil is a negur; but I believe one colour
"is as much akin to him as another.

"I did not keep my second wife long; she
"was a giddy young goose, fond of dress. She
"wore a ruffled smock; and on a Sunday put
"on such sharp-toed shoes, that the points of
"them would have knocked out a mosquito's
"eye. If her children had not been right
"black and right ugly like myself, I should
"have suspected her vartue long before I had
"a real cause.

"I had made *Dinah* a present of a little lap-
"foist; a right handsome dog as you would

* Food resembling hasty-pudding.

"see; and one Saturday, at negur day-time,* a
"mile before I got to *Elk Ridge,* the little
"foist came running up to me. Hie!
"thought I, *Dinah* must be out gadding, and
"looking forward I saw a man and woman
"run across the main-road into the woods. I
"made after them, but I was getting in years,
"and a walk of twenty miles had made my
"legs a little stiff. So after cursing till my
"blood boiled like a pitch-pot, I walked on
"to the tavern.

"I found *Dinah* in the kitchen; but the mu-
"latto fellow was not there. She ran to me,
"and fell on my neck. I hove her off. Be-
"gone girl, says I; no tricks upon Travellers.
"*Dick* in his old age is not to be made a fool
"of. Did not I see you, with *Paris,* Mr. *Jack-*
"*son's* mulatto? Lack a daisey, *Dick,* says
"she, I have not stirred out of the house. I
"swear point blank I have not. I would kiss
"the bible, and take my blessed oath of it!—
"Nor the foist either! says I. Get you gone,
"you hussey, I will seek a new wife. And so
"saying I went up stairs, and made her gowns,
"and her coats and her smocks into a bundle,
"took the drops out of her ears, and the shoes
"off her feet, and walked out of the kitchen.

"I trudged home the same night. It trou-
"bled me to be tricked by a young girl, but it

* A cant term among the negroes for night; they being then at leisure.

"was some satisfaction to know that I had
"stripped her of all her cloathing. Fine
"feathers makes fine birds; and I laughed to
"think how she would look next Sunday; for
"I had left her nothing but a home spun suit
"that she had put on when she got back.

"I now said to myself that it was right fool-
"ish for an old man to expect constancy from
"a young girl, and I wished that my first wife
"had not got her mouth full of yellow clay.
"Half a mile from *Annapolis,* by the road-
"side, is a grave-yard. It was here my poor
"wife was buried. I had often heard tell of
"ghosts, and wanted to see if there was any
"truth in it. I stole softly to the hedge that
"skirted the road. *Hoga,* says I, does you
"rest quiet? *Hoga* does you rest quiet? Say,
"*Hoga!* and quiet old *Dick!* I had hardly
"said the words when the leaves began to stir.
"I trembled as though I had an ague. *Hoga,*
"says I, don't scare me. But in less than a
"minute I saw a black head look over the
"hedge, with a pair of goggle eyes that flamed
"worse than the branches of a pine tree on
"fire. Faith, says I, that can't be *Hoga's*
"head, for *Hoga* had little *pee pee* eyes. I
"took to my heels and run for it. The
"ghost followed quick. As luck would have
"it there was a gate across the road. I jumped
"the gate and crawled into a hedge. The
"ghost did not follow. The gate had stopped

"him. But I heard him bellow mightily, and "when I peeped over the hedge, I saw it was "'Squire *Hamilton's* black bull.

"My master at *Annapolis* being made a "bankrupt, there was an execution lodged "against his negurs. I was sent to *Alex-*"*ander,** and knocked down at vendue to old "'Squire *Kegworth*. I was put to work at "the hoe. I was up an hour before the sun, "and worked naked till after dark. I had no "food but *Homony,* and for fifteen months did "not put a morsel of any meat in my mouth, "but the flesh of a possum or a racoon that I "killed in the woods. This was rather hard "for an old man, but I knowed there was no "help for it.

"Squire *Kegworth* was a wicked one; he "beat Master *Tommy*. He would talk of "setting us free; you are not, he would say, "Slaves for life, but only for ninety-nine years. "The 'Squire was never married; but an old "negur-woman kept house; who governed "both him and the plantation. Hard work "would not have hurt me, but I could never "get any liquor. This was desperate, and "my only comfort was the stump of an old "pipe that belonged to my first wife. This "was a poor comfort without a little drap of "whiskey now and then; and I was laying a "plan to run away, and travel through the

* *Alexandria.*

"wilderness of *Kentucky,* when the old
" 'Squire died.

" I was now once more put up at vendue,
" and as good luck would have it, I was bid
" for by 'Squire *Ball.* Nobody would bid
" against him because my head was grey, my
" back covered with stripes, and I was lame of
" the left leg by the malice of an overseer who
" stuck a pitchfork into my ham. But 'Squire
" *Ball* knowed I was trusty; and though self
" praise is no praise, he has not a negur on the
" plantation that wishes him better than I; or
" a young man that would work for him with
" a more willing heart. There is few masters
" like the 'Squire. He has allowed me to
" build a log-house, and take in a patch of
" land where I raise corn and water *Melions.**
" I keep chickens and ducks, turkeys and geese,
" and his lady always gives me the price of
" the *Alexander* market for my stock. But
" what's better than all, Master never refuses
" me a dram, and with the help of whiskey,
" I don't doubt but I shall serve him these
" fifteen years to come. Some of his negurs

* *Dick's* log-hut was not unpleasantly situated. He had built it near a spring of clear water, and defended it from the sun by an awning of boughs. It was in Mr. *Ball's* peach-orchard. A cock that never strayed from his cabin served him instead of a time-keeper; and a dog that lay always before his door was an equivalent for a lock. With his cock and his dog, Dick lived in the greatest harmony; notwithstanding the pretentions of a white man to superiority over a black one neither the cock nor the dog would acknowledge any other master but Dick.

" impose on him; there's *Hinton,* a mulatto
" rascal, that will run him into debt; and
" there's *Let,* one of the house-girls, who will
" suck the eggs and swear it was a black snake.
" But I never wronged Master of a cent,* and
" I do the work of *Hinton,* of *Henry,* and
" *Jack,* without ever grumbling. I look after
" the cows, dig in the garden, beat out the
" flax, curry-comb the riding nag, cart all the
" wood, tote † the wheat to the mill, and bring
" all the logs to the school-house."

Such is the history of the life and slavery of *Dick,* the negro, as he delivered it to me word for word. It will, perhaps, exhibit a better picture of the condition of negroes in *America,* than any elaborate dissertation on the subject. But it aspires to more credit than the mere gratification of curiosity. It will enable the reader to form a comparison of his own state with that of another, and teach him the unmanly grief of repining at the common casualties of life, when so many thousands of his fellow-creatures toil out with cheerfulness a wretched life under the imprecations and scourgings of an imperious task-master.

Mr. *Ball* was son-in-law to Counsellor *Carter,* of *Baltimore,*‡ who had formerly re-

---

* The hundreth part of a dollar.
† *Tote* is the *American* for to carry.
[‡ Spencer Ball, m. a daughter of Robert Carter, (1727-1804), called 'Councillor,' of *Nomini Hall,* Westmoreland County, Virginia. It was in the family of Colonel Carter that

sided in the woods of *Virginia*, and emancipated the whole of his negroes, except those whom he had given with the marriage-portion of his daughter. Of this he afterwards repented, and in a fit of religious enthusiasm wrote a serious letter to Mr. *Ball*, exhorting him to free his negroes, or he would assuredly go to hell. Mr. *Ball*, whose property consisted in his slaves, and whose family was annually augmenting, entertained different notions; and with much brevity returned answer to the old gentleman's letter, " Sir, I will run " the chance."

But the period is hasting when I must leave Mr. *Ball* and the worthy families in his neighbourhood, and another page or two will conduct me out of the woods of *Pohoke*. I had been three months invested in the first executive office of Pedagogue, when a cunning old fox of a *New Jersey* planter (a Mr. *Lee*) discovered that his eldest boy wrote a better hand than I. Fame is swift-footed; *vires acquirit eundo;* the discovery spread far and wide; and whithersoever I went, I was an object for the hand of scorn to point his slow unmoving finger at, as a schoolmaster that could not write. *Virginia* gave me for the persecutions I underwent a world of sighs, her

Philip Vickers Fithian was Tutor for a year, whose *Journal & Letters* (1767-1774) is one of the most interesting books of that period. See p. 71 of that book.]

swelling heavens rose and with indignation at old *Lee* and his abettors. The boys caught spirit from the discovery. I could perceive a mutiny breaking out among them; and had I not in time broke down a few branches from an apple tree before my door, it is probable they would have displayed their gratitude for my instructions by throwing me out of my school-window. But by arguing with one over the shoulders, and another over the back, I maintained with dignity the first executive office of Pedagogue.

I revenged myself amply on old *Lee.* It was the custom of his son (a *lengthy* fellow of about twenty) to come to the *Academy* with a couple of huge mastiffs at his heels. Attached to their master (*par nobile fratrum*) they entered without ceremony *Pohoke* Academy, bringing with them myriads of fleas, wood-lice and ticks. Nay, they would often annoy *Virginia,* by throwing themselves at her feet, and inflaming the choler of a little lap-dog, which I had bought because of his diminutive size, and which *Virginia* delighted to nurse for me. I could perceive the eye of *Virginia* rebuke me for suffering the dogs to annoy her; and there lay more peril in her eye than in the jaws of all the mastiffs in *Prince William County.*

" Mr. *Lee,*" said I, " this is the third time I " have told you not to convert the *Academy*

"into a kennel, and bring your dogs to school."
Lee was mending his pen "judgmatically."
He made no reply but smiled.

I knew old *Dick* the negro had a bitch, and that his bitch was proud. I walked down to *Dick's* log-house. *Dick* was beating flax.

"*Dick*," said I, "old Farmer *Lee* has done "me much evil—(I don't like the old man "myself, Master, said *Dick*)—and his son, "repugnant to my express commands, has "brought his father's two plantation dogs to "the Academy. Revenge is sweet——

"'Right, Master, said *Dick*. "I never felt "so happy as when I bit off *Cuffey's* great toe "and swallowed it——

"Do you, *Dick*," said I, "walk past the "school-house with your bitch. *Lee's* dogs "will come out after her. Go round with "them to your log-house; and when you have "once secured them, hang both of them up "by the neck."

"Leave it to me, Master," said *Dick*. "I'll "fix the business for you in a few minutes. I "have a few fadoms of rope in my house— "that will do it."

I returned to the *Academy*. The dogs were stretched at their ease on the floor. "Oh! I "am glad you are come," exclaimed *Virginia;* "those great big dogs have quite scared me."

In a few minutes *Dick* passed the door with his slut. Quick from the floor rose Mr. *Lee's* two dogs, and followed the female. The rest may be supplied by the imagination of the reader. *Dick* hung up both the dogs to the branch of a pine-tree; old *Lee* lost the guards to his plantation; the negroes broke open his barn, pilfered his sacks of *Indian* corn,* rode his horses in the night— and thus was I revenged on *Alexander the Copper Smith*.

Three months had now elapsed, and I was commanded officially to resign my sovereign authority to Mr. *Dye,* who was in every respect better qualified to discharge its sacred functions. He understood Tare and Tret, wrote a copper-plate hand, and, balancing himself upon one leg, could flourish angels and corkscrews. I, therefore, gave up the " Academy School " to Mr. *Dye,* to the joy of the boys, but the sorrow of *Virginia*.

Virginia bewailed my impending departure with tears in her eyes. " Alas! " said she, " I " must now quit my *French,* my poetry and "*English* grammar! I shall be taught no " more geography! I shall no more read in "*Paul* and *Virginia,* but be put back into "*Noah Webster's* horn-book! I shall (sob- " bing) do nothing but write and cypher. I

[* Parkinson, *Tour in America,* Vol. II, p. 432,—" As I have travelled on the road, I have made it my business to converse with them, (the negroes), and they say " Massa, as we work and raise all, we ought to consume all," and to a person who does not contradict them, they will declare their mind very freely."]

"wish Mr. *Dye* would mind his own business. "I wish, instead of coming to teach school, "he would go and work at the crop."

I now once more seized my staff, and walked towards *Baltimore*. It was a killing circumstance to separate from *Virginia;* but who shall presume to contend against fate?

I still, and shall ever, behold *Virginia* in my fancy's eye. I behold her fair form among the trees. I contemplate her holding her handkerchief to her eyes. I still hear a tender adieu! faultering on her lips; and the sob that choaked her utterance still knocks against my heart.

Phyllida amo ante alias; nam me discedere flevit! *

[* Virgil: *Ecloga* III, 78.]

NOTE.—The Editor wishes to make acknowledgments to the Secretary of the South Carolina Historical Society, to the officials of the Library of Congress and of the Lenox Library.

www.ingramcontent.com/pod-product-compliance
Lightning Source LLC
Chambersburg PA
CBHW071107160426
43196CB00013B/2497